THE
RIVER
IS
MINE

Printed in the United States of America by Local Color Press, Ltd.
526 West 26th Street, Suite 506, New York, NY 10001, January 2002
http://www.localcolorpress.com
e-mail:localcolorpress@aol.com

Excerpt from "The Dry Salvages" in FOUR QUARTETS,
copyright 1941 by T.S. Eliot and renewed 1969 by Esme Valerie Eliot,
reprinted by permission of Harcourt, Inc.

Book Design by Brooke Hellewell and Don Ledwin
Photos by Ardian Gill

Library of Congress Control Number: 2001127143

ISBN Number: 0-9716607-0-0

THE
RIVER
IS
MINE

JOHN WESLEY POWELL'S 1869 EXPLORATION
OF THE GREEN AND COLORADO RIVERS
AND THE GRAND CANYON

a novel by
ARDIAN GILL

FOR RUTH

I do not know much about gods; but I think that the river

Is a strong brown god — sullen, untamed and intractable,

Patient to some degree, at first recognised as a frontier;

Useful, untrustworthy, as a conveyor of commerce;

Then only a problem confronting the builder of bridges.

The problem once solved, the brown god is almost forgotten

By the dwellers in cities — ever, however, implacable,

Keeping his seasons and rages, destroyer, reminder

Of what men choose to forget. Unhonored, unpropitiated

By worshipers of the machine, but waiting, watching and waiting.

T.S. ELIOT

On May 24, 1869 ten men in four boats left Green River, Wyoming, intending to travel the entire length of the Green and Colorado Rivers to the Gulf of California, a journey of a thousand miles. The vast middle of this distance, including its course through the Grand Canyon, was largely unexplored, and considered to be impassable. This was the last great unknown territory in the westering United States; a successful transit would represent a feat comparable to the exploration of Lewis and Clark, but without an Indian guide.

Three months later, six half-starved men in two boats emerged at the mouth of the Rio Virgen, in Nevada, then still a Territory. This is their story as gleaned from their diaries, letters and later accounts. These records were often conflicting and sometimes self-contradictory, so that descriptions of every major crisis were often tantamount to seeing *Rashomon,* Kurosawa's film told from four different points of view. The daily journal of Sergeant George Young Bradley is the most complete and consistent version and is generally relied on when there are different versions of the same event. Bradley's optimism and veiled criticisms made it necessary to resort frequently to other sources for a realistic picture of events. Wherever possible I have used actual phrasing from the diaries, including much of Bradley's eccentric spelling. This is, however, a work of fiction and, in James Dickey's words, "No artist is bound by the truth." Thus, some events are changed chronologically and much of the action and conversation is invented.

Most accounts of the journey rely entirely on one of the several versions published by the leader, John Wesley Powell. A serious problem with the Powell narratives, written as late as 1875, is that they collapse the experiences of an aborted second trip in 1871 into his description of the first trip and contain much that is misremembered, fictional or promotional. He wrote the most complete version to help his petitions to Congress for funding. In that report he did not mention any of the men from the second trip and often forgot who did what on the trip that is the subject of this book, even scrambling the crews of the boats. In his last version, *The Exploration of the Colorado River and Its Canyons* he switched from the past tense to present tense, and produced a remarkably evocative, poetic and exaggerated description of the merged journeys.

PART ONE

DEPARTURE

The great dragon that lieth in the midst
of his rivers, which hath said, My river is
mine own, and I have made it for myself.

EZEKIEL 29.3

It fell to me to wake Major. He was staying in a room over Jake Field's saloon, instead of in tents down by the river with the rest of us. I couldn't see the room was much improvement, though. Plain rough-sawn boards we'd have cut up for firewood back in Massachusetts. Nailed up green, too, I guess, cracks between them you could put your thumb in if you had no better use for it. Just one small window, high up, so you couldn't slip away without paying Jake for the room, I suppose, glass so dirty you wondered how the sun could stand to come through it.

He slept pretty sound, did Major, and I hated to wake him, so I just watched him for a while. It may sound like a dull thing to do, but when I was in the army up to Fort Bridger I can tell you it was duller, made watching Major sleep seem lively as a parade. He had more hair on his chin than he had on his head, a plentiful beard, full as moss on a cypress, while the top was wanting in the front, near as far back as his ears. But I had to get on with it.

"The boats are down, Major," I said, and shook him just a touch.

He woke up with a snort, like a colt tugging at the reins and maybe rearing up a little. Had his feet on the floor in a jiffy, reached out quick and tipped some water from the porcelain pitcher on the wash stand into the basin, and with his head almost in it, brought up some water to his face, then with that same hand ran his fingers through his hair, such as it was. I don't usually stay and watch a man dress, but he waved me into the one hard chair, so I sat while he snaked his trousers on over the long johns he'd slept in and snapped the suspenders to, over the shirt he'd likewise worn through the night. Makes things easier in the morning, I'm sure. I was uncomfortable through that business, but I wanted to see him tie his shoes, as the boys said he could do. Takes practice no doubt, but he twisted the laces up around the hooks, made the single knot and bow just as good as if he had two hands.

"Now, Sergeant, how do the boats look to your practiced eye?"

He calls me "Sergeant," which is correct as far as it goes, but I was a lieutenant in the war, same as he was a major. They do the ranks over in peacetime, so when I re-enlisted, there being no work at home, they gave me a sergeant's rank, best they could do, they said. So Major might have ended up a lieutenant, had he stayed. Still, they say he was made a colonel just at the end, when he went back into the war with but the one arm. You can do that in the artillery, I guess, but the cavalry wouldn't have had him back, that's for sure.

"Well, they're sturdy enough, Major, at least the big ones are," I told him, "but those Chicago builders never rowed out for codfish in rough water, I can tell you that. We're recaulking them all with oakum and we'll tar over that, then we'll repaint them. After a day in the water, they'll swell up tight as a tick."

"Hearing you say 'watuh', no one would have to guess you were from Massachusetts. Lost your 'r's' somewhere near Boston, I'd judge."

"Newburyport," I told him, "just a little north."

We were downstairs, passing through Jake Field's saloon, still reeking of smoke and whiskey from the night before, when he asked, "You ever been on a river, Sergeant?"

I lacked the time to answer before Mr. Fields arrived and handed Major some black coffee in a tin mug, grey, speckled with white, like it had been caught in a sideways snowstorm, steam coming off so it looked like you'd scald your throat if you tried to drink it. But Major took a hearty slug, just like it was spring water. Didn't bother him none.

"Thankee, Jake," he says, "I'm in need of it."

So was I, since Billy Rhoads hadn't got the coffee to the boil before I left camp, but maybe sergeants don't qualify for coffee rations, or maybe I just wasn't a paying guest.

"And I'm in need of some moccasins, Jake, if you have any in your store. These shoes will be a nuisance on the river."

"You're welcome to the coffee, Major, and yes, I surely do. Come by when you're ready."

"It'll be tomorrow most likely; we'll be busy with the boats today. And I'll be wanting a sack of rice, if you have such a thing."

"I'll get ye some from Chung Chen. He's still feeding some of the coolies left over from building the railroad."

"I'd be grateful."

When we were out in the fresh air I answered Major's question: "Can't say as I've ever rowed a river of any consequence, Major. I've rowed on the Merrimac and on ponds and bays around Cape Ann. And in the ocean, of course, when we hauled in the nets, but never a real river. Seems to me going downstream would be a joyride, but upstream somewhat toilsome."

"Well," he said, "you may find even downstream on these particular rivers somewhat toilsome. Can't say for sure, as not even the Indians have explored it downriver of Brown's Hole or upstream from Grand Wash."

"Major, I'd gladly explore the river Styx to get out of the army."

"Ah mee," he mocked me, but I could see he meant it in fun. "You'll have your discharge before we finish our trip, Sergeant. President Grant said he'd see to it personally. In fact, he sent a note to the adjutant when I visited him in Washington."

"He must have done, Major. My discharge was signed out at Fort Bridger the day before I left, the telegraph being that fast. The paper's in my pocket, and there I'll keep it so I can look at it every night before I sleep and smile at it again every morning when I wake."

"I'd advise you to keep it safe or they'll send some troops after you, same as they did for Billy Rhoads, or Hawkins, as he calls himself when it's more convenient."

We made our way through Green River City, a name that overdignifies the place, there being nothing much left there except a clutch of crumbling adobe houses, huddled together like new-hatched chicks, and a few dozen board shacks, some with just tarpaulin for a roof. Yellow-brown adobe dust kicked up with every step, like you were being tracked by a will-o-the-wisp, tumbleweeds scattering like stray cats. There used to be about two thousand souls living in the town, they tell me, down to about a hundred now, most likely "soulless." Drifters, free trappers and hunters, waiting out the weather or drinking up the rest of their money, a few Indians and Chinese coolies, now functioning as squatters, some like Billy Rhoads staying one step ahead of the law.

The chief feature of Green River City as I saw it was the railroad bridge the Union Pacific built across the river. About a hundred-foot span I judge, just about the last link in the two railroad lines built from each coast until they met in Promontory, two hundred miles northwest of the bridge. They say the tracks were joined there with four spikes of gold and silver. I bet. Well I bet the spikes were pulled up almost as soon as they were driven, if not by the railroad fancy Dans then by the likes of the swells in the shacks of Green River City.

We'd covered most of the distance to the bridge, not talking, Major drinking his coffee, me watching the weather to judge if the rain would hold off long enough for us to paint the boats, when Major undertook to tell me about the river. "It rises in the Wind River Mountains, north and east of here. The trappers called it the 'Seedskeedee', maybe out of fun, though it's probably a corruption of an Indian name."

I didn't know you could corrupt a word, but I didn't say that. Instead I asked him why they called it "Green River" when it's so clearly brown.

"Oh, it's probably green at times when the snow-melt isn't tearing at the banks, the way it is now. But more likely it's like the naming of Greenland, to entice settlers." I guessed that he was right the second time, as I'd seen local newspapers sent east booming the snow-wrapped mining camps of Montana so that they seemed to resemble the sun-bathed beaches of Florida.

We reached the railroad yard and the siding where the flatcar with the boats had been shunted at dawn that day. Our crew had off-loaded them from the flatcar, then rolled and levered them down the slope to a little gravelly beach, where they were launched and floated downriver a few hundred yards to the small park where our camp was.

"Where's the freight car with our supplies?" He looked around the yard, empty except for our flatcar, as if a freight car might be hiding somewhere. I couldn't help him, knowing nothing of the subject. Then he clambered down the slope to the river, thinking the car had sunk, I suppose, until I saw he'd spotted a little home-made boat with a solitary rower just easing down toward us. He hailed the boat and the man rowed to shore. He was a strange looking feller. At first I thought he was a middle-aged man, and I guessed Major felt the same, as he called him "sir" when he asked for a ride down to camp. He was just a youngster though, barely eighteen or nineteen, but he had an older man's head, as if he had inherited it from an uncle and stuck it on his own shoulders. His eyes were deep-set, the dark blue of Cavalry trousers, and his nose was hooked as a hawk's. He was what you'd call "carrot topped," and freckles dotted his face. When he told Major his name was Andy Hall and he'd be pleased to carry him in his "wee skiff," I heard a hint of Scots burr behind the western drawl. I could see the river had picked up a little speed from yesterday, though the tide was still slow enough so we could row back up to the railroad yard and load our supplies. That is supposing we found the freight car.

Major eased himself onto the back seat of the boat, making the little thing lift up at the bow as though it was about to fly. Major had about two inches of freeboard at the stern and his shoes were in leak-water up to the hooks. They were knee-to-knee so that the boy had to take short strokes to keep from shipping water or pushing Major over the stern. You could see he hadn't had much practice in boat-building. Or rowing for that matter. As they started downriver they made a comical sight, like a loon running over the water before taking to the air.

As I arrived where we were campt, Billy Rhoads was hauling the prow of the little boat onto the gravel shore, nearly tipping Major over the stern. Billy was maybe twenty-two years old with a long, bushy moustache, probably blond under the tobacco-stain, drooping on both sides of his chin like parentheses. He didn't look happy. "Major, they tell me you want me to be the cook for this trip. Now that's no job for a free trapper, Major."

Major turned to the boy, "You can row, Andy, can you cook?"

"I've made flapjacks."

"Coffee?"

"I can boil coffee."

"How'd you like to come along with us, help Missouri here with the vittles?"

"I'll tell my mother."

"You've got an assistant, Billy, now let's see how your coffee is this morning," and he handed Rhoads the tin cup.

Well that beat my record; Major had only known me for an hour when he asked me along and agreed to get me out of the army in exchange, but he'd signed Andy on in twenty minutes. He hadn't offered Andy any compensation so far as I could see, but I knew the trappers were determined to work out some kind of salary or payment in kind, not wanting to be out a year's earnings from trapping beaver.

When Billy came back with the coffee Major was waving his one arm in some sort of dudgeon at Jack Sumner, who had been with Major in 1868 on a trip in unknown territory near the White River and was appointed chief boatman for this venture. Jack was a few inches shorter than me, maybe five foot six, about the same height as Major, but when they talked it seemed like each raised himself on his toes a little, so that he appeared a bit taller. Jack had a mustache of fine blond hair, running to his chinsides, and weather in his face; otherwise he'd have appeared a mite delicate for a woodsman. Jack was explaining about the freight car.

"They shunted the flatcar with the boats onto the siding up there and while we concentrated our full powers of attention on that one, the other one got away, went west with the train and the westering sun. Howland's got the railroad agent telegraphing everybody from here to San Francisco, and maybe China if the tracks run that far." 'Westering sun' sounded peculiar to me as the train had arrived at six that morning and left twenty minutes later, but Jack has a way of adding color to a tale.

"Any word back yet?"

"Not a whisper, Professor, that the river ain't drowned." I could hear the river's constant gurgle in the pause he made for effect. "But Oramel's still up at the railroad agent's, burnin' up the wires."

"Come on, Sergeant, let's see how the caulking is coming." Major's shoes squished on the gravel as we went over to where our four boats were resting on makeshift cradles or were careened onto tarpaulins. Before I went to wake Major, I'd shown Bill Dunn how to caulk, and he was at work on the little boat, showing Seneca Howland and Walter Powell, Major's brother, how to do it. There's no secret about it. You take the oakum, which is just hemp rope soaked in thinned out creosote, and you cram it into the seams, keeping it regular, and where it's cut, you take care to nest the new one snug up against its neighbor. Just takes a little practice, is all, and it helps if you've got a caulking tool, something like a broad-bladed screwdriver. Bill Dunn was using a blunt piece of wrought iron he'd found in the rail yard. Bill was a queer looking duck, crow-black hair down to his waist, a full beard half as long, wearing buckskins he'd had on so long they were nearly black and had an oily shine to them. He was possibly good looking under all that foliage, but as it was, he had a wild, apparition-like look that could unnerve a stranger. Took a little getting used to, but he was a decent sort, all the same. He was even taller than I am, maybe five foot ten, and strong as a bull. Didn't say much.

Seneca Howland was another story altogether. He looked younger than he was to about the same degree that Andy Hall looked older, but he was about twenty-five, give or take. Had apple-cheeks, spoke softly with a twang you'd know was Vermont if you grew up in the East as I did. Seemed to worship his brother Oramel, the oldest in our party, beating Major to the honor by six months or so. I suspected he was prepared to transfer some of that affection to Major, given half a chance.

Captain Walter Powell figured he'd mastered the craft of caulking and was flat on his back poking oakum into the seams of one of the three big boats when Major and I caught up with him. He was using a sheath knife, lacking any other tool. A big man, Walter was, over six feet and solid as oak. Looking at him then you'd never know he came out the Confederate prison at Sorghum a near skeleton. He'd got his weight back but not his wits. The Rebs had treated him pretty rough, so he went mad, or nearly so. He was a mite touchy, unpredictable as the weather, and even Major was a bit tentative with his "Good Morning, Walter."

"I'm fine, Wes, fine. I'll have this boat done today. Bill Dunn here showed me how."

"That's good, Walter. Bradley here says it'll be 'tight as a tick' when you're through."

At first I thought the remark had angered Walter as his eyes seemed to be aflame, but he spoke calmly enough. "That's a good one, I guess, but I've seen a hell of a lot of ticks and none of 'em drank whiskey so far as I could see." Then he laughed at his own joke, a sort of wheeze, like a horse snorting. "Can't say the same for myself." The snorting wheeze again.

"You may as well go in this boat you're caulking, Walter. And I'll put Sergeant Bradley here in with you."

Walter seemed about to object, "A sergeant," he said, and I'd have been happy had the objection stuck, but the Major cut him off, "He was a cavalry officer in the war, and he's the best boatman." Then he saw his mistake as Jack Sumner had come up, "Except for Jack here, of course, so you'll have a good man, Walter."

I don't know if the Captain was mollified. He just went back to caulking, mumbling what might have been a complaint, or maybe a song.

"You and the sergeant think of a name for your boat," Major told him as he turned to take a fresh cup of coffee from Billy. Walter showed no sign of having heard. I'd already chosen "Maid of the Canyon" for my boat but I was afraid it would take some doing to get Walter to agree. When I got around to asking him, he just said, "'Long as it floats."

When Billy brought the coffee, there was this feller tagging along behind, dressed like a snake-oil salesman, with a swallow-tail coat and a string tie, hat that could have been beaver but wasn't, if you looked close. "He's a scientific duck from back East," Billy whispered to Major, "been camping with us for a week while you was in Chicago seein to the boats.

The feller advanced to Major like he might run him through with his extended right hand, didn't see his mistake until the last minute, then switched to his left hand, but Major ignored the gesture and the feller just let his hand fall, gradual like it was a leaf dropped from a tree. "Captain Samuel Adams, Major, Samuel Adams. Secretary of War Stanton has sent me out to take charge of this expedition."

Major's head snapped back a little just then, "Stanton hasn't been Secretary since Johnson fired him in the last administration and was impeached for his pains. Rawlins is Secretary."

Captain Adams didn't pause any more'n a rock falling off a bluff, went on like a barker I heard once in a carnival. "I've got letters here from the Secretary and from Congress, putting me in charge, to look out for the Government's interest. Best interests, protect their investment as it were."

Major stiffened a bit and though he wasn't near as tall as Captain Adams, he looked to be staring down at him. Major's eyes were blazing like Walter's, so I guessed it was a family trait.

"There is no government money in this expedition, *Captain*." He came down hard on the man's lower rank, which I suspect was as bogus as his hat. "There is only my own money and that of friends in these boats and in our provisions. A few barometers and such have been loaned to me by the Smithsonian Institution. I'll see those letters if I may."

The captain dug out a few papers from an inside pocket, had the look of a dog chewed 'em. You could almost see him wiggle saying, "Let me read them to you," in a voice would suit a Boston Brahmin pouring tea.

Major snapped them out the captain's hand like he was catching a fly mid-flight, "I can read."

Turns out they were just letters from Congressmen wishing the captain good luck in his proposed trip down this river. "Good-bye, Captain, and you can pay Rhoads here a dollar a day for your grub."

Adams just turned on his heel and stalked off, stiff as a scarecrow. "You haven't heard the last of me, Major, and the food wasn't fit for a pig." I knew then he was no Captain 'cause he'd never had army food.

Billy just chuckled, "He didn't eat with us much. Didn't think the grub was up to Eastern standards. Now here's another one wants to see you. He's got a funny way of talkin, but he didn't eat our grub. Stayed up to Chung Chen's with the Chinee."

Up came this feller had a face as red as if he'd come in from a blizzard. Big, too, belly like a pregnant sow. He didn't seem to want us in on their conversation so I drifted off with Jack and Billy to help with the boats. I saw him talking up a storm, though, Major shaking his head, the feller waving his hands palms up until he reached in his pocket and thrust something at Major. At first Major waved it away, then he snatched it and plunged it into his pocket. When he brought the man over to where we were standing near my boat, Major said to Jack, "You've met Frank Goodman, Jack. He's just joined our party." Major had taken Frank on in five minutes, even beating Andy Hall's record.

"Jolly glad to be aboard," he said and I knew right then he was English. Any American would have been satisfied with being glad. Or jolly, but it's a waste of words to be both.

There's not much to amuse a body in Green River City, and so our little party had become the chief entertainment of the entire population. They'd begun to gather in our clearing, carping about the boats, how the big ones made of oak were too heavy and would sink and how the little one made of pine was too flimsy and would break up on the rocks. A policeman from Pigot told us we'd drown before we got to Brown's Hole, a miner from Breckenbridge said the Indians would kill us like they did the Gunnison party, and I don't know what all. But we just went on with our work and shrugged off the noise until Oramel Howland pushed through the crowd, which had grown to twenty or so, blocking the way between us and the town. He headed for Major, and we naturally gathered around to hear the news of the freight car with our supplies and provisions.

Oramel was tall and gaunt, thin as a sheath knife, and he was covering ground with strides almost the length of a fence rail. He had on these printer's overalls, denim straps over his shoulders, a pencil in the bib-pocket, a vast and shaggy beard blowing left and right as a gust of wind caught it. He looked like mad King Lear pictured in a book of that name that I'd read up at Fort Bridger. Oramel reached us pretty quick, but he started talking before he quite got to us.

"They found the car in Promontory, John. Thought it was want- ed in Salt Lake City. The agent had a bitch of a time but they final- ly agreed to have it back here tonight on the eastbound train." His voice was much like his brother Seneca's, but the Vermont twang had lengthened out a bit by his years as printer for the Rocky Mountain News, as if there was more room for words to spread out in the West.

"Good work, Oramel. We'll be off tomorrow then."

"I don't think so, Professor," Jack broke in, "Bradley here says we've got to repaint the boats, then the paint's got to dry and then they have to soak and be pumped out. Then we have to reseal the water-tight compartments. But with the luck of an Irishman, we'll be off the day after."

"Day after tomorrow is *Sunday*," I pointed out. But Jack just chuckled. "Sure, that's another reason for stayin. It'll be livelier than the Fourth of July here on Saturday night. Jake Fields has got a couple of can-can dancers coming from St. Louis on the morning train, call themselves 'Kitty Clyde and Her Sister.'"

I thought to maybe delay the painting or caulking so we didn't get to leave on the Sabbath, but that would have been un-Christian of me, so I didn't do nor say anything else about it, but I suspected we'd do penance in some way I couldn't predict.

Oramel had another man along with him, neat looking feller, buckskin jacket, cord pants, plaid shirt open at the collar, a sight more appealing than Sam Adams. Oramel introduced him to us, "Mr. Jed Dawes, works for Bill Byers as a writer of the *Rocky Mountain News*. We used to work together in Denver. Jed is wanting a story for his paper, about the trip, if you have the time."

"If you've come all the way from Denver, I'll make the time. By the way, Mr. Dawes, I know your editor, Mr. Byers. We climbed Long's Peak together. Fire away."

It seemed a remarkable thing to say, for a man who'd lost his arm being fired at in the battle of Shiloh. I wasn't going to stay, but when I heard Mr. Dawes first question, I could tell he'd put Major off.

"Why are you undertaking this adventure, Major?"

"It's not an adventure," Major said, a little louder than was strictly necessary for Dawes' hearing. "It's a scientific expedition. We expect to measure latitude and longitude, direction, distance run. In other words to produce a reliable map. We'll also collect specimens of flora and fauna, try to determine the geological origins of the land. We'll examine fossils which will help to determine the age of the formations. In short, everything you'd expect from a scientific expedition."

"Who will get this information when you're through?"

Major started to answer but he was cut off by a rough in the crowd, "They ain't gonna get through," he shouted at us, "Won't get no further'n Brown's Hole. The river'll swallow 'em up."

The laughter was general in the crowd and another rough yelled out, "There's a hole in the river will just suck you in." And another yawped, "The walls go straight up down there. Once you git in you cain't never climb out."

There were two in that crowd deserve mention. One was a deaf-mute boy, about ten years old, maybe twelve, and another boy a bit older, most likely his brother. The brother was trying by signs to explain to the boy what the man had said, that the river would swallow the boats and that we wouldn't be able to climb the vertical walls. When the deaf-mute boy understood, he began to act it out, a man desperately trying to claw his way up a clift and falling back each time, then sinking, gasping for breath and drowning. He kept doing this over and over, while his brother was holding his sides laughing.

It didn't sit too well with any of us, but Walter Powell took it more amiss than most. He rose from his work, his eyes blazing and his sheath knife in his hand, and started for the boys. Major stepped in front of Walter real quick, nodded to Jack and Billy, and they led Walter off to the campfire, gave him some coffee and started a song. In a minute Walter picked it up. He had a fine voice, deep and resonant, like a bullfrog been schooled proper, and he soon filled our little park with sound,

> *Oh ya, ya, darkies,*
> *Laugh away wid me*
> *De white folks say Ole Shady am free*
> *Don't you see dat de jubilee*
> *Am coming, coming, coming*
> *Hail! Mighty day*

It put everybody in the crowd quiet but the deaf-mute, who couldn't hear the song, of course. He just kept on with his act, falling, gasping, make-believe drowning, didn't even notice his brother had stopped laughing, didn't hear the others at the campfire join in the chorus,

> *Away, den away, for I can't stay any longer*
> *Hurrah! Boys, hurrah! for I am going home*

I wished then that the deaf boy could hear it, maybe go home himself, for I admit his pantomime left me a little quivery in the lower limbs.

I decided the best thing for my state of mind was to get busy, so I went back to my boat. Major led Mr. Dawes along in the same direction, so as to get out of the crowd's hearing and heckling and so's they could hear over the singing, and Oramel came along.

Dawes picked up right where he left off, didn't miss a stroke, "What do you say to that, Major. The Indians say there's a great hole in the river. That's why they won't go near it."

"I've heard them say that, 'Heap swallow everything,' You ever see a hole in a river?" I thought that Major's answer was right smart, but it didn't faze Mr. Dawes, and he stayed right with it. "My experience is that Indians are given to colorful descriptions. I expect they're talking about a whirlpool. But you haven't told me just who will benefit from all the scientific information you plan to bring out?"

I thought there was a touch of sarcasm in the way he asked that question, but Major came back pretty sharp himself, "The whole country will benefit, just as they did from the Lewis and Clark expedition thirty odd years ago. It's the same thing, exploration of the unknown for the good of the country. Perhaps you haven't heard that the country is opening up to the west. The canyons of the Green and Colorado Rivers are the last great unknown in America. We plan to make them known."

"But the government sent Lewis and Clark."

"And they damn well should have sent me." I'd not heard Major use a cuss word before, but he seemed comfortable with the vocabulary. "The Illinois State Normal College and the Smithsonian Institution will both be the beneficiaries of our research. They've donated a little money or loaned us some instruments when the Congress declined to appropriate funds for the expedition."

"Captain Adams says Congress did appropriate funds for your trip."

"Adams says Stanton is Secretary of War."

"But you do have some government money behind the trip, isn't that true?"

I could see Major was running out of patience, "Not a red cent with an Indian on it. The only thing Congress would authorize is drawing supplies from army posts, and there aren't many of those on the river."

I could see Mr. Dawes looking over at the crew sitting by the fire or poking oakum in the boats and while I can't say what went through his mind, I suspect it was much the same as would have been in mine in his position and, truth be told, was then anyway: A demented captain singing a slave song, trappers with more hair than most women, a red-faced Englishman, a boy with a man's head. About as loose a collection of scientists as you're likely to find anywhere.

"Who in this group of scientists will draw your map?"

"Oh, Howland here is our cartographer."

I could see Oramel's eyebrows raise almost to meet his hairline, and Dawes' near as far, but he wasn't the type to back off. Goes with the newspaper trade I guess.

"Our readers will want to know how you'll determine latitude and longitude in primitive circumstances."

It was probably the "primitive" that got to Major, for you could see a shade of carmine start to fill the void between beard and brow. "We'll use a sextant, we'll shoot Polaris, Beta Ceti, the moon at night, use calendar charts for lunar distances, set our clocks by the sun at its meridian." He just rattled them off like he was a schoolboy saying the alphabet, or maybe a teacher teaching it. "We'll have a chronometer set to Greenwich mean time. The earth rotates fifteen degrees every hour, so every noon we can determine our longitude by simple multiplication. It's an old science."

Jack Sumner came up just then with Walter Powell, who went to work on the other side of the *Maid of the Canyon*, about as fine a name as a boat ever had. Jack shook Dawes' hand and said if he needed any detailed information he'd be happy to oblige. But Dawes had a question or two more before he finished with Major, or could be it was t'other way round.

"And who besides you, Major, can use a sextant?"

"Oh, Sumner here is expert at it."

This time it was Sumner's eyebrows went up, but just a little as you could see he saw the humor in it.

"One final question, Major Powell. Are you sure this trip hasn't been done before? There have been newspaper reports of a man named White going down the entire length of the river on a raft."

"Knowing the accuracy of newspapers, I find that reassuring, Mr. Dawes. It means we'll have a pleasant journey. And now I must wish you the same, as we have work to do." And Major took Oramel and headed off to the fire with his coffee cup at the ready.

That left Jack to deal with Dawes, and by the time the battle was over, there was some doubt in my mind about the victor.

"Mr. Sumner, you seem like a sensible man. What possessed you to go along with the idea of spending a year exploring a thousand miles of unknown river under the leadership of a one-armed, greenhorn botany professor from the East."

I knew my mission, and I'd just heard Major tell his, but I didn't know Jack Sumner's. So while I'm not partial to eavesdropping on another man's conversation, I stopped my poking oakum to hear Jack's answer.

"Waal, you got a few things ain't quite right there, Mr. Dawes. First off, it warn't precisely the Professor's idea, and he ain't exactly leadin it, and he ain't exactly a greenhorn." I could hear Jack was in his storytelling mode, another reason to listen in.

"What do you mean? He's in charge, isn't he?"

"Surely, surely. He's surely in charge of the science, and welcome to it. But I'm the chief boatman, and I'll see to it that we get down the river somehow while he does his botanizing and geologizing and makes his maps, same way I was in charge of things when we climbed Long's Peak or went out on the Berthoud Trail or wintered on the White River. He pretty much takes my advice, just like he did for this trip."

"You mean it was your idea?"

"Let me give you a little history. I been out with the Professor two years runnin now, and I could see he warn't all that interested in those plants and things his wife and those college students were bent on picking up. His mind was elsewhere and I saw right away it was the rivers that took his fancy, especially those that white men hadn't traveled yet. Hills, too, if they hadn't been climbed. Of course that didn't come 'til after I led him up Long's Peak, and he learned to get used to the heights."

"You mean he was afraid of heights and you cured him?"

I could see Mr. Dawes was entertaining some doubts, but Jack went right on. "Waal, he ain't exactly cured, but leastways he ain't crawlin on his hands and knees any more."

"*Hand* and knees," Dawes said, and I heard Walter snort on the other side of the *Maid*.

I began to guess Jack might have met his match because he broke stride just a little then, but he went on readily enough, "I guess he had a right to be a little skairt when we was gettin to the top of Long's Peak, as it warn't never climbed before, leastways by white men. When I see him crawlin along behind me, I just took him by the hand and said, 'follow me', and he did. Mrs. Powell too." Walter snorted again and I guessed it was a trait of his I'd best get used to if we were to spend a year sharing a ten foot space.

"Anyways, last year when I had him down to explore the White River, we got to talking about rivers, and he wanted to know what river I thought would be the hardest to navigate. I told him about the Grand River, or the Colorado as the politicians want us to call it now, a river which the Green here joins, and which no man, Indian or white, ever navigated upriver from Grand Wash, Arizona Territory, or downriver from Brown's Hole. Told him I was planning to take Bill Dunn and make the trip, trappin, huntin, lookin for gold or silver, maybe even map out a route for a railroad, no tunnels, no bridges, just a rail-bed flat as a plain.

"Waal, that got his interest all right. He'd hardly talk of anything else all winter but that river, he was that desperate to join me. His wife wasn't so keen on his going when he sprung it on her, but when she heard I was leadin it, she felt comfortable enough.

"Come to the question of boats, he couldn't think what sort of boats would stand the pounding against the rocks nor sink beneath the billows." I stopped all pretense of work then and sat up to listen as it appeared Jack was just getting up to his natural gait and rhythm.

"So I drew out my design for him. Told him how there ought to be a small pilot boat to scout out the way and bigger boats to carry the freight. When it came to keepin 'em afloat in the wash, I designed those compartments, front and aft, you see there. Sealed tight so the water can't get in."

"I think the phrase is 'fore and aft,'" Dawes said, but Jack seemed not to take that advice to heart and just went on. "You can see that little pine thing over there, eighteen foot long, just as I planned, and floats like a feather. The big ones are oak so strong you couldn't break 'em with a cannon ball, twenty-one feet fore to stern."

"I think 'stem to stern' is the phrase you want. Or you could say, 'bow.'"

"Don't know as I'd say it, but I'll take a bow for the design. The professor took my plans to Chicago, had 'em built to my specifications by the Bagley Boat Works, none better. They won't sink, they won't roll, they won't break. Finest boats ever put on a river. You can ask the sergeant there, fixing up the caulking like I showed him."

"I'll take your word for it Mr. Sumner. Now let me ask you something else: The Major says you can use a sextant."

"Oh surely. Hadn't been for me knowin how to use a sextant, we'd still be lost on the Berthoud Trail."

"Tell me about that."

"Waal, we was on what they call the 'Berthoud Trail', though it was so little used you could call it 'lost'. I was leadin the party. We had the professor's brother, your friend Oramel Howland, my trappin partners, Bill Dunn and Billy Hawkins, or 'Missouri Rhoads' as he called himself until he got out of the purview of the Missouri constabulary. Had Mrs. Powell on her little piebald pony, weepin and carryin on the way she allers did when the professor warn't around. 'Oh Mr. Sumner,' she says, 'We are surely lost and done for without the Major to find the way.'" Jack's imitation of a meek female voice would have done credit to a jay bird.

"She called him the Major?"

"Oh yes, and she could salute pretty as you please. I said, 'Don't you worry, little lady, I'm never lost, and when the snow stops and I can shoot a star with my sextant, we'll be back on the trail as soon as you can say 'General Grant.'" And so I did and soon we were back on the trail, smart as you please."

I heard Walter snort again.

"What star was it that you shot, Mr. Sumner?"

"As I recall, it was one of those in O'Brien."

"Is that Patrick O'Brien?

"No, just O'Brien. Don't know as he had a first name, being a mythical figure, you know. It's a clutch of stars called a 'constellation.'"

"Thank you, I was wondering about that. One last question, Mr. Sumner: Who's paying for your services as chief boatman?"

"Oh, there ain't no pay. We're all volunteers, goin just for our grub and whatever minerals we might find, maybe a beaver skin or two if we're lucky."

"Thank you Mr. Sumner, and good luck."

"It won't be a matter of luck, Mr. Dawes; the trip's in good hands. You can bet a year's salary on it."

"I wouldn't take the risk, Mr. Sumner." Howland told me later that Dawes didn't have a salary.

I asked Jack, "Don't you have some concern that the Major will read Mr.Dawes' story and maybe take minor exception here and there?"

"Oh that won't get into print," he said, "Paper's owned by my brother-in-law, Bill Byers. Bill will recognize a yarn when he hears it. He'll print a story of his own makin." And Jack went to join the boys at the fire.

"Wasn't west, was Sumner. Wasn't Sumner was Keplinger."

Walter seemed to want me to know something, now that Sumner and Dawes had gone their separate ways. But I didn't know Walter's habits then, so I just let it go by, until he said again "Wasn't west." So I asked him, "What wasn't west?"

"No, not west, Wes, the Major."

"You call him Wes, not John?"

"No, Wes. Call him John if you want to get him mad. In the family we call him Wes. Wasn't Wes 'cooned it on Long's Peak. Was Sumner. Got so scared he couldn't stand up. Crawled like a raccoon with Wes ahead and Emma Dean behind trying to keep up his spirits, telling him he couldn't fall, just don't look down. Feller's a liar."

"Suspect he's just a storyteller," I told him, "but you said it wasn't Sumner, it was Keplinger?"

"Wes' student. He was along on the Berthoud Trail. Emma Dean wasn't even there. I was leadin the party, Sumner and Hawkins leadin the mules. No snowstorm neither, but we was lost just the same. Young Keplinger looked at this star with his sextant, said 'got to go northwest,' so that's where I led the party, Sumner gripin about our gettin worse lost. Found the trail soon enough. Hawkins didn't come up for some time. When he did we was shy a mule. Got away in the dark, Hawkins said. Feller's another liar. They stick together." And he started off singing to himself and poking at the oakum with his Bowie knife.

Andy Hall came back with his kit, wasn't much, just a bedroll, blanket, extra boots looked like they'd been retired on disability pension. He wanted me to write a letter to his mother so she'd know why he wasn't by for a while. I told him to write it himself and I'd look it over when he was through.

It took him longer to write it than it did to pack his kit and it was just a short little thing when he handed it over:

Dear Mother;

I am going down the Colorado River to explore that river in boats with Major Powell, the professor of the Normal College in Illinois.

You need not expect to hear from me for some time ten or twelve months at least. You can write to me at Collville, Arizona Territory give my love to all.

Yours till death
Andrew Hall

I told Andy any mother would be proud to receive such a letter. Said she surely wouldn't worry, his being with someone both a professor and a major. When I pointed out "Collville" should be "Callville," he said, "No matter. Mother can't spell either."

It reminded me I'd better write to my own mother but as she'd have to ask somebody to read it, I'd best write to Lucy instead. But I could see the weather was thickening up, so I postponed it and got on with the caulking. Sumner spotted Andy and sent him up to Jake Field's to scare up some paint. By the time he got back we had the boats pretty well caulked up, with tar spread over the lapseams, and ready for painting. We'd left the tops of the buoyancy compartments unsealed as we'd have to bail them out after the boats took on water in the swelling.

Major came up with Howland just then, and we got a taste of what we were in for, taking Andy along. "What colors do we have, Andy," said Major.

"You'll have your choice, Major sir, for Mr. Fields has a fair supply of both white and white."

First time I'd heard Major laugh, "White'll do fine, Andy. Now you and Billy Hawkins take that big boat there and choose a name for it. Oramel, I'll put Frank Goodman in with you and Seneca in that last boat."

"That's a sight of extra weight, John. He's fat's an old boar hog."

When Major said, "I expect you'll manage," I judged that another man's comfort didn't occupy his mind over much.

We got the boats painted a desperate pure white and to my mind they looked spanking and neat as a Scotia double-ender and near as big. Odd enough, the little pine boat looked smaller, though pretty, almost lady-like.

Just in time, too, as evening brought soft rain. We got tarpaulins spread over the boats so the paint wouldn't suffer and bunched ourselves up under another tarpaulin stretched over poles near the fire, where Billy and Andy were fixing supper. You could see Andy was new at the game and he was taking a little ribbing from Jack, with Bill Dunn calling discouragement from the sidelines. Andy got a little flustered by the process and didn't think it through

when he took the lid off the Dutch oven with his bare hand. He
dropped it quick enough and we won a lesson in how to curse in
Scotch. I couldn't tell you the words now, but it wasn't about any
"wee timrous beastie".

While we could follow Andy's line of thought, Frank Goodman
seemed to know the words and he followed on with a Scots song:

> *John Anderson, my jo, John*
> *When we were first aquent,*

Walter was familiar with the ballad and he piled his bass onto Frank's
baritone, near drowning it:

> *Your locks were like the raven,*
> *Your bony brow was brent*

Andy thought to make it a trio and whipped right in with a voice
like a buzz-saw. It wasn't his last attempt at song, but it came near to
being. Walter figured he was being made sport of and made a swipe
at Andy, but him sitting and Andy standing it didn't come to anything. It did raise a ruckus, though, everybody jumping up and
yelling at once, so much noise that we didn't hear the train until it
blew those four mournful notes,

> *woooooooooooooooo, woooooooooooooooo, wooooo, wooooo*

and went through Green River City, whipping along at what I judged
to be about thirty miles an hour.

It got that quiet then that we could hear the train all right,
clacking like a brood hen 'til the noise was drawn off east. Andy
had a song for the occasion, and even Walter had to laugh as Andy
rasped it out:

> *Don't you see that passin' train*
> *Goin round the bend*

Major didn't laugh, though. He was fit to be tied that our freight
car with the supplies wasn't dropped off, but I was thinking there
might be a reason, for the Lord works in mysterious ways, and it
might mean we wouldn't be leaving on the Sabbath after all.

The next day dawned bright and clear and with the sun came our car, shunted off by the westbound morning train while we were still taking in some of Billy's coffee and biscuits. Frank Goodman had joined us and Billy gave him a share of our grub. Frank said the coffee tasted muddy, no surprise since it was made with river water. Billy said, "Just you let it set a spell. The silt will settle out with the coffee grounds."

The hot desert sun had the paint on our boats more or less dry by late morning when Jack came down from town with a sign painter he'd dug up somewhere. Feller had a pot of green paint and a clutch of brushes, a pencil behind his ear, white overalls polka-dotted with paint-drops in a variety of colors, green dominant. Looked like he'd prefer another occupation but was too old to change. Major touched the hull of the small pilot boat, judged it dry enough, "We'll call this one the 'Emma Dean,' after my wife." Feller just nodded.

I told him we'd chosen "Maid of the Canyon" for my boat. He ticked the letters off on his fingers, "Fifteen letters," and he measured out the space he'd need on the hull with the handle of one of his brushes, shrugged. "You're only gettin it on one side."

Billy told him he and Andy had settled on, "Kitty Clyde's Sister" for their boat. "Seventeen letters. Cain't you do with just 'Kitty Clyde'?"

"Her sister's prettier."

"Then use *her* name for tarnation's sake."

"It's Sister we want to get into," Billy said with a smirk and Andy gave a big guffaw. "Oh, sir, he meant the boat," he said with as innocent a look as his comical face could conjure.

The feller seemed resigned when he gestured toward the last boat, "That one book-length too? I ain't got all day."

The Howlands and Frank had not settled on a name for their boat before Major sent them up to the freight yard with orders to start sorting out the supplies, so Major said, "Oh, no name on that one."

Then I heard the cook's cry, "Bull's in the corral, chain up the gaps" and joined the others at the fire for our noon meal. We were just finishing about a half hour later when Frank and the Howlands showed up and you could see Oramel was in a state. I figured something was amiss with our freight car, but it turned out it was another matter altogether. "Lookee here," he says and marched off, and we all followed. We got to his boat just in time to see the sign painting feller finishing the last "E" in "No Name" on its hull. We had a good laugh at that one but Oramel fumed and fussed and said it was bad luck to have an unnamed boat, but Major said, "Well it's got a name, Oramel, though it is a bit unusual, I agree." Jack said, "It's only on one side, Oramel."

We spent the afternoon organizing the freight for the big boats. First we went to Jake Field's root cellar, the coldest place in Green River City, where Major had stored the bacon. Jake had a regular circus of things down there: jars of canned string beans left by Noah when the waters receded, a sack of black-eyed beans spouting away in the dark, a lump of something that could have been a dead dog but wasn't. I suppose it was cold enough in there for bacon in December but it being May and nearly June, I'd have left it in the river, except maybe for thieves and coyotes. We brought it out along with the sack of rice Jake got for us, wouldn't be needed for the coolies now the railroad was built, and some dried apples, weren't dry any more. But we took them along anyway for want of anything better was offered right then.

Piled up by the river we had hundred pound sacks of flour and rice, fifty pound sacks of coffee, bags of dried apples, beans, sugar, whole sides of fat bacon, pistols, rifles, shotguns, saws, augers, barometers, sextants, duffel bags, my valise and the cast iron mess-kit I'd brought down from Fort Bridger. As the *Emma Dean* was to carry only some instruments along with the three passengers and their duffels, the rest of the freight was divided into what Howland said were, "more or less equal parts."

"Rather less than more," I said, but it didn't do any good as Howland said he had Goodman as a passenger and couldn't carry as much freight as the rest. Seemed to me I got the worst of the division when they added the whole heavy iron mess-kit to my stores. But Major just said, "We'll try it and see."

We thought Mr. Dawes had taken the morning train to Denver, but there he was with his pad and pencil, walking around through our piles of provisions, noting everything down like he was a supply sergeant himself. You could see he was doing some calculating, maybe dividing the stores into ten parts for the ten men and ten again, for the number of months we'd be on the river. "Major Powell," he said at last, "is this what you expect ten men to live on for ten months?"

"There are fish in the river and game in the canyons," Major told him. "Several of the men are professional hunters, crack shots. Why Dunn here once shot an eagle out of the air with a rifle at two hundred yards."

"A little stringy, eagles," Dawes said, and you could see Major wasn't all that tickled by the remark. "Will you be able to add to your supplies at any point along the river?"

"We'll be able to reach an Indian agency some thirty miles up the Uinta River, but they aren't likely to have much. We're depending a good deal on the skill of our hunters."

Dawes slowly looked around at our stores and focused his gaze on our arms. We had six Colt revolvers, one double barreled Le Mat pistol, which is half shotgun, four Henry and six Spencer repeating rifles, and three Remington shotguns. "I suppose you could storm Fort Bridger if all else fails," Dawes said. He was a witty feller, all right, but Major didn't seem to be in the mood for fun, and I found out why when Oramel showed me the contract he'd written out and got Major to sign. Oramel had a fine hand, and I admired the writing. Probably something he picked up working for the *Rocky Mountain News:*

Major J. W. Powell (party of the first part) William Dunn, John Sumner, O. G. Howland (parties of the second part) contract as follows:

He spelled out how the men were to care for the scientific instruments and assist in taking readings. Major had to grant them five days at a stretch for prospecting, *if not too often,* and *thirty days for hunting and trapping between 1st September and 1st December, 1869, and*

*sixty days between 1st January and 1st June, 1870... Party of the first part
to pay $25 each per month for the time employed... and the annexed price
for all skins procured.*

> *Bear: Grown grizzly $10.00 (cub $1.00)   Grown cinnamon $5.00
> Grown black $3.00*
>
> *Sheep: $1.25   Beaver: $1.00   Elk: $2.00*
>
> *Wildcat: $.50   Deer: $1.25   Otter: $3.50*

*Party of the first part to furnish boats, provisions and ammunition
for up to a year.*

Oramel said Major tried to get them to agree to pay a dollar a day
each for board, but Oramel said they'd have to add a schedule of
payments for the meat they shot, so Major dropped the subject.
Oramel didn't crack a smile but I could see the mischief in his eyes
when he said, "I fully expected the Major to ask for room rent, too."
Then he asked if I wanted him to draw up a contract for me. "My
army discharge is pay enough," I told him.

We put the boats in about sundown. The red sunset bouncing off
the white hulls made a pretty picture, and they tugged at their
mooring ropes like they were colts wanting to run. I admit I wanted
to run, too, wished we could get on the river instead of messing
around in Green River City, where everybody who could walk or
talk was making sport of us. I just wanted to get going.

Billy fed us supper early so the boys could go watch Kitty Clyde
and her sister do dances they should be ashamed of, and I was
assigned to keep guard over the supplies. I didn't mind as it gave me
a chance to write my letter to Lucy:

> *Dear Sister,*
>
> *Except for our leaving on the Sabbath, it will be a relief to
> be off tomorrow, for this crumbling adobe village is a miserable
> and sinful place. What a contrast it is with that green and
> flowery hillside where we parted over a year ago. But I take
> my family and friends with me. I have tintypes of mother and
> Aunt Marsh, Eddie and Henry, Chas. Palmers, E. Marston's,*

Porters, etc. And of course, Lucy! I have two of you. They will keep me from being lonesome, though the men are good company, if a bit rough. I don't know yet what kind of officer Major is, but he got me out of the army so I count myself lucky to be on this journey.

I plan to keep a diary of the voyage whenever we are campt and I have time, so we can share the fun of it when I return home next year. Please assure mother that I am well and in excellent spirits. You can write me through Mr. Heard to the Ute Indian Agency.

Your loving brother

Major's a good sleeper, or maybe the noise from the saloon below kept him awake 'til late. Anyway, the sun was well up and I was hungry as a hibernated bear by the time he arrived at the freight car with a mug of coffee in his hand. He didn't offer me any, no surprise, so I set off to get some at camp. No coffee there either, except some cold from the night before, which I drank, sharing Frank's view that the taste of mud was dominant. Nobody up, snores in every key and pitch, so you could fairly feel the ground shake. I shook Billy Rhoads 'til he came full awake, "Bulls in the corral, Missouri. We got to get the boats upstream. River's rising." He didn't welcome the news, but he pointed me to where I might find a Mormon church service. I came in late and missed part of the sermon about the later saints, but the hymns were fine, if sung a little off-key.

I got to camp just in time to hear the cook's, "Roll out! Roll out! Bulls in the corral! Chain up the gaps! Roll out! Roll out! Roll out!" The men crawled in some sort of slow-time from the tents, blowing off gas and puffing out fumes of bad whiskey. "We tried to drink up all the whiskey in Green River City," Jack told me, "but Jake Fields persisted in making it faster than we could drink it." I think it was a tight race by the way they moved as if groping through a fog. Oramel Howland forgot to stop leaning when he went to wash his face in the river and had to be hauled out by his brother, Seneca.

We wolfed down some bacon and biscuits and drank copious amounts of bad coffee, Frank taking his share but making out like it was a chore to drink. Then Jack ordered us into the boats, "Board your piratic craft or spend the rest of your lives in this miserable place of sin and frolic." Oramel wasn't interested in carrying Frank upstream, so we sent him off on foot to tell Major we were coming.

The *Emma Dean* pushed off first and I could see Jack and Bill Dunn knew how to handle a boat. They kept her neat as you please in the slow water near the east bank and made solid progress against the tide. I went off next, Walter Powell in the bow and me in the stern rowing hard to keep the *Maid* steady as she wanted to yaw without ballast of freight to keep her steady.

Kitty Clyde's Sister came next and I was glad I was rowing backwards and could watch the show. You could tell Andy and Billy were more used to laying a whip across the back of a lazy ox than they were of pulling an oar. Billy would pull first on one oar then the other while Andy pulled them both together. They tangled oars and got crossways to the tide and grounded themselves on a sandbar in the middle of the river. The *No Name* came up behind and by the Howlands tugging on the oars on one side while Billy and Andy pushed off on the other, they got *Sister* free. She headed for the bank and kept right on going 'til she encountered it. Billy shouted out, "She won't gee nor haw worth a cuss." And Andy said, "She ain't broke yet!"

The good citizens of Green River weren't missing the fun. They'd assembled on the trestle bridge and were jeering and shouting to beat the band but the deaf-mute wasn't there and truth be told I didn't miss him. The bridge loomed up in black silhouette against the morning sun, red with dust, so it looked like the bars of a cell in a prison that has caught fire. It made me a little uneasy, and I was glad to get to the little beach and start loading our supplies.

We put a few hundred pounds of instruments, clothing, Major's inflatable life jacket, and some small tools in the *Emma Dean*. Each of the big boats got roughly a ton of tools, clothing and provisions tucked in two cuddies, fore and aft, with some odds and ends sitting under our feet in the open compartment. You could see my *overloaded* boat was lower in the water than the others. "About a hand lower than the other mules," Jack said, but Major wasn't in a mood to make any changes. Then Major told us how the trip was to be run and showed us his intended flag signals. He would go ahead in the pilot boat, scouting out the way. We were to maintain a distance of one hundred yards between boats whenever we could and especially when making landings. "A flag waved to the left means keep to the left of the *Emma Dean*, a flag to the right means keep to the right. If I wave it to the right, then to the left, then straight down, it means, 'danger, land at once.'" I could see Howland wasn't taking this all in, and he confessed later to having "a head bigger'n a beaver dam" and wished for simpler signals.

Jake Fields gave us the noon dinner, buffalo steak and eggs, grateful I guess for the money he'd made off the crew with his whiskey. He offered us a parting glass, but I declined, it being the Sabbath. Major declined too, saying it smelled like an army hospital. "Hair of the dog," says Jack, and the other men partook of the mongrel stuff. When we left, Howland did some business with Jake, passing money and taking something I couldn't see before he hid it in the bib of his overalls, except to know it was blue.

When we came back to the boats, there were a dozen or so townsfolk gathered nearby, and just about the entire remaining population was clustered up on the bridge. Dawes had come to shake the crews' hands all around and wish us luck. As we pushed off the *Maid*, Walter pointed to a small man with reddish hair, "Irishman, name of Maguire," Walter said. "Took him at poker last night." Maguire was trying to lay bets on how far we'd get before the river got us. I guess he wanted to get even. "High field is any place below Brown's Hole," he called out, but nobody was willing to bet we'd get that far. As we drew free of the shore, Maguire said to Dawes in a near shout so we could hear, "There they go, six drunks, a boy, a cripple and a loony."

"That's only nine," Dawes said, "They've just signed on an Englishman as well."

"Sure it's two loonies then!"

Walter went for his Bowie knife, but he was at the forward oars and we were afloat, which probably saved him the embarrassment of being hanged and us some delay in departing. A harmless "Son of an Irish bitch" was all he could fling at him. And Maguire flung back, "A hex and a pox on ye, you cheatin barsted," so I reckon they scored it about even.

We eased out into the river, the *Emma Dean* first, my boat a hundred yards back. As each boat crossed the slow water near the shore and got to the middle, the tide picked it up, the way a mother cat does a kitten, and drew it downriver at six or seven miles an hour. When the *Emma Dean* went under the bridge, the crowd shifted to the downstream side, hooting and jeering or calling, "Godspeed", about half and half. When we passed under I could see the deaf-mute had joined the group. He was being egged on by his brother and was doing his dumb show of scaling imaginary walls, falling back into imaginary water, gasping for breath, sinking beneath imaginary waves. Over and over. Over and over. We all saw it except Major, who was facing downstream and who just waved back over his shoulder at the crowd with his little flag. The brother's laughing was the last thing I heard before the growing gurgle of the river around our hulls drowned out the sounds of the crowd.

The bridge, black against the sky, reminded me again of a prison cell and, as I was leaving the army behind, I told myself that it meant I was getting *out* of prison, but I wasn't totally easy with that conclusion. *Sister* grounded again on the same sandbar.

We made maybe ten or twelve miles on an easy stream when we went into camp. There isn't much to do at night when you're camping. After you set up the tents, make a fire, eat your supper, about the only thing left is swapping lies, that and singing. That first night everybody was gay as a gull from easy floating or from Jake's whisky or, like me, just plain glad to be moving. It seemed everybody had a story to tell. Walter Powell bragged about how he skinned that Irishman at poker, drew three kings and beat the Irishman's three queens, laughed that snorting laugh of his. I don't hold much with card playing so I only half listened and thought about what I'd write in my journal come morning, when the men laughing got my attention, and I saw that Andy and Billy were doing a demonstration of the can-can dancers they'd seen at Jake Field's. But it was Jack Sumner's story that got us all to laughing the most.

"Now there was a feller at the bar, name of Hook, John, Theodore, Frederick, whatever. He had more aliases than Missouri Rhoads here and was just as shy of the sheriff." Billy just grinned, took it like a sport and Jack went on, "Hook's a miner. I come across him once out near Long's Peak where I was trappin one winter. He and a dozen or so other rough stock had a little silver mine they was workin. Vein ran out and they come down to Green River City a few days back to assay what ore they had and get some grub, look for a new venture and such like. Well he most naturally had heard of our trip and knowin I'd panned for gold from time to time, he couldn't get it out of his head that we was goin down the river prospectin for gold. Said nobody would risk such a trip just to make a damnfool map. The longer the night went on, the drunker he got and the more him and his cronies got fixed on the idea that they should go down the river too, stake some claims before we snapped 'em all up or them two prospectors did, left in a boat just a few days ago. Said if a one-armed greenhorn from the East could do it they surely could. I asked him where he was goin to get his boats, seein we had ours built in Chicago. He said, 'Bulls and taters, man. There's a hundred empty shacks here in Green River City, got plenty lumber in 'em.'"

When Jack was finished, Frank said, "They should have retained Andy here to help with the design." Maybe it was the way the English talk, but he didn't excite much laughter from the men and none from Andy, who gave him a look and muttered something I couldn't hear.

Major said pretty much what I'd been thinking, "They're probably sober by now and have thought better of the idea. Otherwise, they'll overtake us if we continue at today's pace. Let's get some sleep and be off early tomorrow. Billy, you get the fire going at first light."

It seemed that Walter hadn't heard him for he just started in singing in that deep rumbling voice:

Ya, ya, Darkies, laugh away wid me...

I suspect he went through Old Shady from stem to stern, sitting alone there by the fire, rocking back and forth, sometimes looking up at the three quarter moon, but I can't fully attest to his finishing, seeing I was asleep before the second verse was fully accomplished.

ROCKY MOUNTAIN NEWS

DENVER, COLORADO.   MAY 25, 1869.

RIVER PIONEERS ENTER THE GREAT UNKNOWN.

—

GREEN RIVER, WYOMING - MAY 24.

To the wild cheers and cries of "Godspeed" from the good citizens of Green River City, Wyoming, a party of ten brave men, led by Major John Wesley Powell, a hero of the battle of Shiloh, set out today to explore the Green and Colorado Rivers to their mouth in the Gulf of California. The Colorado has been explored and found navigable from its mouth upstream as far as Grand Wash, Arizona, but above that point, Lieutenant Joseph Christmas Ives, who led several pioneering expeditions in the area, has declared that, "It seems intended by nature that the Colorado River, along the greater portion of its lonely and majestic way, shall be forever unvisited and undisturbed." It is Major Powell's intention to put the lie to that assertion, but if he is to succeed it will require traversing nearly a thousand miles of unknown and unmapped country, on a river that has been seen at only a few crossing points between the mouth of the Uinta River and the Rio Virgen. It is known that the Grand and Green Rivers join to form the Colorado River, but not even that junction has been discovered.

Major Powell's crew consists of his brother, Captain Walter Powell; five free trappers, including his chief boatman, John Sumner and Sumner's trapping partner, Wm Dunn; Sergeant George Bradley, recently of the Cavalry at Fort Bridger, and Mr. Frank Goodman, a British subject. Among the trappers is this newspaper's erstwhile printer and sometime editor, Mr. O. G. Howland and his younger brother, Seneca. Two young bucks, Andrew Hall and Wm Rhodes, round out this brave band.

The boats, built in Chicago to Major Powell's specifications, consist of three twenty-one foot oaken craft, powered by two sets of twelve foot oars and steered by an eighteen foot sweep oar at the stern. It is estimated that the boats weigh five hundred pounds each and will carry a ton of cargo, including provisions sufficient for ten men for a year, if supplemented from time to time by fish and game killed by the hunters.

An eighteen foot pilot boat is made of pine and is similarly oared. Each boat has two watertight compartments bow and stern, so they cannot sink, and two cuddies for cargo. The pilot boat will carry Major Powell, Mr. Sumner and Wm Dunn. It is the Major's intention to scout out the river ahead with this boat and determine how to proceed from that point. His conclusions will be communicatred to the other boats by flag signals using the wigwag system brought to perfection during the late war between the States in which every American in the party, saving the then too young Mr. Hall, was engaged.

The stated objective of the journey is to provide reliable maps of the river and its canyons, the height and composition of the cliffs and otherwise to open up the last Great Unknown in the United States and its territories.

Major Powell's trip is sponsored by the Smithsonian Institution and Illinois Normal University, but is privately funded. Some of those funds derive from Captain Powell's skill at the poker table where he separated a handsome sum from Green River City's resident Irishman.

PART TWO

MIDDLE PASSAGE

To trace the history of a river is to trace the history of the soul, the history of the mind descending and arising in the body. In both, we constantly seek and stumble upon divinity, which, like the cornice feeding the lake and the spring becoming a waterfall, feeds, spills, falls and feeds itself over and over again.

GRETEL EHRLICH

"Roll out! Roll out! Bulls in the corral! Chain up the gaps! Roll out! Roll out! Roll out!"

Truth is, I'd rather come from sleep by myself, gradual as dreams allow, but Billy Rhoads' call to breakfast was anyway better than an army bugle, and waking to a day on the river beat almost anything else I could think of. The rhythmic rolling sound of the water in my sleep was like a low lullaby, and that morning there were sounds of geese overhead, looking for a day's resting place, meadow larks and doves behind us in the trees and, on the river, grebes, dressed like they were going to a fancy ball, black with a white breast, a white stripe down the middle of the back, a white beak, pointed as a whittled branch. They didn't seem to mind my being nearby washing my face in the river, just glided along with perfect grace, heads bobbing, hunting forage. A great blue heron pumped his way down the river, his wings flapping so slow it didn't seem possible he could stay aloft, grace of a different kind, taken easy. His legs stuck straight out in back, like they were a steering rudder, and his neck was the shape of a sink-trap, so you wondered how he ever worked a fish through it.

Breakfast was only coffee and biscuits, "Major's orders," Rhoads said, "so we can be on the river timely." I could have done with a bit more sustenance, but the biscuits were fine and the coffee acceptable. At least I found it so, but Frank complained again that it tasted muddy. It struck me that the English should stick to tea. When Major came up to camp from downstream, he still had Jake Field's grey, white-flecked coffee mug ready for a refill. Whether purloined, given or neglected return, it's not for me to say, but he'd acquired it all the same. "He's attached to it," Sumner said, "surgical removal the only answer." Major said he'd walked down the river a mile or so and found it was clear of rocks and falls, so it looked like a good start to our first full day on the river.

When we were about to launch the *Emma Dean*, a strange thing happened, at least a thing I'd never seen before. Two peregrine falcons came down from somewhere, almost wingtip to wingtip, skimming the river, with their little beaks making furrows in the water, and glided downstream 'til they were out of sight. Major signaled for us to stop the launching, and just stared after the birds, then he said, "The gods are sending us a good omen. We'll have a good day." As there is only one God, I didn't hold much with Major's omen.

Andy said he thought "Perry green" might refer to the color of the feathers, but Howland told him, "Peregrine means pilgrim, and we are making a pilgrimage." Howland had a sort of twinkle in his eye so I mistrusted he was serious. I'd been thinking about Andy's slight schooling since I read his letter and hoped Major might see it too and take him in hand, him being a professor and all. The falcons came and went, but it seemed every time we turned a sharp bend, there they were, until in mid-morning they found an updraft convenient and soared out of sight.

It was almost as if our luck flew off with the falcons, because that's where our troubles began. I was steering easy, drifting with the tide wondering how my *overloaded* boat would fare in a rapid when I saw the *Emma Dean* fetch up short on a sandbar. Major tried to signal danger with his little flag, but he was knocked off balance, and the *No Name* and *Sister* grounded behind him. Being last, I had space to slip around the other boats and pass without touching. Walter and I rowed the *Maid* to shore and had some amusement watching and calling to the other boats while they tried to work free with the oars, first pushing one side then the other while Andy shouted, "Gee" and "Haw," but it was no good. They were stuck solid, and as the water was full of snow melt, it was of a temperature suitable only for beavers, which inspired a certain reluctance to plunge into it. Finally, Major ordered Andy and Seneca into the water. They pulled off their boots, jumped in and pushed off all three boats in turn, yelling "Hoo, hoo," like they were owls crossed with doves. "The boats don't drive like a mule but they're just as stubborn," Billy Rhoads said when he got down to us.

We eased our way down the river for another hour or so, the tide slowing and the river widening, until Andy and Seneca began to complain of being chilled from their wetting, so Major ordered a halt and we built up a driftwood fire so they could dry their clothes. Billy boiled some coffee and fried up some fat bacon. Now, bacon is supposed to be strips of fat laced with lean, fried up crisp, but this bacon was three or four inches thick, all clear fat, no way to make it crisp. When Frank complained, Billy said, "There's an old American custom, Frank. If you find any lean in fat bacon, you get to kiss the girl of your choice, same as if you'd found a red ear of corn at a huskin bee."

"Bacon's villainous," Jack said, "you boys got to see about getting us some game here." That might have been another omen because just then five mountain sheep appeared on the edge of the clift above our camp. The boys let out a whoop, Jack and Frank and Andy all grabbed repeater rifles and started blasting away, but the sheep just ran straight up the clift and disappeared. Then one old ram reappeared for an instant looking down on our camp as if daring us to catch him.

The men took out after them and were gone for several hours, came back with two breadpans Jack found in an abandoned cabin and a small rabbit. Billy Rhoads had better luck, though of an unusual kind. He found a small lamb asleep on a clift above camp, grabbed it by the heels and flung it down to camp. Bill Dunn butchered it so quick I thought he was going to eat it raw, right then and there. Sumner said the lamb was probably dead when Billy found it. That's what they call "sour grapes," I guess.

I said I thought it remarkable that the sheep could run up such a steep slope of solid rock. Jack said, "Waal, you see, mountain sheep have cupped hooves that are sharp all the way around, so they can get a grip almost anywhere." I thought, let them shoot one and we'll see, but I didn't say as much.

We waited out an hour of heavy rain under our ponchos, then embarked again. After another eight or ten miles, the boys began to agitate to stop and cook the lamb for supper, though it was only four in the afternoon. Major gave the order to go into camp, we made up a good driftwood fire and Rhoads cooked the lamb. We ate our fill and had a smoke. We were content to doze away the afternoon, but Major was restless and decided to climb the clift on the west bank looking for fossils. The clift was kind of black and menacing looking, so I followed along to help should he get into trouble what with only one arm to hang on with. He did fine though; at one place he inched up a narrow crevice by pressing his back against one side and his feet against the other. I followed using the same technique, but truth be told I wasn't comfortable with it, wondered what would happen if the crack widened and I ended up horizontal. Next, Major let go a handhold on one side of a three-foot wide crevice, jumped across to a six inch shelf on the other side and grabbed a cornice there, looking down on four hundred feet of empty space. I took the long way round. It doesn't bother me to look down on deep nothing, but I'd rather get there safe. Major seemed to look on the whole thing as a kind of game, see who could win, him or the clift.

We arrived at the top at about the same time, me puffing for breath, Major breathing easy as if he was asleep, and we saw something that stole my breath in a different way. It was a sight more unusual than the falcons, and that was the view. There was no end to it in any direction, just faded off to nothing. To the north and east we could see the rightly named Green River bad lands, desolate and treeless, mesas and buttes with shapes man couldn't conceive of carving, but the wind did, and in every color, crosswise bands of red, brown, grey, blue, black, like God was a painter. To the south, stretching all the way to a snow-capped, limitless east-west line of mountains, we saw verdant forests, vast valleys, unexplored canyons and snow fields glittering in the rose light of sunset. I asked Major if they had names. "Except for the Uinta Mountains you see there, no," he said, "but they will, Sergeant, they will."

Back at camp Major described the view as, "Three hundred sixty degrees." Jack asked me later what that meant and I told him, "full-circle." He said Major could have said that in the first place. He went on to say, "I don't see the recreation in climbing, like it fine down here at the river's edge. See no need to look down and see it smaller. I'd be pleased to look on the view, but would prefer it be brought down to me, instead of t'other way round."

We would have dozed the day away, but Major ordered another launch. We floated along on flat water, drifting with the tide, me steering with the big sweep oar and Walter rowing a little whenever my *heavy* boat fell behind. The river was quiet but gurgled against the walls when they came in close, like the sound of sea around a sailboat's rudder when she's trim and sailing true. It was about as pleasant an experience as you could want of an afternoon following a heavy rain. I didn't even mind the crows nattering at us, but I guess Andy did, for he shot one out of the air, and we watched it tumble to the river like an acrobat turning cartwheels. "Waste of ammunition," Walter said, "not a bird you can eat." "We'll be eating crow soon enough," I told him, "if the hunters' aim doesn't improve." I thought better of it as soon as I said it, thinking Walter was a hunter and might take it wrong, but he just snorted and squirted some tobacco juice over the side.

There was a bend up ahead and as we approached it the sound of the river grew louder and louder. Just before we reached the bend, Major signaled with his flag that we should land, but he'd waited too long again and the *Emma Dean* struck a sandbar, *No Name* doing the same right behind her. I was next but had enough distance to figure I could slip around like we did before and show how it was done, but "pride goeth before a fall" and we went hard aground a few dozen yards downstream of the others. The boys in *Sister* had more sense and landed upstream of the other boats. Walter and I tried tugging and pushing with the oars but it was no good, so we both jumped into waist-deep water, freed the *Maid* and froze ourselves, the water so cold it made my head hurt.

Bill Dunn got in the river and pried off the *Emma Dean*, his oily buckskins shedding water like a duck's feathers, but the *No Name* was another matter altogether. First Seneca got in the water and pulled from the front, but he couldn't budge her. Then Frank jumped in too, pushing from behind. Still no go, so Oramel joined them in the frigid water, and they began to rock and push and pull and it still didn't work until the Howlands took the oars and pried the boat from the side. Frank was pushing and lifting from the back, puffing like a blowing horse, when the *No Name* broke free and ran down with the tide. The Howlands grabbed the gunwales and mounted all right, but Frank was caught off guard and just had time to grab the long steering oar and was drawn along behind, flapping like a caught fish. We got all the boats to a small beach and hauled Frank in like he was a trout on a line. While we were building a fire and talking about the groundings and Major was scouting out the rapids ahead, Howland whispered that Frank was "Useless as tits on a boar hog, can't fathom why John took him along." Jack said, "I did. Saw some folded greenbacks pass but one way. He's a paying passenger."

When Major came back he said it looked like rapids ahead and we'd best wait 'til morning to tackle them. Then he lit into me, "When I signal to land, then by God you land." It was just like being back in the Army, but Walter told Major, "Boat's got too much freight, Wes; 'thout that we would have got down all right."

This time Major listened, so I thought maybe it paid to be demented, and he ordered our barometers and half the mess-kit transferred to the *No Name*. "It's a mistake, John, we've got too much weight already, what with three men in crew," Oramel said, but Major wasn't in a mood to listen, or he didn't like being called John, for he narrowed his eyes a bit when he looked at Howland and said, "You'll manage if you keep your wits about you."

Then Jack said, "I suspicion the other boats are too close behind to follow your signals, Professor, 'specially since they can only see 'em by looking over their shoulders rowin." Major tugged on his beard a little bit like he was pulling out a thought, "All right, from now on we stay two hundred yards apart." Howland said, "Can't see that far, John." Then he added that he wasn't going to be the last in line if he could help it. You could see the remark didn't please Major; he stared at Howland for a minute, like he couldn't figure the man, then he walked away.

When Billy got the fire up to a respectable flame, the other boys who'd got themselves wetted stripped to the buff and dried themselves at the fire, but I don't hold too much with public nakedness so I went behind some willows and changed into my other outfit. Andy said he figured out I didn't want to show the other boys up, said I probably "had twelve inches but didn't use it as a rule." I thought it wasn't Christian to be so crude, but I'd heard worse in the Army, so didn't say anything.

It looked to be coming on rain again, so we campt for the night. We spent part of the time while Billy and Andy were making up supper trying to judge how far we'd come on the river, and how far if it was straight and flat like a prairie, so Howland could do a map, a job that Major assigned to him for no good reason I could see. Major said he guessed we'd come eighteen miles, I thought twenty-five, and Jack said twenty. "That makes it twenty-one by water," Oramel declared and Major wanted to know how he got to that figure. "Can't put three guesses on the map, John, so I averaged them out." Major declared that we'd do that every night, and Howland would make his map that way.

I was thinking mapmaking on a river was a job I was pleased to leave to somebody else. You can think of a river running north and south or east and west, but it's a rare day that it does either for very long. A river has a mind of its own and it meanders, like thought, wherever the mood strikes it, sometimes this way, sometimes that. I couldn't figure how Howland was going to handle that on his map with nothing but water distance to guide him, then I saw the logic of it: A boat is rowed backwards if you think of how the oarsman sits. He can only see where his boat's going if he looks over his shoulder. It's hard enough to recall how directions change when you're looking straight ahead, but if you're facing backward, east is west and north is south and it's like a game of blind man's buff, being spun round and round and having to guess where you're facing when you stop. Now, as Howland's boat had three people in it, only two sets of oars, he could face forward, like Major, and he could take a compass reading at each bend, if he wasn't in a rapid or otherwise stressed. So he could split up that twenty one miles into fractions he had in his head on how far we'd gone between turns. I could say my times table pretty good, and I'm easy with fractions of halves and fourths and eighths, there being two pints to a quart, four quarts to a gallon and eight quarts to a peck, four pecks to a bushel, but beyond these and some few of the thirds, fractions are a source of some discomfort for me.

Andy Hall walked up a ravine a ways and found a nice little stream with sweet tasting water that ran from a gully in the clift side, rain runoff no doubt, and he brought a couple of buckets for use in the making of supper. When Walter saw the clear water he asked Billy for the use of a kettle to boil his socks in as they had got full of river mud when he was pushing off the *Maid*. "You ain't puttin' them things in my cookpots," Billy told him. "Fetch yourself a bailing can and park 'em by the fire there, next the coffee pot." Billy gave him some fresh water, and Walter did as he was bid.

With a fair amount of time to prepare supper, Billy and Andy had cooked up a fine meal, bacon, the rest of the lamb, beans, biscuits, stewed dried apples, all washed down with sweet stream water. It was dark by the time we got to our coffee and Frank complained again about it tasting muddy. Billy said, "That's funny. Andy, didn't you make the coffee with fresh water?" Andy said he had; then Billy took the lid off the coffee pot, reached over it with his Bowie knife and fished one of Walter's socks out of the bailing can next to it. He held it dripping and hissing over the fire, saying, "Now who in hell put his muddy socks in the coffee?" We had a good laugh and I think Frank took it all right until Andy said, "Beastly behavior," in Frank's accent, and that didn't seem to go over very well, Frank raising up his head a bit and staring at Andy in a way no stranger would call friendly. Frank got up then and I thought maybe he was going to go for Andy, as a man might if he was touchy. His big frame in the firelight cast a long shadow that seemed aimed at Andy, but Frank just went off to his tent. That kind of broke up the evening and we all retired.

We didn't sleep long though, for we had a night of it like I haven't seen since cod-fishing in the Atlantic. The rain came down in bursts like cannon fire and the wind blew so hard my tent-pegs pulled out on one side, so I spent the night wrapped in canvas like a mummy. Most of the boys had paired up in tents to keep warm, but I'd brought my own tent down from Bridger and preferred to bunk alone. Dunn was alone, too, as his trapping partner, Jack Sumner, was tenting with Major. Frank was sharing Walter Powell's tent but I didn't think that would last long, because Walter was inclined to wake up yelling, from the war I expect, and Frank was big enough to fill a tent by himself.

In the morning the wind had died but the rain kept on and it turned cold as April in Maine. Though the river was swift, I was glad to get going, just to shake the cold by rowing. In a short time we came to the first rapid you could rightly call by that name and ran it without stopping, or thinking for that matter, even Major concentrating on being warm instead of scouting out the safest course. *Sister* grounded again, as the boys hadn't yet figured how to hoe the same furrow, but it wasn't serious, just Billy Rhoads in the river, where it was probably warmer anyway.

The clifts began to get higher and near vertical and the river got narrower, maybe a hundred feet wide where it had been two hundred fifty. It had the same amount of water in it though, and the water was surely going to get where it was going. What the river lost in width it had to make up by getting deeper or flowing faster. For a time it chose depth then switched around to speed. It didn't do it quiet though; in that narrow space, with the walls getting steeper and closer together and the water roaring through, you'd think a mountain was crumbling in on you. Still, it had a feeling of safety about it, like lying on a battlefield when you know the artillery is going over your head. I guess Major felt the same way as he just sat there, holding on with his one hand and looking downriver as calm as if he was out rowing of a Sunday with his wife. Jack said it helped to face forward and maybe Major's wearing a life preserver had something to do with it. As for himself, Jack said that between looking over his shoulder for rocks and looking up to see if the clifts were falling in, he felt like one of those dolls with the heads that bob whenever you pick them up or set them down.

When we stopped for dinner, Jack and Major made a great show of looking at the sun through some colored glass and judging when it was exactly at its zenith and setting their watches to twelve o'clock. I didn't own a watch but thought we ought to keep the same time we started with, to know how long we'd been gone. Major said we needed to keep changing our watches to figure out longitude and when we got to Henry's Fork, which he thought we'd reach in a day or two, he'd show us. He'd hid a chronometer, a sextant and another barometer and some flour in a cave a few months before and intended to pick them up. Figuring latitude and longitude was something I could wait a while to learn, if I ever could learn it, but Howland was keen to know so he could put them on his map.

Then Jack and Major got out our barometers and checked them over. The glass tube was broken on one of them and the mercury was lost, but Major said he had more of each cached at Henry's Fork and that he'd teach Jack how to repair it when we got there. It looked like Henry's Fork was going to be a regular classroom for things I wasn't anxious to know. Major took a barometer reading and said, "The altitude here is 6025 feet above sea level. Since we're going to the sea at the Gulf of California, we have just that amount to descend. The mouth of the Rio Virgen is seven hundred feet above sea level, so we have about a mile to descend to that point." When I asked him how far we had come down already, he said, "Fifty feet." We had a ways to go.

While Billy and Andy were making dinner I climbed the clift with Major, taking a barometer, so we could measure the height of the clift. Major explained that if you take a reading of the barometer at the river and another at the clift top at the same time, you can tell how high the clift is by subtracting one altitude from the other. He told Jack to take another reading at one o'clock and we would do the same at the top of the clift.

When we got to the top we could see the river twisting and

turning for miles and I could see how the thing was laid out. It didn't lie snug and cozy between banks like a low stream but seemed to be attacked from each side by breaks in the clift walls, runnels, gullies, ravines, crevices, canyons until if you saw it like a bird did, it would resemble the tap root of a great pine, with roots branching off at random, some half its own size, some smaller, but all with their own rootlets and so on until you were down to some just the size of a hair. It put me in mind of a medical chart I once saw in a surgeon's office showing how the blood circulated out from the heart through arteries and back through veins. Same thing with the water running to the river, like blood in the veins, running to the heart.

The river ran south where we were, slicing through a mountain running east and west, and that meant the sun would drop behind a clift like a falling stone. We'd have an early sunset and a late sunrise. When the river runs east and west for a stretch, the sun will tarry and slip into the river slow and quiet, red as our camp fire, and we'll have a long day.

Major got the barometer out and took off the little leather flap that held the mercury in the glass tube. Then he hooked on a little basin or pan and upended it. When the mercury flowed into the pan the air pressure left most of it still in the tube. Major read off the inches of mercury and noted it In his book. Then he took the temperature and wrote that down. When I asked him how high the clift was, he said, "About 1200 feet, but we won't know exactly until we get to camp and compare my readings with Jack's." I decided not to pursue the point then, but when we got down to dinner, I saw the reason of it. He told us each inch of difference between his reading and Jack's was 900 feet. When I asked him what the temperature reading was for he said that if there was a difference in temperature between the river and the clift top, he'd have to change the 900 to some other number from a little chart he had, but it would always lie between nine hundred and a thousand. I saw no need to research this further.

With the sun bright and warm over us for much of the afternoon it was almost as good as boating to a picnic. We made another twelve miles ("Only ten," Sumner said) when we could see the night was coming on so we began to look for a campsite, and there the hunters got lucky. Flocks of Canada geese and mallard ducks came downriver looking for their own camping place. Dunn brought down a mallard and Sumner got a goose. Andy Hall blasted away and missed every time. Walter said in a voice could have been a crow's, "We'd better teach the ducks to caaaw, then maybe the boy can hit one." Second time I heard him make a joke, so I thought maybe being in the same boat with him would have some merit after all.

Two birds among three shooters wasn't a record, but I thought there might be hope after all of having fresh meat now and again. I was less disposed to that idea when we campt in the early dusk and saw a blacktail deer grazing. Frank Goodman blasted at it with a Spencer rifle, but it just bounded into a cottonwood grove like nothing had happened, and of course it hadn't.

"He's too swift for ye, only stayed a quarter hour," Andy said. It seemed to me the pot was calling the kettle black, so I was glad when Frank came back with, "I note the mallard population did not suffer from your efforts."

Billy made a green wood spit for the birds, turning it from time to time while the beans were baking, and by dark we had a fine meal, goose, duck, beans and biscuits. Nobody had any tall stories to hand so Frank gave us some sea shanteys sung in a clear baritone that had a kind of plangent edge to it. He sang mostly English songs and one of them he said was called *Leaving Liverpool*:

> *Farewell to thee my own true love,*
> *I am going far away.*
> *I am bound for California*
> *But I know that I'll return some day.*

Andy mumbled, "I hope not," but Frank heard him and stopped singing. He gave Andy a look that would wither a plant and said, "You sing then, little man." But Andy seemed to lose his voice.

I expected Major to say something, for there was a silence that wasn't truly comfortable. He didn't, so I tried out my idea about the river being like blood in our bodies, and Howland said, "De motu cordis et sanguines," which he said meant, "The motion of the heart and blood." Jack said, "Oramel, you'd save yourself a heap of trouble if you spoke American in the first place instead of French."

We judged the rain was over for the night so we didn't bother with the tents, just laid our blankets over some willow branches and had a fine sleep. Until the rain came again. It was a bitter-cold, biting rain, like a Fall line storm in New England, and by morning we were all cold and wet and cranky as a crone, nobody saying much, except for Billy cursing the wet firewood. He didn't get much of a fire made, but he managed to boil some coffee and fry up some bacon, and we had last night's leftover biscuits. When he went to take a plate to Major, as he had been doing regular, he stumbled over Walter's boot and spilled some hot coffee on him. That wasn't popular with Walter who cursed Billy and leaped to his feet. If it hadn't been for Bill Dunn and Seneca Howland jumping between them, we'd of had a fight on our hands. Major just chuckled, but Walter wasn't ready to let it go, "I'll tan your hide fer ya," he told Billy, but Billy just said, "And I'll pizen yer damned coffee."

As if the rain hadn't already done it, the quarrel put a damper on things, and there wasn't much conversation in the boats that morning, which I guess we wouldn't of heard anyway, being two hundred yards apart. Walter was sullen and bent to the oars as if he needed the exercise. It was all right with me because he supplied power for both of us, so I sat easy, just wagging the steering oar from time to time. The only excitement was some yelling from *Sister*, and when I looked where they were pointing I saw a cinnamon bear loping up a trail on the west side, too far away for the hunters to get a shot, as if they'd have hit it anyway. By late morning we fetched our first landmark, Henry's Fork, where Major's instruments were stowed. When we landed and saw signs of an Indian camp, Major said he was afraid the instruments had been plundered. Jack said, "Barometer tubes make good beads, you break 'em up right. And you take them little wheels out'n the chronometer, you got yourself some fine hair ornaments." And Andy said, "Sextant heap bad medicine, you throw 'em in river."

Major was already nervous as a long-tailed cat in a roomful of rocking chairs, but he near threw a fit when Andy let out a loud war whoop. "Dammit, Andy, you'll excite every brave in hearing distance." Thing is, Andy had been an Indian fighter with the Cavalry, and he could see the camp was a long way from new.

No damage had been done to the instruments, but the sack of flour had been invaded by packrats and we had to leave it. We found a sextant, a chronometer, another barometer, some extra glass tubes and a jar of mercury. It being dinner time or nearly, Billy made up a fire and Major told those who'd listen how to determine longitude. He said there were three hundred sixty degrees in a circle and he swept his one arm around over his head like the sky was a school slate and he was writing on it. "Now," he said, "since the earth rotates once every twenty-four hours, that means it rotates fifteen degrees every hour. So you set your watch by the sun at its zenith and you find out what time it is in Greenwich, England, where the longitude is zero degrees, and figure the hours in between. Then you take that number and multiply it by fifteen. That gives you degrees of longitude right where you are."

Howland looked troubled, "How do you know what time it is in England?" "That's where the chronometer comes in," Major told him, "It's always set to Greenwich, England time." "But it ran down while it was in the cave," Howland said. "How are you going to set it to Greenwich time now?"

"Oh, I know the longitude here," he said, "so I can figure the time by working backwards. It's the rule of three. If I know the two times I can determine longitude. If I know the longitude and one of the times, I can determine the other time." Howland was probably the happiest about this information, but I could see Jack Sumner was keen on it too, so I guess he'd taken his scientific duties to heart.

After dinner, Major took away whatever good feeling Howland had by storing the new-found instruments in the *No Name* and waving off Oramel's protests that he was already overloaded, "taking into account Frank's poundage." "They don't weigh much," was all Major said.

MINNIE CLYDE,
KITTY CLYDE'S SISTER.

MAY 27   ASHLEY FALLS

We drifted lazy on smooth water all afternoon, passing a Mormon ranch and some other places showing signs of civilization until we came to a canyon nobody could have seen before without telling of it, and it wasn't on the Fremont or Warren maps Major had got from Army Ordnance. The canyon walls were sheer and smooth and were a handsome bright vermilion in color. Major signaled us to land on the right, and when we had the boats beached, we just stood there admiring the color. Just then a flock of a hundred or so white pelicans wheeled in silhouette against the canyon wall in a formation so perfect and so tight the spaces between looked like opposing red birds. It was a fine sight, and we campt for the beauty of the place.

On the canyon walls between bands of hard red granite, there were layers of the softer limestone, buff and grey, that in places arched down to the river's edge. Major and I were able to find hand and footholds in them where the wind and rain had carved ridges out of the soft rock. Major wouldn't take any help and, truth be told, he didn't need it. He had a kind of little dance, leaping from handhold to handhold, letting go one and swinging his one arm up in time to grasp the next one. It made my stomach jump up nearer my throat to watch him, so I gave it up, concentrated on my own navigation.

We got to the top and saw a view that was grand beyond

conception. We looked down twelve hundred feet to a river that seemed as deep and calm as a lake, gleaming in the sun, winding like a silver serpent through vertical clifts of flaming red rock. I confess I lost my powers of voice when I looked on God's handiwork. Major said, "We'll call this 'Flaming Gorge'" but to me it was more like Eden, and I thought, *And whatever name He gave them, that was the name thereof.* An eagle soared between the clift tops, and a whole herd of deer scampered over the plateau, wolves trailing them. I thought, if Adam hadn't named these creatures already, Major would do it now.

Standing there marveling at God's handiwork, I couldn't help thinking of how things had changed for me in the short time since I'd been garrisoned at Fort Bridger, where they'd made me the supply sergeant. As most of the garrison was out every day guarding the men building the railroad, there wasn't much call for supplies, and I mostly sat waiting for something to do. I had the good luck to meet the local judge there, and he let me use his library to put in the time. He started me on poets like Milton and Burns, and I liked them fine. Then he tried me on Shakespeare, and it was a different matter. Mostly they were a struggle, except for *King Lear*, of course. Anybody whose heart doesn't break for the old king in the storm doesn't have a heart. I worked my way through a few of them and liked the stories well enough, but the man's spelling was none too good and he used a lot of sayings I'd heard before. The judge could see my mind wasn't truly set that way, so he switched me over to geology. I was reading *The Testimony of the Rocks* in the Judge's library when Major came to visit.

The Judge told Major I had learned a lot of geology from his books and had found fish skeletons in the rocks. Then he blew things up a bit telling Major I knew all about rock formations and such and was a true expert on fossils, though all I knew was in that one book, and I hadn't even finished reading it. One thing led to another and there I was on Major's expedition, Major having me climb with him to find fossils. Well, we'd found only one or two worth looking at that day when it came on to rain and we took shelter under an outcropping of rock. Conversation being our only amusement, I asked Major how it was he came to spend his time in the West, going down rivers and collecting fossils and such like.

He said, "It didn't start out that way. My father wanted me to follow him into the ministry, to become an ordained minister in the
Methodist Church."

"Your father was a preacher, then?"

He looked straight at me, as though he'd just discovered I was
there, "A preacher, oh yes, and more. He was a devoted - no even a
fanatic Wesleyan, and that's how I got my given names. He came
from England to spread John Wesley's gospel here in the States. God
did everything in our household. If a spoon fell on the floor, or if
cabbages rotted, it was God's will. When I was old enough to think
for myself, I could see too many things that didn't fit. These rocks
and rivers, for example, billions of years in the making, but my
father was adamant that six days did the whole thing."

I said, "*The Testimony of the Rocks* says...," but he cut me off. "I
know, Sergeant, I know. And if you read John Wesley as I had to,
you'll find a rationale for every cruelty, every injustice, every con-
tradiction between science and the Bible. But I couldn't swallow it.
Even the small congregations we had in upstate New York found my
father's views too extreme. We moved west, first to Ohio, then to
Illinois, Wisconsin, Kansas. My father took up farming, though he
kept preaching wherever he could get two people together. I sat
through it all, but I knew there were books other than the Bible,
and there is more philosophy in nature than in John Wesley."

It's not my nature to quarrel, for every man is entitled to his
opinion, but discomfort with Major's views led me to ask, "Who
taught you that?"

"When I was about ten years old, we moved to Jackson, Ohio and
my father enrolled me in the common school. We were abolitionists
and the ruffians in the school were pro-slavery. They drove me out
of the school. Then I had the good fortune to meet a kind and intel-
ligent man named George Crookham, a great self-educated scientist
and teacher. Crookham said if he could teach himself, so could I. He
let me use his library, took me into the field, taught me botany and
anthropology, made me read Hume and Gibbon and explained them
when I couldn't understand. He introduced me to his friend,

William Mather, who was the state geologist. Mather taught me geology, about the formation of Ohio and west, about the inland seas, the great uplift, the volcanoes, the earthquakes. Fire and water made the west, Sergeant, not God.

"Once Crookham took me to a lecture by his friend, Charles Grandison Finney, who was president of Oberlin College. I was only twelve years old but Finney's talk persuaded me that science was supreme, though I'm sure he didn't intend it that way. If I had any thoughts of bending to my father's will, Finney's talk washed them out of me the way a flood will take away a river bank.

"Crookham set up a free school in his house for children who couldn't go to the common school because their parents weren't pro-slavery, but that didn't last long. The pro-slavers burnt his house and library and drove him out of town. When that happened to that good man, and God let it happen, I put religion and John Wesley behind me as you, Sergeant, would Satan."

"I've always been told John Wesley was a great teacher. You took nothing from his teachings?"

The wind had shifted and the rain was blowing into our narrow shelter. Major didn't seem to notice, just wiped his face with his bandana and brushed back his hair, though there was hardly enough there to justify the effort.

"Not from his teachings, but I did from his life. I took his determination to follow his calling which he came to in a moment of revelation. I had my own moment of revelation in science at Finney's lecture."

I said, "In my opinion, Major, you needn't leave God out of it," and I told him what I'd read in one of the judge's book of plays, "There's a Divinity that shapes our ends, rough hew them how we will."

Major said, "Let me tell you how a chemist named Boyle put it. Boyle said, 'I do with some confidence expect a revolution whereby Divinity will be so much a loser and real philosophy flourish, perhaps beyond men's hopes.' What we're learning here is part of that revolution."

When Major said that, I knew why we were on the river.

Philosophy and science had merged, but philosophy was the junior partner. Major would climb these clifts, scramble around in the rain on this mountain, examining the strata or collecting fossils or just naming the colors he saw in the buttes, risking his life to get here and risking his health to sit sodden where we were, with the same determination his father brought to preaching the word of John Wesley.

I said the rain was letting up so maybe we should start down.

We'd been gone so long it was nearly dark when we got back to camp. Jack was scornful, "Tramped around all day in the mud and rain to get a few fish skeletons," and he showed us a bushel of fossils he'd picked up at the river's edge. To Jack, one fossil was as important as another, and his fossils were all pretty much the same, tubular worms mostly and a few snails, common stuff that didn't tell us much. I made up my mind to lend him the book that the judge presented to me when I left Bridger, but not 'til I'd worked my way through to the end.

That night Frank asked Billy Rhoads how he came to call his boat *Kitty Clyde's Sister*. "An odd sort of name now isn't it?"

It looked like Billy didn't want to tell him about the can-can dancers with Major present, for his face turned as red as the fire he suddenly decided needed poking. Then, with a twinkle in his eye, he said, "You tell him, Andy." Andy shook his head and found a thread in his shirt needed pulling. When it seemed somebody had to say something, Billy started, "Oh well, it's this way..." But Major broke in, "I guess you don't know the song, Frank. Walter, sing *Kitty Clyde's Sister* for us."

Walter always seemed happiest when he was singing. I guess knowing what words came next was a comfort to him, for he rarely said more than a few words at a time, and those took some doing. He roared right into it:

> *Oh, long have I sung of sweet Kitty Clyde,*
> *Who lived at the foot of the hill;*
> *And 'tho that sweet pretty bird has flown,*
> *Another is living there still.*

She's blithe and gay as the robin that sings
On the trees by the old mill-side;
And if ever I loved a girl in my life,
'Tis the charming, sweet Minnie Clyde
Oh, Minnie Clyde, she is my pride,
And sure I am no jester;
For if ever I loved a girl in my life,
'Tis Minnie, Kitty Clyde's sister.

"About as dumb a song as I've ever heard," Jack said, but it didn't stop Walter:

I think her eyes are brighter than Kitty's,
The dimple in her chin is deeper,
I would be imprisoned the rest of my life,
With Minnie Clyde for my keeper
In the festive throng she sings a sweet song,
With the lowly alike she is meek;
Her eyes are the windows of her soul,
Thro' which Minnie's heart would speak

By this time we were all converted to Jack's view, but Walter plugged on and with considerable laughter we managed to join in the chorus:

"Oh Minnie Clyde, she is my pride, and the rest.

I saw the meaning behind the boys' working over the sign painter when Walter ended with:

The birds all chant their notes to Minnie,
The angels above have caress'd her
But you have the angels and you have the birds,
And I'll have Kitty Clyde's sister.

"I already did," Billy said, and we ragged him and Andy a bit about the name, then Jack proposed we make up our own words to the song.

We all had a go but nobody topped Jack's:

Oh Kitty Clyde, I'll tan yer hide
And give you quite a blister
If you tell your ma or your pa
What I did to your sister.

It was a good note to end the day on, so we went to our tents. I said my prayers and then I did some thinking. The way I reasoned it, Major got me out of the army to do a job, and aside from just steering a boat, which was more fun than work anyway, that job was to find fossils. Exploring one side of the river with scant results left me feeling I had to do more, go acrost the river and try my luck there. At that point in the trip, I would have done anything for Major.

He chuckled the next morning when I told him I thought we ought to explore the other side, "You go, Sergeant, and take Walter with you. I want to work on my notes and Howland's map." That might have been true, but Walter was walking around camp in circles and every once in a while bursting into prayer or a scrap of song, and I think maybe Major wanted some peace and quiet.

The tide didn't amount to much where we were campt, the river slow enough so I could have swum acrost it. Anyway, it wasn't a chore for Jack when he rowed Walter and me acrost right after breakfast. "Fossils always better on the other side of the river," he said when he'd landed us at the foot of what looked like a place to climb the clift. Walter took one look at where I expected to climb, snorted and got back in the boat with Jack. Each man to his own fears, I thought, but I was glad to part company for Walter made me uneasy: I never knew what he might say next. Or worse, what he might not say when he'd been asked a direct question.

Jack said, "You call out, George, or whistle. I'll come and fetch you." I poked around all morning jumping over crevices, hammering at rocks with Major's little wedge-shaped hammer, working my way down the river. After four or five miles I decided to call it a day and tried to find a place I could climb down to the river, meaning to walk up along the shore until I was across from the camp. Trouble was, every time I started down I'd hit a place I couldn't climb down any farther. I'd worked my way back upriver a mile or so in this way when it began to rain. It was nothing at first, just a soft drizzle, then a hard downpour, then a regular waterfall of rain; rivulets formed, grew into streams so a place I'd walked or jumped over earlier was now a torrent to ford, and as I couldn't see the bottom, maybe an opportunity to be washed off the clift. The appeal of that outcome was limited, so I headed back away from the river to higher ground. The rain came down in sheets so bad I couldn't see but a few feet in front of me, and by mid-afternoon I was persuaded I was lost. I came to another clift then, maybe a hundred feet high, and found a way up, away from the washes. I waited out the hard rain, wet and shivering, and when it had eased off enough for me to see the river, I spotted a way around the flood. I walked as fast as I could in the driving rain, and just as it got dark, ended up at the river in the place where I'd started in the morning, tired, hungry and mad as a bear. I could see the men in camp by the firelight and I hallooed until they heard me. Jack rowed over and collected me.

When I got to the fire Andy gave a signal and all the men sang out:

> Git out the way ole Dan Tucker,
> You're too late to git your supper
> Supper's over and dinner's a cookin
> Old George Bradley, standin' there lookin

But Billy had a Dutch oven full of biscuits and some beans in a pan, and the coffee was still hot. Andy teased me, "Take off your clothes, Sergeant, dry out by the fire," but I declined the offer.

The next morning it was still raining and we were still in camp, huddled under tarpaulins, writing in our diaries or playing poker, Walter winning more than most. Major was showing Jack how to repair the broken barometer. As Jack said, it was a "tetchy" job. The job was to get mercury up a fine glass tube. He had to ease it in a few inches at a time then boil it over a spirit lamp which I guess chased the air out. Jack said it was like working a string through a straw. When he got the last of the mercury in and sealed it with the leather flap, Major was excited as a boy at a circus. "Now Jack," he said, and he seemed to be rubbing his one hand against the absent other, "Now, Jack, we are ready to measure mountains."

After dinner Major led Seneca and Andy and me up the river about five miles and we made what he called a "section," which is a drawing of what a place would look like if you sliced it through with a sharp knife, as though it was a wheel of cheese. We had to climb up and down making measurements with barometers, directions with compasses and distances with a ball of string as big as my head. It was hot, tiring work but better than sitting in camp watching the wind shift or waiting for a snake to crawl by for amusement.

You could see the boys were restless and burning to move on when we got to camp because all the boats were loaded and the men standing by them. The thing was, we didn't know what was beyond the mouth of Flaming Gorge because the river seemed to end soon after it entered, so it had to twist one way or the other, and we could hear the water singing louder just beyond the twist. We were all itching to see where it was going to take us. Major was in no hurry, though, and he had Howland dig out his papers from the cuddy and sketch in the section from the figures we brought back. Oramel had an artist's fine hand and as he was that quick about it, we were ready to get on the river by about four o'clock. We stripped off our boots and coats and headed due west, straight into the unknown.

For a time it looked like the river was just going to be swallowed by the clift, and I thought maybe we'd come to the hole in the river we'd been warned about back in Green River City. But just when I thought we were going into the clift or into a hole, the river twisted hard left and we'd no sooner rounded that bend when we came on a chute and the river took us, speed unknown but fastest yet, and we knew we were in for a ride. The water was plenty deep and there weren't many rocks, so we just barreled along through the chute which had a fall of about three feet in a hundred. I could hear Andy whoop as *Sister* shot through like an arrow from a bow, my boat right behind her, closer I confess than Major had ordered.

We came through the chute dry and excited and shouting like schoolboys. Then, before we could catch our breath, the river whipped off still further to the left and began to roar like a displeased schoolmaster. The pilot boat ahead hit a boil of foam in swift water between two giant boulders, hit the rapid so hard and quick it knocked Major off his seat into the bottom of the boat as the *Emma Dean* plunged into the fastest part of the fall. I lost sight of the little boat and fixed my attention on *Sister* which was following it close. *Sister* was weaving in and out like a needle basting a hem and I was following the same moves, steering with the sweep oar, the *Maid* bobbing like a bottle in ocean surf. First our prow would disappear under a wave and when it figured it was deep enough, it would rear up and pop out of the water like a risen bubble, and the stern would sink as if they were the two ends of a see-saw, and it was all I could do to keep the long sweep oar in its oarlock. This kept on for what seemed like an hour but was truly much less, until we hit smooth water and had covered about five miles, ending up facing east, the direction we'd started from, and probably not more than a mile away from there by land. We'd run our first really dangerous rapid which Jack said was "Crooked as a street in Boston."

We stopped as soon as we could, to catch our breath, bail the boats and talk about the experience. Major told us, "There was once a vast inland sea where we are now. There was probably a great uplift millions of years ago, when the land rose out of the sea." I figured he was right because God said, *Let there be firmament in the midst of the waters*. Well, just like when the canyon narrows, the water had to go somewhere and it decided to make Flaming Gorge. Major said, "It probably hammered away for eons until it got to the granite heart of the mountain and could go no farther. It couldn't go back because more water was pushing in from behind, so it did the next best thing and looped around and worked its way back out, to try again later."

I'd have had trouble with Major's ideas before I read the Judge's book, because the Bible says the world was made in six days, but the *Testimony of the Rocks* explains that those days weren't "natural" days of twenty-four hours, as they are now, but "prophetic" days that could last millions of natural years. When I told Jack this, he said, "In that case the Lord must have had Himself a nice long rest on the seventh." I'm doubtful Jack is a believer. Major named the canyon

"Horseshoe Canyon."

We were wet but we were a bit wiser. We'd learned that the eighteen foot steering oar was worse than useless in rapids. The span from rock to rock or wave to wave was too short and the turns too quick. Worse, the long oar was likely to snag on a boulder or be floated free of its open-topped oarlock. Unless we were in flat water, we were going to have to steer by pulling hard on the side oars. All right if you had three men, like the *Emma Dean* and the *No Name*, so that the odd man could call out directions, but the rest of us were going to have to steer looking over our shoulders and that could be awkward. When we campt, I cut the *Maid's* sweep oar down to fourteen feet and tied a length of rope across the oarlock to keep the oar from floating out the top.

When we came out of Horseshoe Canyon the river was swift but deep and rockless. The walls went straight up and the canyon narrowed to maybe eighty feet. It's the way I like to travel, no rowing, moving fast, just using the sweep oar a little here and there, like flicking a buggy whip over a horse's flank when he starts to slow. We rounded a sharp bend and came upon a herd of mountain sheep. Howland and Billy Rhoads pulled out their Spencer rifles and let loose volleys that made the canyon ring, but it was no use, the sheep just scampered up a steep slope and disappeared. "Couldn't hit the broad side of a barn with birdshot," Walter said.

A small, clear creek came in from the right, out of a narrow side canyon and we eased to shore to see if it would do for a campsite. Where the stream entered the river a belted kingfisher was sitting on a branch of a dead willow that hung out over the water. He had his head cocked, staring with one eye at the water. "Look at him," Jack said, "He's watching that finny tribe with the determination of purpose of a politician watching for the spoils of office."

Major named the stream, "Kingfisher Creek" and the canyon, "Kingfisher Canyon" and a grassy open field, "Kingfisher Park." Jack said, "Now there's a bird has gained notoriety."

We campt opposite a high limestone point coming out of the clift wall that had been shaped by wind and weather to the form of an old-fashioned straw beehive. Swallows by the thousands found it a congenial place to plaster their mud nests. Flitting in and out and around they looked like bees around a hive. Major named the place "Beehive Point." We started an elk drinking in the stream, kneeling on his forelegs as if in prayer. Frank Goodman grabbed a Henry repeater rifle and fired away but missed, though a kneeling elk is not the swiftest runner in the wilderness. Maybe his prayers were answered, for the Lord sees the meanest creature. I started thinking about whether animals have souls, and that led to maybe so did birds and plants and insects, but then I left off; I could see where that was leading me. Before you knew it I'd be assigning the river a soul.

Andy brought down two Canada geese and Billy and I tried to shoot some beavers, but it seemed every time I pulled the trigger they were gone under the surface. Billy claimed a hit, but the evidence dove out of sight. Howland said, "It wasn't a palpable hit." Billy asked him what that meant and he said, "Oh, just something I read. I misremember where." Jack said, "You can't ever shoot a beaver. They have a sixth sense that lets 'em dodge a bullet just as it's about to hit." I was never sure when Jack was informing or when he was speculating on our ignorance. But I thought if beavers had that power, they may have souls.

Our camp was beneath a clift that rose in terraced steps of glowing red sandstone to a height of fifteen hundred feet, give or take. On each step cedars grew, so that the whole effect was like a vast vermilion amphitheatre, with a green audience watching the river perform through all its seasons. Major said he felt like he was on a great stage. Howland said, "All the world's a stage, John, or so I've read."

"So have I, Oramel, and I mean to play a major role."

"Nice pun, John, but I don't see how you're going to do it out here on an unknown river."

"That's the point, Oramel. It won't be unknown when I'm through. It'll be known by the map we're making. And this is just the beginning. Half the West is unmapped, there's a vast part of this great country to be made known. We could spend our lives exploring and mapping it and still not see it all."

"You'll have to do it without me, John, I'm going back to

printing. I can't do without a salary."

Major gave Oramel a look like maybe he pitied him. "Oh, when we finish this trip, Congress will *shower* money on us for any exploring we want to do. Think of the money they've spent on Army explorations and railroad surveys, and none of them has mapped this river or its canyons. None of them. We've floated off every map that was ever made. This river will be ours, Oramel. We'll map the whole thing, do more important work than Lewis and Clark."

Howland said what was running through my own mind just then. "Why are you so bent on making a map?"

"I am drawn to far places," Major said. "If I see a map of a place where I've never been, I want to go there. If I see a map with a hole in it where no one has been, I *must* go there, if only to show those who come after me what's ahead of them."

"No man knows what's ahead of him," Oramel said, "and what man would want to?" It was a hard question Howland put, and I was just as pleased I didn't have to answer it. I guess Major felt the same way, for he didn't choose to say anything more.

That night it was still light when we finished supper, and whether it was Howland's question or Major decided we needed improving, or maybe he just wanted to get in ahead of Walter and *Old Shady*, but anyway, while we were having our coffee Major got out a book and started to read to us from *The Lady of the Lake*.

We listened a while with only Oramel and Seneca seeming to be taking it in, besides me and maybe Walter, though it was always a chore to guess where Walter's mind was. Jack said he'd prefer hearing about a woman wasn't so much a lady, Billy fell asleep at the fire and Andy said he was tired too, and that ended *The Lady of the Lake* forever, and I never did get to know how it all fell out at the end.

The next morning we'd been on the river a week and Howland reckoned the distance at sixty-nine miles. When he went to write the miles down in a blank book Major had brought for that purpose, he couldn't find it and thought he'd left it at a stopping place about two miles upriver. Well, nothing would do but we had to go and get it, though it was the Sabbath and we should have rested. Major

ordered Bill Dunn and me to row him back up the river to look for
it. I said I thought Howland ought to go, him being the one that lost
the book, but Major said, "No" and sent Howland and Goodman to
the top of the terraced clifts to sketch out the countryside and
improve the map. Bill Dunn and I launched the *Emma Dean* and
pulled and pulled against the tide and got Major back upriver the
two miles, my arms sore as toothaches. We looked everywhere but
there was no book. "Coyotes," Dunn said, "needin something to
read at night."

"The book was blank," Major said.

"Coyotes don't know the difference," Dunn told him. I don't
think Major saw the humor in it for he looked at Bill with total
puzzlement.

I found some interesting rocks which I took along to examine
later, and we headed back downstream. There came a lone falcon
skimming the water ahead of us and, high up, a great blue heron
flapping along. Major said he looked like a "Terror dactyl," which he
said is a dinosaur with wings. I guess they were pretty big wings or
the dinosaur was a midget.

When Howland and Goodman came down from their climb, we
broke camp and started down the river again. After about an hour
the canyon grew narrow and the water fast, and we raced like the
wind for three or four miles. Then, of a sudden, we heard a sound
like reboant thunder and didn't need a signal from Major to tell us
there was trouble ahead. We went ashore on the right, and Jack and
I and Major scrambled downstream along the talus slope to scout
things out. When we got to the head of the rapid the sound of the
water was so loud we had to communicate with hand signals or
shout in each other's ears. The rapid was two hundred yards long
and had a fall I judged to be ten feet. There were boulders everywhere in the rapid, but I thought we could thread our way through
them and said I'd take the *Maid* down first. But Major said it was
too dangerous and Jack agreed with him. "Be foolish to try it,
George," and after another look I thought maybe he was right, but
still I'd have chanced it, nothing ventured nothing gained.

When we got far enough upstream to hear each other easy again,

Major said, "Now you'll see what the ropes are for," and he explained how we would fasten a line to a boat's stern and walk it downstream. "You know any good knots, Sergeant?"

"Bowline would be best," I told him, "but how are we going to keep them off the rocks?"

Major said, "We'll put two men in the boat to fend off with oars," and I thought that would be the next best thing to running the rapid and looked forward to it.

I asked if he was worried about our holding the big boats, seeing each held a ton of cargo. Major just shrugged, "We've got seven men for the rope."

So we shipped and secured the *Emma Dean's* steering oar and Bill Dunn and Jack got in her, each holding a rowing oar, one on each side. I tied a bowline on the ringbolt that was on the rearmost of the double sternpost and we walked along the talus, letting the tide take her downstream, slowing her a little. She yawed and bucked and tugged on the line like she was a colt trying to break free of a tether, Bill and Jack fending off as best they could, which wasn't perfect. The little boat took a few good knocks and at one point I was sure she was stove in. She went over the falls smooth enough, but when she struck the pool that lay just at the foot of the falls, she dug her prow in, and Bill Dunn was thrown into the water and disappeared from view. I was running along the shore readying to go in after him when he showed up bobbing in the pool some twenty yards farther downstream. He swam to shore easy as walking. "He's a fine swimmer," I said to Major, and he said, "I wish he'd swim more often, in his buckskins." Then he added, "He's a dirty devil." I thought there was something to the idea of cleaning Bill up a bit, but it wasn't as though any of us took a hot bath every Saturday night.

We found that seven men on the line were too many for the rocky scree; we kept stumbling over each other, so Major sent Billy down to start dinner, and the rest of us let the *Maid* down. We added a line on the bow to steady the boat, so now we had two men on that line and four on the stern and two in the boat, and it worked just fine, Walter and me fending off with oars, Andy calling out, "Whoa, girl, whoa, easy now...," so we made good sport of it. Even so, it was hard work and took us better than two hours all told to get the big boats down. It was hard on the boats too, but we were pleased as a new bride and confident that now we could get through any rapid by letting the boats down on lines, just so long as there was some shore to walk along.

After dinner we had a run of eight or nine miles in fast, smooth water, me steering with the big sweep oar, Walter singing one of his Scotch songs, *John Anderson My Jo*, I think it was, until I was some sick of it, so I asked him how Major lost his arm. At first I thought he didn't hear me: he just stopped singing and staring at me until I thought I'd asked a touchy question, then I heard what he'd been concentrating on: the sound of the river had changed to a roar, getting louder every foot, and it was a sound started my heart thumping so I thought the pounding in my head could be heard over the river's roar. Major signaled to land on the east shore and we all put in.

We set out to scout out the rapid and I saw a sight that stunned me. For about three hundred yards the river raced through a narrow channel, maybe eighty feet wide where it had just been two hundred. It didn't take any science to know the water had to speed up to get through it. The noise and the foaming were frightening enough, but the red sandstone had tumbled in, making a rough dam clear acrost the channel, and there was a sharp fall where the water rushed over it. The clift dropped sheer to the water on the east side of the fall, so if we were going to let the boats down on lines, we had to do it on the other side, where there was a narrow rocky beach. Trouble was, we couldn't row acrost where we were without being swept over the falls.

Because the river narrowed all of a sudden, the water couldn't all rush through and some had to ease back upstream to wait its turn, so there was an eddy along the shore on each side, where the river ran back against itself. We unloaded the Emma Dean's cargo and took her upriver by wading in the eddy to a point where the river widened out to about two hundred feet. Frank said, "If they let out a line behind, we can use it to tow the other boats over." It wasn't a good idea as our ropes were only 120 feet long, but I thought Andy's remark was uncalled for, "Sure, then, with you on the end of it for ballast." Frank nodded his head and sort of winked at Andy as if to say, "Just wait."

With Bill Dunn and Jack grimly gripping the oars of the *Emma Dean,* we shoved her off. They rowed their hearts out and got the little boat across the river, with ten yards to spare from going over the falls. They'd got the hang of the thing though, so they unloaded, eased the boat upriver in the eddy and rowed back. We kept loading the *Emma Dean* and used it to help ferry cargo from the other boats, she making five trips in all, and the big boats making two trips each. In this way we got the boats and all the cargo over on the west bank, and it was a journey I hope never to repeat. We decided to rest for the night and let the boats down over the falls in the morning. Billy Rhoads spotted a deer and blasted away with the usual result. "You shoulda got him by the legs, Billy" was Jack's advice. So we had fat bacon and stewed apples for supper.

As the night was clear, there was no need for tents and we just stretched out on the ground wherever we happened to be. I'd had three cups of coffee and the moon shone right in my eyes, but I fell asleep in the middle of my prayers.

At dawn I was awakened by the shriek of a blue jay and by Major yelling at the same time. "Thought it was a minié ball," Walter told me when we were back on the river. Major didn't say much all morning. I guessed he had a dream where he lost his arm to a minié ball again. Everybody in the Union Army hated the minié ball rifle bullet the Rebs used. It made a shrieking, high-pitched noise when it came at you on the field. I could see that in Major's sleep the blue jay's call could sound like it, but to me the sound of a minié ball was like the scream of a frightened child.

When we got back on the river, I asked Walter again how Major lost his arm. At first he didn't say anything, as though he was collecting scraps of thought rattling around in his head. "Shiloh," he said finally, "April '62." What Walter told me came out in fits and starts, but pieced together it went like this:

"No orders; artillery a separate command, no orders from Grant;

'not down yet' they said. Wes took it on himself to bring us to a place called Duncan's Field, men runnin everywhere, rebel fire hotter'n Hades. Minié balls screaming all over the place. Men runnin away from battle is what I mostly recollect. Wes took it on hisself. Just set us up on the north end of the field, square in front of the Rebs. We were unlimbering the guns; troops came running by us, not retreat, just runnin away scared to death. Didn't have a preacher's prayer of where they was goin. Some just kept runnin but about half of 'em stopped in a little copse in the woods at the south end. We'd lost a gun but saved the horses so Wes moved us down there. He found General Wallace and General Prentiss just standing there. Wallace said he couldn't give us any orders, but Prentiss set us up behind the 8th Iowa under Colonel Geddes. We let go one barrage, made the trees shake and the leaves fall off. Then it happened, Wes was pushing me on the shoulder, sending me off to the right where a caisson had got knocked over, when he caught that minié ball. Caught it in the hand and it ran up his wrist to his elbow and buried itself there."

Walter was quiet a long time then, maybe trying to gather his thoughts together the way you'd rake up the coals of a fire, maybe remembering the moment Major was wounded, his hand on Walter's shoulder, maybe thinking another inch it would have caught him instead. Would he have been happier if it had, I wondered. We ran a few small rapids in silence, just the river splashing, a thump here and there when a rock bruised our hull, but mostly just the quiet and the river's steady murmur.

Just when I'd decided there wasn't going to be any more, Walter said, "Left two fingers on my shoulder, like they was my captain's bars."

It was a backbreaking day. We had to portage the cargoes, carry them around the falls on our backs, a ton each in the big boats, and as the shore was all big boulders and tide pools, we had a wet and weary time of it. Then we had to let the boats down with a line on each end and men standing on shore or in the water with oars to keep the boats off the rocks. I was the only one to stay in the boat, as I thought it would suffer less damage that way. But it was a trip, I can tell you. The boat bobbed like a balloon borne along the ground by the wind, and if I was ever subject to seasickness I'd have had it then. But I got her through with less pounding than the others. This didn't mean there were no leaks, for all the boats took some hard knocks, but mine less than some, the *No Name* in particular being near stove in.

While we toiled, Major scouted. He climbed the clift and brought back the news that the river got narrower ahead, which meant even faster water, for the river will not wait on its journey to the sea. We were nervous about fast water what with our boats some battered. We couldn't careen them where we were and anyway we had not brought tar to seal the leaks with, for we never imagined the boats would strike the rocks with such force that the caulking would be knocked out. We tore some strips from one of the tarpaulins and stuffed them in the worst leaks, screwed up our courage and set off. It was fast and all frothy in the rapids, and we could hardly see the *Emma Dean* for the spray as she went through, but there were no distress calls so we followed in the big boats, only a few yards between. Below, the river was fast but the rocks mostly stayed out of the channel and we raced along a good ten miles through high and boisterous waves. We went through one rapid that was a narrow billow of foam and mist so that the spray in the sun made a rainbow. When we stopped to bail the boats, I could see the flour sack in my boat was wet and I feared for my tintype albums which I'd stowed beneath it, but Major ordered us right back on the river so I couldn't attend to them.

We were learning about the river as we went, and for me that meant forgetting a lot of what I'd learned on the sea. I was used to the waves in an ocean, which are always moving and have a force and speed that go in the direction of the water, so you use their power, don't go against them, ride with the tide. River waves run contrary. Except where they rebound from the canyon walls, they are always in the same place, and they have a vee that points upstream, like an arrow aimed at you, and they go against the movement of the water. We had been veering around these wave heads and shipping water, sometimes near getting broadside and broaching. We found that by hitting the vee at its point and splitting it, pushing the water to either side, we were in the deepest water and could tame the river one wave at a time.

If you've spent any time at sea you know that a sailor is always sensible of the speed and direction of the wind and the motion of the waves. On the river we became aware of the sound and speed of the water without thinking about it. We had just run one rapid and its roar was fading behind us when we became aware of a new and louder sound ahead. The *Emma Dean* in the lead came to a bend and started around it, and Major signaled a landing, but we already knew by the rising sound that there was bad water coming up. When I rounded the bend and landed the *Maid*, I hit a wall of sound.

We could hear but we couldn't see what lay before us, so Major had Bill Dunn and Jack ease the *Emma Dean* down the slow water near the shore to the source of the sound. They studied things out for a while, then Major signaled the rest of us to come down and land behind them. When I got the *Maid* down, my heart sank. I was looking at a rapid with a fall of ten feet in twenty five, which Howland said was forty percent, but I took no comfort in his mathematics. There was a thirty foot long boulder sitting in the middle, about five feet of it out of the water, and on each side fallen rock broke the rapid into sheer falls, two on the left, three on the right, one right after the other. I didn't see how we were going to navigate this one, there being nothing but big boulders along the shore, strewn about like the remains of a wrecked fortress.

And neither did Jack, saying, "We'll never be able to hold the big boats against that current, Professor, even if we had a dozen men."

"Then we'll have to portage the cargo around the falls."

"Still don't think we can hold 'em clear to the bottom," Jack said, "That last fall's a bitch, drops faster'n a fish."

Major said, "There's clear, flat water below that big rock." We could pivot the boats around if we could get a man on it with a line," and Major looked at Dunn.

"A bird, maybe," Bill said, "but not a man. Leastways not this man."

But the idea took hold and we worked out a plan to let down on the right where the three falls broke the drop into three smaller ones. After we unloaded the cargo from the big boats, I made a line fast to the *Emma Dean's* bow, making a round turn on the ringbolt and two half hitches on the standing part of the line. I then walked the other end of that line downstream below the last falls and made a rolling hitch around a rock. That way the little boat couldn't escape downstream of the third falls, if we got her that far. Billy and Andy came with me and I showed them the knot. Billy got it all right but Andy couldn't master it.

I took another line and made one end fast to a rock at the head of the first falls in the same way. We passed the other end of that line through the *Emma Dean's* stern ringbolt, and four men took hold of it. We pushed the *Emma Dean* into the stream and the men walked downstream along the shore holding her back, paying out the line as they went, letting it slip through the ringbolt. Two men stood on rocks in the river with oars fending off as best they could. We got her through the first two falls that way without too much damage, but then we couldn't hold her any more and we just let the line go. As the tide took the little boat, the line buzzed through that ringbolt like it was a bee heading for its hive and the *Emma Dean* rushed over the third falls, running free. Arrested by the bow line below, she swung around like the last child on a snap-the-whip game and ended up bobbing in the calm water below the big rock. Billy and Andy hauled in the line and beached her. There was some damage to her port side and a few bruised shins among the men, but it had worked. Work was the word for it, hard work, and we were wet and cold and tired. Major wanted to get the other boats down, but we were too worn out for more labor and left them 'til morning, just bringing down enough provisions so Billy could make supper and breakfast.

Breakfast was a sorry thing, just stewed apples and coffee, and it didn't provide enough nourishment for a working man, but Major didn't do the work and he'd be content to live on coffee anyway. I never saw a man drink so much coffee, muddy river water in its makings or no.

I wanted to stay in the *Maid* when we let her down to keep her off the rocks, but Jack said we'd need extra hands on the line for the heavy boats, and I saw he was right. We were worried about holding her and put five men on the line. A man stood by each of the three falls to keep her from broaching and that left Andy and Major below to haul her in. It turned out her weighing more than the *Emma Dean* meant she steered a truer course through the rocks and didn't bob about like the little boat. So she swung around on the end of her tether as pretty as you please and was soon nested on shore with the *Emma Dean*. It was but a little beach so we didn't dare let the other boats down for fear of a collision. That meant we had to portage the cargoes of the *Maid* and the *Emma Dean* down over the boulders, reload the two boats and move them downstream to make room for the other two. I decided I didn't need to portage the interesting rocks I'd collected back up the river a ways and left them.

We got *Sister* and the *No Name* down in the same way, then stopped for dinner and a smoke, and Major told us a story:

"Last Spring I had a conversation with an old Indian named Pariats, who told me about one of his tribe trying to run this canyon in a canoe. 'The rocks,' he said, his hands above his head, his arms vertical, and looking between them to the heavens, 'the rocks h-e-a-p, h-e-a-p high; the water go h-oo-woogh, h-oo-woogh; water pony h-e-a-p buck; water catch 'em; no see 'em Injun any more! No see 'em squaw any more! No see 'em papoose any more!'"

We laughed as best tired men could, but Frank didn't, so maybe he was tireder than most. Major said that if the Indians hadn't run the river here then it was for sure that no white men had ever done it, that we were the first. Then he said, "I name this gorge 'Red Canyon', after the walls," and he swung his one arm at the red clift. I followed the arc of his arm with my eyes and part way up, under a slight projection, I saw what looked like black writing. "There's writing up there," I said, and everybody scrambled up the scree to see what it was. We saw painted with tar on the clift, "Ashley 18_5," the one number being partly washed away. Most of us thought it was the number 2, but Major said that was impossible, that it had to be a 5, and his brother agreed. Major named the place "Ashley Falls."

It seemed like the river was testing us, and if we passed a test, it gave us a reward, like a teacher awarding a gold star, because after the toil at Ashley Falls we found ourselves on fast, flat water, free of rocks but abounding in big waves, so that we ran half swamped most of the time. At one point two otters raced us along the shore, leaping over waves as our boats did. We tore through one stretch of maybe fifteen, seventeen miles in less than an hour. The *Emma Dean* bucked like an unbroken "water-pony," and we rocked along in its wake, singing, splashing each other like porpoises playing. At one point my boat caught up with the *Emma Dean* and we raced side by side in the fast water until, with some relief, we found ourselves on flat, wide and slow water again. Jack said the ride was "like sparking a dark-eyed girl, just dangerous enough to be exciting."

In the late afternoon we arrived at one of the few places that were on our maps, a place called "Little Brown's Hole," which Major, not content to let the world rest, renamed "Little Brown's Park." I watched the hunters go out for game and figured we'd have bacon again for supper. They came back empty-handed but the one-armed major killed two grouse with the shotgun barrel of the Le Mat pistol. I was too tired to go out for fossils and anyway the ground didn't look right for good ones, having few layers. It came on to rain so we pitched the tents and sat it out until the evening when we got another reward, a most beautiful rainbow arcing across the canyon, about as pretty a sight as I was ever likely to see in this life.

When it got dark and the stars came out, Major decided to teach Jack the sextant. We all gathered around to hear the professor teach some science to the trapper. Major explained how 'sextant' meant one-sixth and that meant one-sixth of a circle, or sixty degrees. Jack said, "Now whose tom-fool idea was that?" Frank said the sextant was an English invention and it was like their money, sixes and twelves and twenties, "Good for the calculating mind," Frank said

"Ain't there no American instrument?" Jack wanted to know.

Major said the English had no claim on the circle, that it went back to the Greeks, and Howland said, "Everything does." So Jack had to get used to some foreign science, and he took it well enough, but said he drew the line at Greeks.

He sighted on a star Major pointed out to him, called Beta Ceti and read off an angle on the sextant. Major looked in a little book of the position of the stars at that date, and Jack figured out we were a hundred sixty miles from Green River City. When Major told him he was right, he was like a schoolboy got a good grade. He was still squinting at the sky and consulting the book when the rest of us spread our blankets beneath two giant pines and fell asleep to the sound of wolves' steady howling and the hoot of an owl somewhere. For all I know Jack was at it all night for he was there in the morning when I was roused by Billy's call, "Roll out! Roll out! Roll out! Bulls in the corral! Chain up the gaps..."

Jack said he'd spent the night "looking through the old pine boughs at the sentinel stars shining from the deep, pure blue sky, like happy spirits looking out through the blue eyes of a pure-hearted woman." Then he said, "As we are guided on this voyage by the star in the blue, so may it be on the next, by the *spirit* in the blue." I said, "Amen," but the way Jack grinned at me I thought again if he was a believer it was of some god other than mine, but he anyway had the makings of a fair poet when he set his mind to it.

Jack said the names of the stars, like Beta Ceti, were tongue twisters and couldn't we call them by our own names, the way Major had renamed Little Brown's Hole. "Sure you can," Howland told him, "Call them anything you like, but be sure you remember the names." Jack said he'd get to it when he had more time.

Billy cooked up a fine breakfast of fried grouse and biscuits, and we persuaded Major to let us spread our outfits to dry in the sun as we had got pretty wet the day before. We figured it would be wet like that from now on and resolved to run the river in our long underwear and shirts. Frank's were both red, and Andy called him the "cardinal bird," said he would scare away all the game. Frank said, "You jolly well couldn't shoot it anyway." He was right of course, but Andy took it hard, stood up like he was fixing to fight when just then Sumner fired away at three sheep to no effect except to frighten them, and they ran up the almost perpendicular clifts as fast as a deer could run on level ground. When the hunters set out after them, I figured I'd better go fishing.

I caught twelve of the finest whitefish I ever saw. The cook took them from my boat and it was all he wanted to carry as some of them weighed four pounds. They weren't like any fish I'd ever laid eyes on before. Five of them were trout-like except for their humped backs, and the other seven bigger fish had thin backs and a bump just behind the head.

The hunters returned without enough game to make a grease spot. Jack came in a little after the others, been looking for bread-pans, I expect. When he saw my fish he said, "These with the bump look like a mongrel of mackerel, sucker and whitefish, and the others are an afflicted cross between a whitefish and a lake trout. Doubt they can be eaten by a human who expects to live more'n a minute; you better fry up some bacon, Billy."

But Billy dredged the fish in flour and fried them up in bacon fat, and we had a feast, sweetest tasting fish I ever had. The other men agreed, but Jack said, "Now you take a piece of raw pork and a paper of pins and make a sandwich, that gives you the first kind. Take out the pork and you have the other kind." More sour grapes; if we'd depended on his hunting for subsistence we'd have been fat as Job's turkey in a week.

The fourth of June and Major figured our altitude as 6000 feet, so we'd dropped only seventy-five feet in ten days. Howland said, "At that rate, John, we'll require 800 days to get down to sea level." You could see that Major wasn't pleased with the arithmetic. He ordered us onto the river early, before the sun had climbed over the high canyon wall to the east, so we were shivering in our shirts and long johns when we started to run rapids. We ran fast most of the morning, rowing hard to keep warm and maybe we got a little too close together. When we heard a shout from Major and saw the *Emma Dean* ground on a sandbar, we all started to row away from the little boat, some to one side, some to the other so our oars tangled and we got acrost each others bows. In the end we all grounded together up against the *Emma Dean* in a muddle of mixed up oars and a chorus of curses. Everybody (except Major of course) had to get into the water, biting cold as it was, to get the boats off the bar, and we'd no sooner done it than we grounded again, as there were many small islands, and each seemed to have its own sandbar just under the water where we couldn't see it. So we tugged and cursed and waded and eventually stopped at an island where we were able to build a fire and make dinner.

We wanted to stay the afternoon and maybe camp for the night, taking the time to get warm and dry our clothes but Major wouldn't have it. He said we had to keep moving and when we didn't jump to it he made us a little speech:

"We must move on. We have an unknown distance yet to run; an unknown river yet to explore. What falls there are, we know not; what rocks beset the channel, we know not; what walls rise over the river we know not."

Howland stood up then and wrung some water out of his shirt-tails, making the fire hiss. "And how to row we know not," he said. A little mist rose up from the fire but not enough to mask the anger on Major's face, red as the fire. "It's time you learned, Oramel. It's an ancient skill." "Ayuh," Oramel said, "even the galley slaves learned it."

We launched the boats and after about twelve miles in mostly deep water we passed a little stream on the right. We were surprised to see a flat-bottomed rowboat tied up near its mouth and went to examine it. Jack said it was the boat of two prospectors who left Green River City a few days before we did, "Stone cold sober, too." Major didn't believe him at first, but Walter said he recognized the boat, so Major had to accept the idea that the small and rough-built boat could have come down where we did in our big Chicago-built boats. "Boat's pretty light, professor," Jack said, "They probably carried it around most places where there was rough water." I think Jack had it right but still they had to have run some rapids, no mean feat in that little boat. We examined their skiff and found some lines and tents so figured they'd gone up the creek exploring. We hallooed for a while and fired off a rifle, but there was no answer and we moved on.

A few miles farther on we came across a wide creek that came in from the east. It was blood-red and had an odor like old socks. Frank Goodman tasted it and said it was an improvement on Billy's coffee.

We toiled on, lining where we had to, running when we could, until we came to a place where a spur of red mountain cut across the river, which had carved a canyon straight through it. Rowing through in the boats we found the canyon was cool as a tomb, and there was red all around like we were inside God's bloodstream. Major wanted to call this one Red Canyon and change the name of the other one which wasn't quite as red, but finally he settled on "Swallow Canyon," as there were many swallows flitting about where they had plastered their mud nests against the clift.

When it clouded up some, looking like it was going to come on to rain, we stopped for the night, Major and Jack unable to make an observation with the sextant, the sky being so dark. We campt beneath a huge cottonwood tree that could have sheltered two hundred men. "Provided they don't take up so much space as Frank," Andy said. Frank laughed with the rest of us but maybe not as loud. We saw on Warren's map that this was a place called "Brown's Hole." Naturally, Major renamed it. He called it "Brown's Park." White men had been to here by land, and it looked like Ashley may have reached it by water, but this was where the country descended into the unknown, the point beyond which no one in Green River

City was willing to bet the Irishman that we'd survive.

We put up our tents on a sandy beach down by the river, expecting rain, but Frank said the cottonwood tree would be enough shelter and just spread his blanket under it. The next morning we were awakened at dawn by a shrill and deafening chorus of birds in the giant cottonwood tree, so dense the tree fairly quivered with sound: warblers, finches, flickers and, in the grass, meadowlarks; ducks and geese on the river, a loon somewhere. Major said we had our own Jenny Lind, and Jack said the birds and the scent of wild roses was "Lovely as a poet's dream." He said he'd dreamt that he was "just wandering into paradise, could see the dim shadow of the dark-eyed houris..." I don't remember the rest because at that moment Frank Goodman emerged from under the tree and joined us at the river. He was a sorry sight, his red long johns and shirt spattered all over white from the droppings of birds that had roosted in the tree. Though I pitied him, I couldn't help laughing. Andy thought it was comical too and said, "Oh Frank, you do look pretty in polka dots." Frank was in no mood for jest, "You're asking for a spot of trouble, you are, you little shit," and he started for Andy.

Andy seemed ready for a scrap, but Major stepped between them, "That's enough," he snapped, sounding like a major should. Frank went to the river to clean up and Andy went to start the fire for breakfast.

When we'd eaten, Major sent me and Andy along with Oramel Howland to measure Brown's Park and make another section. He wasn't in the habit of sending Andy, who had cooking chores, so I figured he was trying to keep him away from Frank. We found a verdant park that ran three and a half miles back from the river until it got to a high bluff, and we guessed it went downriver about fifteen miles. Then we heard Billy's call to the noon meal and started back, but I stopped when I heard a buzz too loud for a bee and saw a rattlesnake coiled on a rock just a few feet away. I don't recall thinking about it but just drew my pistol and shot it in its gaping mouth, didn't even stop to count the rattles.

Andy said it was luck, my hitting it with one shot. Maybe he was right, but he wasn't bit neither. He wanted to take the snake for its skin but Oramel stopped him, saying he'd heard of men being bit by a rattler after the snake was dead. It sounded like something Jack would make up, but I'd seen chickens try to fly after they'd had their heads chopped off, so maybe it was true. When we got to a clear little stream and saw some trout swimming around, I thought to show Andy my marksmanship. I fired four shots and didn't hit a one, so I guess pride got in the way again or they had the same power to dodge bullets that Jack had assigned to beavers.

Jack had had little to do sitting in camp so he'd undertaken to measure the cottonwood tree. "Twenty-three feet around at five feet off the ground," he told us.

Howland said, "She'd have been smaller had you been taller."

After dinner and a nap, Andy and I caught some whitefish, which were more normal looking than the fish I had caught before, and Bill Dunn killed some ducks, so supper was a feast. We were just finishing the last of the coffee around the fire and I could see Walter gearing up to give us *Old Shady* again, so I cut in and told about the rattlesnake. That set Major to telling us an Indian legend.

"A witch, which the Paiute's call teguai, stole a baby and a little girl from a village and ran away into the wood. The Indians from the village tracked the teguai into the wood, where they found her asleep. They rescued the children and chased the teguai away. The teguai was afraid the braves would come back and kill her, so she snatched her own children and ran to her grandfather, the rattlesnake, which they call togoav. She asked the togoav to protect them, but all he could think to do was swallow them. Now, this made him so sick he asked them to crawl out again. The little children were able to crawl out, but the teguai was too big and got stuck inside. Togoav then crawled out of his own skin, leaving the teguai in it. She crawled into a crack in some rocks and hid. The village braves came looking for her, calling, *teguai, teguai*. She would call back to them, *teguai, teguai*, and anything else they yelled, she would yell back, mocking them, but they couldn't find her. Since that time all teguai live in rattlesnake skins, and what we call echoes are the teguai mocking us. Each repetition in an echo represents one of the teguai's rattles."

When Major finished, Jack said, "About as far-fetched as the parting of the waters."

Jack said he'd be content to take up residence at Brown's Park, and there was no denying it was a fine piece of land. He said we could bring some cattle up from Texas, probably raise a thousand head. For my part, as pleasant as Brown's Hole was I just wanted to get on down the river, which was slow and wide here, hardly any tide at all. If I closed my eyes I might have been on a pond in Massachusetts, but without the mosquitoes. I wanted to get into some territory no white man had seen or been to, and the sooner the better.

It seemed to be working out that if there was measuring or map-making or science to do, Major had all the time in the world to do it, but if the crew was wet and cold, time was short and we must move on. It wasn't until the sixth of June that Major let us stop measuring the world and get back on the river. We found the going troublesome, though. The wind turned contrary and we had to row straight into it. I missed the pull of the tide and the thrust of the water against the oars in the rapids. A whole day of toil brought us to camp only seventeen miles downriver, by Oramel's average. Major said it was only twelve, but he was a passenger. My guess was nearer twenty.

When we campt at the head of another canyon, Andy and Major tried their hand at fishing. It looked like Major was taking Andy in hand as I had hoped, or maybe he was just keeping him and Frank separated. Andy caught three trout and the one-armed major caught five. Andy told me they didn't use hooks, "Just shot the fellers between the eyes with a pistol, Sergeant Bradley."

The river ran south just where we were, so the sun set early, and I was pleased to be abed early after the hard day's rowing. The Bible tells us, "The sleep of a labouring man is sweet," to which I say, "amen". We rose late the next morning, following the practice of the sun, and it was ten o'clock before Major and Dunn set off up the clift to measure altitude. But first Major checked his watch against the chronometer. His wife, Emma Dean, had given him the watch when he left on the trip, and it was a pretty little thing. Silver, with chasing all the way around the outside rim, sort of a vine pattern, and on the back there was etched a flower stem and leaves set up so that the winding stem looked like it was the flower, maybe a thistle. On the front there were two doves so close together they might have been holding hands, or wings I guess I should say. When Major pressed the winding stem down, the front opened and the watch played a few bars of a song he said was "The Indian Love Call," but I couldn't tell from the little it played.

The face of the watch was of the whitest white, and between the white and the silver you could fair be blinded when the sun hit it just right. Inside the cover was something in Latin, or so Howland said. I didn't ask him what it meant as I figured that was Major's business strictly. When Frank told Major the watch was "spot on," he was pleased as Punch in the Punch and Judy puppet show.

I patched up the caulking of the *Maid*, replacing the tarpaulin strips with oakum, and gave Billy some oakum for *Sister* which was hauled up next to my boat. Having nothing better to do, Jack was helping Billy poke in the oakum. "She's in pretty good shape considering the thumpin she's takin," Jack said. Billy squirted out a stream of tobacco juice adding a little more color to the yellow in his moustache. "Yep," he said, "Sister can stand more thumpin than Kitty ever could."

When Major returned and finished his calculations, he said the clift was 2086 feet high, so we were most near to a half-mile in the earth.

After dinner Major said, "Sergeant, let's climb up to the top here and see if we can find any pine pitch. Billy looked up from where he was scouring out a pot with sand and said, "What is it you want with pine pitch?"

Jack said, "I suspect the professor just wants to add a little flavor to your cookin."

"It's to seal the caulking on the boats," Major told us. We have no tar, and pine pitch will serve the same purpose. Come along Sergeant." I went gladly, for I knew the oakum would just fall away if we didn't seal it in somehow.

We didn't find any pitch worth mentioning, for pines were in scant supply there and as a pine only makes pitch if it's wounded, there wasn't much to collect. Mostly it's when lightning strikes a tree or when wind breaks off a branch that a pine will make pitch. First the wound bleeds a brown liquid not much thicker than blood. Then that liquid clots up some the way blood does and once it's made a knot about as thick as your fist, it stiffens up a bit so it can be spread like coal tar. If there are other times a wound proves useful, I don't know of them. We sliced off the few knots that there were and dropped them in a bailing can, but they were scarcely enough to flavor Billy's cooking.

We stood a while at the clift's edge and had a look at what we were going to be up against the next day. The river completely filled the channel, wall to vertical wall, as far downriver as I could see. Then it opened to a wide mouth at the entrance to the next canyon. The walls at the canyon mouth were red, shading to green and grey where lichens had taken hold. Ferns grew in clefts in the walls, and hundreds of rivulets splashed silver among the ferns, racing one another down the clift. Of a sudden the sun lit up the canyon mouth, and I felt I was being bidden to enter. It only wanted organ music to make me think I was in a church, looking at stained glass.

Back in camp, night moved in wind-swift behind the canyon mouth, changing its appearance so much it could have been another place altogether. Instead of the red of midday, the walls turned grey, then black, and the air turned cold. We all got quiet then, like a pall had settled over us, full of foreboding. Instead of inviting us in, the gate to the canyon seemed to be a dark portal to a region of doom. Major reminded me of my saying I'd be willing to explore the river Styx to get out of the army. "You may get your chance, Sergeant," he said, "but let's hope we don't see old Charon with his three-headed dog tomorrow." I said "I hope not, for none of the hunters could shoot him." Most laughed but I think I bruised Jack up a bit with my thoughtless remark. I told myself I'd apologize first time I got Jack alone.

Howland surprised us all by having the inspiration to sing, because he usually kept his own counsel and said little, same as most Vermonters I'd met. He sang *The Cumberland's Crew* about a naval battle in the late war to preserve the Union, a battle I'd never heard of:

> *Oh shipmates come gather and join in my ditty*
> *Of a terrible battle that happened of late*
> *Let each Union tar shed a tear of sad pity*
> *When he thinks on the once gallant Cumberland's fate*
>
> *The eighth day of March told a terrible story*
> *When many a brave tar to this world bid adieu*
> *Our flag it was wrapped in a mantle of glory*
> *By the heroic deeds of the Cumberland's crew*
>
> *On the eighth day of March about ten in the morning*
> *The day it was clear and bright shone the sun*
> *The guns of the Cumberland sounded a warning*
> *Which told every sailor to stand by his gun*
>
> *An iron-clad frigate down on us came bearing*
> *And high up above the rebel flag flew*
> *Its pennant of treason it proudly was wearing*
> *Determined to conquer the Cumberland's crew*

It must have been a long battle because the verses seemed to go on forever:

> *Then up spoke our Captain a stern resolution*
> *"We've sworn to defend our beloved constitution*
> *And to die for our country we are not afraid*
>
> *"We'll fight for the union, our cause it is glorious*
> *For the stars and the stripes will stand ever true*
> *We'll die at our station or conquer victorious"*
> *He was answered by cheers from the Cumberland's crew"*

Finally Frank said, "All that for one ship? Why Drake would have jolly well finished off the entire Spanish Armada by the fifteenth verse."

> *Our noble ship fired huge guns dreadful thunder*
> *Our small shot like hail on the rebels did fall*
> *The crowds all stood gazing in terror and wonder*
> *As our shot struck her hull and glanced harmlessly o'er*

> *The pride of the Union could never be daunted*
> *Though our decks with the dead and wounded did strew*
> *The star spangled banner how proudly it flaunted*
> *It was nailed to the mast by the Cumberland's crew*
>
> *Three hours they fought us with stern resolution*
> *'Til these rebels found cannon could never decide*
> *The flag of succession had no power to quell us*
> *Though our blood in the scuppers did crimson the tide*

My attention drifted and I think Howland repeated a few verses, but it ended badly for the Union:

> *She struck us amidships our planks she did sever*
> *Her cruel iron prow pierced our noble ship through*
> *They cried as they sank in that dark rolling river*
> *"We'll die at our guns," said the Cumberland's crew*
>
> *So slowly they sank in that dark rolling water*
> *Their voices on earth won't be heard any more*
> *They'll be wept by Columbia's brave sons and fair daughters*
> *May their blood be avenged on Virginia's old shore*
>
> *Whenever our sailors in battle assemble*
> *God bless our fair pennant of red white and blue*
> *Beneath its proud folds we'll cause tyrants to tremble*
> *Or die at our guns like the Cumberland's crew*

Major and Jack were watching for a star to shoot with the sextant when Morpheus sent me to sleep The sound of the river was like the roar of a train, and I dreamt I was on a train going to Massachusetts, so I guess I missed Lucy and mother.

The eighth of March was the fatal day in Howland's song, so maybe eight is unlucky. Anyway, on the eighth of June disaster struck. We worked hard all morning, stopping every few hundred yards so Major could walk down the river and decide whether to run or line the boats. Mostly he decided to line and about half the time he also decided the boats had to be lightened so they would-n't sit so deep in the water or so we could hold them against the pull of the tide. That meant we had to portage the cargoes along a rocky scree. If it was up to me I'd of run them all, for I believed then that the danger to life was only trifling.

By noon we were all wet and tired enough to sleep again, but Major had us back in the boats after a quick meal of leftover biscuits and coffee. The river grew worse after dinner, full of boulders, all the boats shipping water from the waves and backwashes off the canyon walls, which could swamp a boat that got too close. The *Emma Dean* was leading as usual, and I followed in the *Maid*. The *No Name* was following me, and *Sister* was last. With the boats two hundred yards apart we kept losing sight of the pilot boat and were left to choose our own course. I used the sweep oar to hew to the middle of the river and avoid the backwash off the clift, but it was rocky there and I guess that's why Howland favored the right side of the river. I looked downstream and saw the *Emma Dean* disappear around a bend to the right.

When I looked back up the river I saw the *No Name* get hit by a backwash and half fill with water. I yelled to Howland and motioned for him to steer toward the middle, but I could see he was having trouble just keeping afloat, navigation being a matter beyond his ability at that moment. The *No Name* was moving slow, like a sunken log, and as the tide had quickened where I was, I couldn't slow up to throw her a line. I rounded the bend and saw the *Emma Dean* beached in a little bay on the left. I didn't see Major or Jack anywhere. Bill Dunn was in the *Emma Dean* waving the flag around in a signal that was new to me, but the roar of the water below told me that I had to land, and I angled the bow toward the left bank. When I got to where I could see downstream I saw that the river sort of sagged to the right, gathered force and made a frightening series of rocky falls beneath a steep clift on its right.

I shipped the steering oar and jumped to the other rowing pair. Walter and I had to pull hard to get acrost without we were taken by the strong tide in the sag, so I knew the *No Name* would have trouble, being half swamped and far to the right. Howland was standing in the stern his flowing beard blowing up into his face, trying to steer with the big sweep oar, while Seneca rowed at the forward oars and Frank Goodman at the aft pair, though Frank was flailing more than rowing, looking over his shoulder, saying something I couldn't hear.

When we'd beached the *Maid* next to the *Emma Dean*, I looked back to see Oramel with the steering oar hard over to turn to the left and the other two men pulling with all their might trying to get the *No Name* across the strengthening tide. They got her bow turned at last but now she was broadside and the tide snatched her. I was yelling and beckoning, Dunn was yelling and waving his flag, and Howland was yelling, "Good Christ in heaven, row!"

When *Sister* came around the bend, Andy started to yell too. If yelling helped, we would have rescued her, but the *No Name* broached and began to move sideways downstream, ever faster. Frank stood as if to jump out of the boat, but Oramel pushed him down just as the boat struck a rock and they were both tumbled into the boat's bottom. In the moment that her forward motion was arrested by the rock, the water rushed in from behind, totally swamping her. The boat pivoted on the rock then, giving Frank and Oramel time to get back to their oars, but the long steering oar snagged on another rock and was yanked out of Oramel's hands.

The boat headed bow first downstream and dove over a short fall near the clift on the right, and I saw the oars get ripped from Frank's hands and then from Seneca's, the oarlocks torn from the hull. The spray and foam made it hard to see but I could make out that Seneca and Frank were hanging onto the gunwales for dear life while Oramel clung to the stern. Totally helpless, they entered the next fall, which was longer, maybe forty feet long, narrow and filled with rocks. The *No Name* struck a boulder with her port bow so hard she was stove in, the solid oak plank reduced to splinters. She spun around in a half circle, then struck another rock amidships on the starboard side with such force the boat broke in two, plunging Seneca and Frank into the freezing water.

They somehow clambered back in and the three of them were huddled in the stern section which was mostly submerged from their combined weight. They clung to the boat's remnant as it was knocked from rock to rock like a caroming billiard ball, the waves washing over them again and again. I kept losing sight of them but they continued to be battered that way for two hundred yards or so when the boat collided with another boulder and Frank and Seneca were again thrown into the water. I thought they were done for, but somehow they hauled themselves aboard again, just before the wreck plunged over a six foot fall that would surely have drowned them had they been in the water.

The water pooled briefly at the foot of the fall and there was a sandy island shoal on the left, a sea of spray and foam beyond. Howland yelled something, and Frank dove overboard. The pool was deep, and he sank from sight. Oramel jumped next and in a few strokes made the little island and pulled himself onto the beach. Seneca clung to the hull until he was only thirty feet from a big, boiling fall and certain death. Oramel was yelling and motioning for Seneca to jump. Seneca made what Jack later said was "the best leap I ever saw by a two-legged animal." He said Seneca made the shoal just at its bottom tip only seconds before the remains of the *No Name* dashed against a massive boulder, broke into a dozen pieces and disappeared in the maelstrom below.

When I looked to see what happened to Frank, I saw that the river had carried him to a whirlpool near the clift on the right. He was circling around in it, bobbing up and down in a fashion that would have been comical if it wasn't so serious. Finally he was thrust against a barrel-sized rock not far from the island and got his arms around it, the waters of the whirlpool smashing against the clift and circling back around him like a coiling rattlesnake.

Seeing Seneca was safe, Howland ran to the upstream end of the island, nearest Frank, who was suffering from the cold and seeming like he was about to be torn from the rock into the stream. Howland found a long pine root in a pile of driftwood and pushed it acrost to Frank who let go the rock and grabbed it, and Oramel pulled him in like he was a snagged log.

Jack and Major had left Dunn in the *Emma Dean* to signal the other boats and were downstream scouting the rapid when the disaster occurred. The two of them were then on the left shore, across from the island where the *No Name's* crew ended up. The rest of us scrambled to unload the *Emma Dean's* cargo and lower her down on a line at some cost to our shins and our tempers until we got her to a point opposite the marooned men. Oramel always kept matches in his tobacco tin, and he managed to get a fire going, lighting the pitch of a giant pine log, a blessed thing, for Frank looked about as cold as a body can be and still be alive. He was turning blue and shivering so he couldn't talk, not that I could have heard him over the roar of the rapids. It put me in mind of a time I pulled a man out of the ocean when he'd slipped hauling in a net. He turned blue and his flesh felt so cold you wondered his heart could beat. By the time I got him from our dory onto the mother boat, where there were blankets, he'd stopped shivering and died in an hour.

The log had been split by lightning and there was a pitch-filled crack that ran the length of it on the side facing us, making Oramel's fire a long horizontal line of sputtering blue flame. A rock that had been out of the water when we first got the *Emma Dean* down had nearly disappeared, so I guessed the snow was melting fast in the Wind River mountains, flooding the Green with icy water. It wouldn't be long before it would put out the fire and perhaps even cover the island. We had to move quick. Time would be lacking for a second trip, so the *Emma Dean* would have to be rowed over by one man and back with four, though she was built to be rowed by two and to carry only three. Though I'd learned not to volunteer in the army, the sight of those boys was pitiful, and I volunteered to be the one that rescued them. Andy did, too, but Jack said, "Sorry boys, only the trapper rows the pilot boat. But you can give me a powerful push."

I lashed the forward pair of oars to the gunwales to keep them from being torn away, making a slipknot that could easy be undone. We pulled the *Emma Dean* upstream as far as the rocks permitted and launched Jack toward the island with a push Hercules would have envied. Jack rowed with a will, though mostly the tide took him, and threaded through the rocks to the island with only one solid knock against a rock. Seneca caught his bow near the downstream end of the island, which was getting smaller as we watched, the water below it a foaming boil of rocks and rapids. Oramel and Seneca hauled the little boat up to the top end of the island where

Seneca held the boat while Oramel and Jack managed to get Frank aboard. Frank was still shivering, so I was hopeful he wouldn't die. Then the Howland brothers got into the cold water again and pulled the *Emma Dean* farther upstream until they were in water up to their necks, trying to get as much distance as they could from the terrible rapids below the island.

Frank took Major's seat where there was a strap to hold on to, and Oramel climbed in and took the forward oars while Seneca stood on a rock and held the *Emma Dean's* bow. At a "Go" from Jack, Seneca pushed the little boat's bow into the stream and flung himself over the forward compartment. Jack and Oramel pulled mightily on the oars and the tide pushed on the bow. She turned half a circle towards downstream then hit a rock, her bow pitching up near forty-five degrees, almost throwing Seneca back into the water. The tide took her stern then and swung it downstream, around the rock on the island side.

Jack and Oramel rowed against the tide and slowed their speed some, but they were going downstream sternforemost without making progress acrost to where we were huddled waiting. They were wiggling their way through the rocks but were having trouble rounding them on the side nearest us, and I despaired that they would make it. We'd left the *Emma Dean's* line in her so had nothing to throw them. They were headed straight for the roaring rapid below. Bill Dunn and Andy, in some distress, waded out into water up to their chests, hoping to catch her, Bill's hair flowing like seaweed in the tide. When it looked like they might be taken by the tide, too, Major ordered them to stop. It was touch and go whether the little boat could get to where they could catch her when Seneca on the bow managed to reach into the boat, grab the *Emma Dean's* line and throw it to them. Andy caught it and they hauled the boat in, fifty feet from a perfect hell of foam. With much handshaking all around, Major said he was "as glad to shake hands with them as if they had been on a voyage around the world and had been wrecked on a distant shore."

I wrapped Frank in my coat and rubbed his shoulders to thaw him out while Billy built up a fire. When Frank didn't show any signs that he could move and then stopped shivering so much, I was afraid we were going to lose him. Then after what seemed an eternity, he began to move around a bit and then stopped shivering and finally got up and said, "Bloody cold, that water," which provoked a loud cheer from everybody, even Andy.

Then Frank passed out, his great bulk falling against me and carrying me down with him. He was still breathing and began to snore, so I guessed he'd be all right and thought we should let him sleep, but Major said no, "Wake him up. Keep him moving. Keep the blood flowing." We set about it, Howland declaring, "It's like Sisyphus rolling the rock uphill," but we finally got Frank on his feet and awake enough so we could walk him around and around the fire.

When Frank seemed to be recovering, Jack told Major how the experience of going down the rapids stern-first "might just be the way to do it all the time, Professor. First off, you can see where you're going, and second, you can slow the boat a mite by rowing against the current." Major answered pretty sharp, "Boats are built to go bow first, that's why they have a point." But it seemed to me there was merit in Jack's suggestion and I decided I'd try it some time when Major's boat was out of sight.

I asked Jack if his last ride was still "like sparking a black-eyed girl, just dangerous enough to be exciting." Pulling on his moustache and nodding a bit, he said, "More like being married to one —pure hell."

Major was pretty angry. First he barked at Dunn, wanted to know if he had signaled with the flag. When Bill said he had, Major turned to Howland and asked if he saw the signal. Oramel said, "Saw it all right, John, didn't understand it at first, but it made no difference. We were too far to the right and too full of water to land."

Then we totted up our losses: Half the mess kit, all the outer clothing of the *No Name's* crew, three Henry rifles, one Colt revolver, nearly a ton of provisions, all of Howland's maps and notes and all the barometers. Through some mistake, the barometer that Major usually kept in the *Emma Dean* wound up in the *No Name*, and so did the one mostly kept in my boat. Major was fuming when he learned we'd lost all the barometers, and it struck me that he had more concern about the instruments than whether those three boys had to run around naked.

Leaving the three to dry by the fire, the rest of us went on letting the *Emma Dean* down on lines, hoping against hope that some of the cargo might have been thrown ashore or was stuck on a rock where we could get at it. It was a faint hope and seemed to be a vain one. We let down a quarter mile and there was nothing, another quarter mile and still nothing. Then, of a sudden, we saw part of the *No Name's* rear cuddy stuck on a rocky shoal in the middle of the river, foaming, boulder-studded water in between. Andy and Billy Rhoads volunteered to row over and try to recover it. Major looked at Jack, who would insist on rowing his own boat, and when he made no move Major said, "There's been enough risk of life for one day."

As we passed the island on our way back upstream to the big boats, there was nothing left of it but a narrow strip of sand with the big pine log and its line of blue flame. Just as we came opposite the log, the rising water reached the flame and it went out all at once with a hiss and a pop that we could hear even over the sound of the river, and a plume of steam slipped skyward.

I was talking to Billy about how the high water meant fast water, which could be good or bad. I said, "On the one hand, it will hide the rocks and any strike would do more damage to the boats, but on the other hand, it will cover some rocks to a depth that would let the boats pass over." Billy grinned and said, "Best ask Major to decide. He's only got one hand."

We made our way upstream to the big boats and set up camp, nobody saying much. Even the roaring fire and the smell of Billy's biscuits baking and the bacon frying did nothing to cheer us up. We shared out our spare clothing among the three who lost everything. Nobody had clothes big enough for Frank, so I gave him my blanket as I could sleep in my clothes and use my poncho for a blanket.

Supper that night was a melancholy affair. Major didn't eat anything but drank four mugs of coffee. Frank sat there wrapped in nothing but my blanket, waiting for his shirt and drawers to dry. Billy bustled about the fire, poking it here and there, sending up a shower of orange sparks, though it was doing fine on its own. Jack and Andy tried to loosen things up by joking about the biscuits and bacon, but they didn't spark much conversation from the rest of us. I thought to cheer things up and said that it was always darkest before the dawn and that the sun of another day might bring better luck.

Frank perked up then and seemed to come suddenly from a cold place into the warm; he stopped hugging himself to himself and started a song, which he taught me the next day. He started so low we first thought he was moaning. We had to stop what talk there was and cock our ears. I even wanted to shush the fire of its crackling:

> *Clouds are upon the Summer sky*
> *There's thunder in the wind*
> *Pull on, pull on and homeward hie*
> *Nor give one look behind*
>
> *Row on, row on, another day*
> *May shine with brighter light*
> *Ply, ply the oars and pull away*
> *There's dawn beyond the night*
>
> *Fare where thou goest, the words of love*
> *Say all that words can say*
> *Changeless affection's strength to prove*
> *But speed upon the way*
>
> *Row on, row on, another day*
> *May shine with brighter light*
> *Ply, ply the oars and pull away*
> *There's dawn beyond the night*
> *Like yonder river would I glide*
> *To where my heart would be*
> *My bark should soon outsail the tide*
> *That hurries to the sea*

Most of us picked up the chorus pretty good by this point, and we sang:

> *Row on, row on, another day*
> *May shine with brighter light*
> *Ply, ply the oars and pull away*
> *There's dawn beyond the night*

And Frank supplied another verse:

> *Row on, row on, God speed the way*
>   *Thou must not linger here*
>   *Storms hang about the closing day*
>   *Tomorrow may be clear*

We finished, even Major joining in:

> *Row on, row on, another day*
>   *May shine with brighter light*
>   *Ply, ply the oars and pull away*
>   *There's dawn beyond the night*

The words were uplifting and encouraging to me, but the melody was so mournful it took the meaning to a different, sad place, and it made me homesick. The next day when Frank and I were alone, I told him how I felt about his song, leaving out the homesick part, of course. He said the song's style was a lament, so I was meant to feel sad. I guessed then that Frank was homesick too.

I felt a little better after my prayers, but my spirits were pretty low at the thought of lining and portaging around nearly a mile of roaring rapid. Still, all's well that ends well. But the end was not yet in sight. Then it came to my mind that there would be less cargo to carry, so every cloud has a silver lining, I thought as I fell asleep. I dreamt a train arrived with barometers and a side of beef.

There was no boisterous "Bulls in the corral..." from Billy the next morning. He just went around shaking us awake. I guessed that Major hadn't slept at all, because he had already made biscuits and boiled coffee. The biscuits were hard and granite-like, and the coffee was so thin Jack said, "It's what I call 'versatile', as it could as easy pass for tea." Since we'd lost half our mess-kit in the wreck, we had only one cup between each two men, and when I passed mine to Frank, he tasted it and complimented Billy on his coffee. When Major headed downriver to scout, Billy dumped the biscuits and made another batch, this time with saleratus to make them rise. Andy used Major's biscuits as skipping stones, throwing them one by one out to the middle of the river, where they sank.

When Major came back from scouting the wreck, he told us what he planned to do:

"First, we'll move the big boats down, keeping an eye on the wreck, which looks like it wants to move with the rising water. Maybe it will move to a place where we can get at it. Except for the barometers, we can do without everything we lost until we get to the Uinta trading post where we can probably replace most of it." He said, "I'm authorized to draw supplies from army posts, and I have a letter from the Secretary of War to that effect. I hope and expect they'll honor it at the Uinta trading post as it's a government agency.

"We can reconstruct the map from my notes and from what we collectively remember of each day's travel. But if we can't retrieve a barometer, we can't measure altitudes." He told us he could guess the clift heights pretty good from a method he'd figured out and called, "triangulation," but he couldn't measure altitude at river level. Without the river's fall he really wouldn't have a "portrait," as he called it, of the river.

Not being a scientist I said, "It strikes me the trip justifies itself, as we will be the first to make it, neither white man nor red before us," but Major wouldn't have it. He said, "We're not going on just for the adventure. I'm damned and determined to get to the wreck if humanly possible. I didn't quit the war just because I lost my arm, and I'm not going to quit this river for the loss of a boat. If we can't get a boat over to it where it is now, we'll camp until the river moves it to a better spot. If we can get just one barometer we'll go on with three boats. If we can't get an instrument, we'll camp at Uinta Basin until I can get to Salt Lake City and send to New York for more barometers."

Camping for weeks in one place waiting for barometers to arrive from New York wasn't my style. I like to keep moving, so I made up my mind that I'd *swim* to the wreck if I had to, get the barometers come hell or high water. And the water *was* higher, though it wasn't rising much any more. What it meant was the narrow rocky beach we'd used to let down the *Emma Dean* was now covered with water. To portage the cargo and let down the other boats, we were going to have to build a road through broken rocks and stunted mountain cedars on a talus slope.

Two of us took axes and cut the scrub cedar trees while the rest wrestled the rocks, and with great labor we got a rough road built and lined the *Maid* and *Sister* down to a little sandy beach. After wolfing down the rest of Billy's biscuits and coffee, we set out to move the cargo. We'd got only a small part of it portaged when we heard a shout from Major, who was watching the wreck. The rising water had shifted it fifty or sixty feet to where it lay wedged between two boulders at the head of another small island. It wasn't likely to move again, so Major said, "It's now or never." The wreck was in a better place, all right, but that was a relative thing. When I saw where the cuddy was lodged, I took back my silent vow to swim to it, or even to try to row over, for there was swift, rocky water between, all foaming like a hard-ridden horse. I felt a little ashamed and was about to volunteer anyway when Oramel said, slow and deliberate, "Seneca and I will try to get over to the wreck, John. It's our responsibility."

But Major wouldn't hear of it, brushed Oramel off with a quick wave of his one hand, "How to row you know not, Oramel." He was barely speaking to Oramel since the *No Name* was lost. Then Andy Hall said he'd try it if someone would go with him, but Jack said, "No bullwhacker's goin to pilot my boat."

"Well, Mr. Sumner, you'll be joining me then," Andy said and headed toward the *Emma Dean* where she was beached upstream. Jack followed, after a pause so short you wouldn't have noticed if you weren't looking right at him. It occurred to me that I'd never heard Jack call the *Emma Dean* by name. It was always, "the little boat" or "the pilot boat," or "my boat," and I thought I might ask him why when an opportunity came along.

We hauled the *Emma Dean* farther upstream to where the tide could carry her down to the wreck and eased her into the rushing water. With Andy supplying most of the power and Jack doing the steering, they got over all right but not without a few hard knocks and one near capsizing where they slid over a boulder that the high water had hidden.

Soon they were breaking open the cuddy while we craned our necks to see what they'd find. Andy let out a whoop and Jack yelped like a wolf, and they held up in turn three barometer cases, extra glass tubes, some thermometers and an old pair of boots. I could see Major was touched that they thought so much about finding his barometers, because his eyes teared up a bit. Then Andy held up a blue gallon jug of whiskey and we all let out a whoop. No doubt that was the object Oramel took from Jake Fields just before we left Green River City.

It was a bold thing Jack and Andy had done, not least because they hadn't figured how to get back. They couldn't row back upstream the way they'd come, and downstream the water was fast and rocky. They went off to scout the island and when they came back and started walking the *Emma Dean downstream,* we thought they'd taken leave of their senses. Major shouted to them and they shouted back, but the noise of the water made understanding a thing only to be wished for. The next we saw, they seemed to be hauling the *Emma Dean* up onto the island, behind a few bushes that hid them from view.

We all moved downstream to see better and determined that they had found a narrow cut through the island to the main channel on the far side, where there were fewer rocks. They hauled the little boat through the cut and then launched into the main channel. Rowing hard, they crossed over through a small pool at the bottom of the island and back into the channel on the left. We were all edging the shore with outstretched hands yelling for them to throw us a line, which Andy did while Jack rowed, and we pulled them to shore. When he got out with the whiskey, Jack said, "You looked like a bunch of little children reaching for your mother's apron strings," but I expect he was glad to have come through with just a little wetting. When Major took the barometers and held them clutched to himself, Jack said he "Looked as happy as a young girl with her first beau."

Oramel said Jack deserved the honor of opening the blue jug, and when Jack uncorked it he declared it to have been untapped. Billy whispered to Andy, "About as untapped as Kitty and her sister." I heard it, and I guess Major did, because he looked sharp at Oramel. I suspect he was wondering if the jug might have had something to do with Oramel's seamanship. At least that was my suspicion when I thought back to Oramel's surprising us by singing *The Cumberland's Crew*. He never sang again on the trip.

We all had a drink, and maybe more than one. Major could see that we weren't in shape to bring the rest of our cargo down, so he declared a holiday. Maybe it was the whiskey but anyway for a while I forgot the danger we were in and walked up a little side canyon to see what the land was like. The scenery at that point was sublime. The red sandstone rose on either side more than two thousand feet, shutting out the sun for much of the day while at our feet the river, lashed to foam, rushed on with indescribable fury. I thought how great is He who holds it in the hollow of his hand, and what pygmies we who strive against it. A shiver went through me then and I was taken with a feeling that God would see me safely through this dangerous journey.

While Billy was cooking up breakfast next morning, Major and his brother went downriver to see if anything else survived the wreck. Walter was determined he would find rifles or a pistol which were heavy enough to stay put on the bottom. But all they found from the wreck was three sacks of flour, wedged between rocks and too wet to be of use, and a couple of oars. But they found an old half-buried boat prow, some rusted bread pans and a dutch oven with a broken lid, so we weren't the first ones to come to grief in those rapids. Major said he thought they might have been from Ashley's party.

They brought the cooking utensils back and gave them to Billy. As soon as Major was out of sight, Billy threw them in the river. "Rusted and cracked," he said, "Can't use 'em." Jack went to his boat and brought back the breadpans he'd found in a cabin early on and added them to Billy's depleted mess-kit saying, "I was goin to pan for gold and make us all rich, but shoot, Missouri, your biscuits are worth a ton of gold." He paused a bit then said, "And they're near as heavy."

Major named the place "Disaster Falls."

JUNE 11 SPLIT MOUNTAIN

We went on with three boats. We cut scrub cedars, built roads, lowered the boats, portaged the cargo, and once we had to carry the boats as well, for the fall was a drop of twelve feet and rocks had damned the rest of the river clear acrost. Sometimes we would make only forty yards at a time, lining the boats, at other times we'd line a half mile, then we'd run a short rapid or two, unload the boats, lower again, portage the cargo. Mules have a better life. We were really in one continuous rapid, rather than in a series of them, and it seemed it had no end. This was the first time I was truly discouraged. Judging from the wreckage we had found, it was likely Ashley had drowned here or had walked out. If the rapids went on being impassable much longer I feared we'd have to do the same thing, abandon the river, walk out over territory unexplored and unmapped.

All the boats were being hammered bad on the rocks, and in one place where we were letting the boats down on lines and I was in the *Maid*, fending off, I guess I tried too hard to protect the boat, or maybe I was so tired I wasn't thinking, anyway I slipped, hit my head on the gunwale and opened up a gash over my left eye. That night at supper I was being ragged by the other boys about my caring so much for the boat that I near killed myself. I didn't mind, just wondered aloud if there would be a scar. Andy said, "'Twill surely be a great improvement fer ya, Sergeant Bradley." Everybody agreed and I guess I did too as there isn't much you could do to worsen my ugly mug.

We'd crossed to the west side of the river where there was nothing in the way of beach but a bunch of rocks under an overhanging ledge. The rapids below were roaring like a wild beast, we were tired and cranky, snapping at each other, and Major said we'd wait until morning to pass on further.

I needed rest but couldn't find anything but rocks to sleep on and as I'd given away my blanket, I had no kind of cushion. The Major as usual had chosen the worst camping-ground possible. Oramel asked me, "How do you like the accommodations, Sergeant?" I told him, "If I had a dog that would lie where I have to make my bed tonight, I would kill him and burn his collar and swear I never owned him."

I felt a little better the next day, no thanks to Major nor to a good night's sleep. But it was best to be doing, grueling though it promised to be. The river kept the promise: it was a repeat of the day before, but worse, linings, portages, brief running, more linings and portages until we were bone-weary and beaver-wet. At about three o'clock the roar of fast, rocky water came again, and we found we had another mile-long rapid ahead of us. None had the strength to essay it, so we campt on the east side of the river, and this time we had a bit of luck. Opposite was a notch in the clift that let the sun through, so we would have two or three hours to dry our clothes. I'd always thought of a river being wet and a desert being dry, but here we were on a river in a high desert, so if it didn't rain, clothes would dry in an hour.

The more I looked at that furious rapid the more I had doubts we could get the boats over it. Still there was no retreat. We had to go and I told myself that we would be successful. My eye had closed and turned very black and while it was not very *useful*, it was very *ornamental*.

We were all tired beyond measure from the work, except for Major of course, edging toward despair, anxious to try the worst rapid we'd seen so far, and to know if we'd succeed or fail in the attempt. But Major said he wanted to stop and reconstruct Howland's map from his own notes and our memories. He was hardly civil to Howland, kept snapping when Oramel's recollection was different from his. Every day it wasn't raining we'd taken altitudes at river level three times, and measured longitude at noon and clift heights at one o'clock. We did latitude when Jack and Major could shoot the moon or a known star with the sextant. Jack had kept his own notes of latitude and longitude readings, though he could reel them off pretty good from memory. Howland had taken compass readings at turns in the river and he remembered them pretty well, but Major challenged almost every one of them, "It can't go west there, there's a wall; it had to be southwest...,"or, "I don't recall the river being that wide...," and so on.

It wasn't hard to remember the altitudes at river level because they told us how far we'd descended from the 6075 feet at Green River bridge. So over two days, we pieced together the recordings and Howland drew a fair map of the river to where we were campt. When Major was out of sight, Oramel added a little drawing of a boat crashing at the point where Disaster Falls lay on his map.

I spotted a woodchuck so big I thought it was a fox, and maybe it was, at least Walter thought so. Jack pointed out a badger creeping along a ledge but that was it for wildlife. The ducks and geese had better sense than we did and stayed away, but there was birdsong from time to time, jays and robins mostly and one dove.

We busied ourselves cutting new oars from pine logs with axe and handsaw, a chore that takes no skill but some heavy work sawing and adzing with the axe. What we created bore little resemblance to the lathe-rounded oars we started with, but if they wouldn't win any beauty contests, they would serve. We scraped pine pitch from the trees, patched and recaulked the boats, made moccasins out of tarpaulin, stitched up torn clothes and played cards when we ran out of other things to do. Jack was in a poker game with Walter Powell and Frank Goodman when I was recaulking the *Maid*. I'd lay in a length of oakum, spread pine pitch over it, smooth it down clean with my sheath knife (I'd long since said goodbye to my caulking tool) and move on. Jack was watching me over the top of his cards and when the hand was over he said, "George, I've known cowhands in love with their horses weren't as fond of 'em as you are of the *Maid*." I was trying to think up a reply when Walter broke in, "Many a man been in love with a maid," he said, all solemn like. Then he burst out in that snorting laugh of his at his own joke. But that wasn't enough, he started a song:

> *Come where my love lies dreaming...*

He hadn't got any farther when Jack yelled, "Sheep!"

He and Frank jumped up, grabbed their rifles and started blasting away at the sheep, with the usual result. Walter scooped up the pot he'd just won and the three of them set off after the sheep, leaving their cards where they'd been playing. Thinking that the wind might carry them off, I went to gather them up. I looked to see what cards Walter held when he won the pot. It was three kings. Then I looked at Jack's hand. Three queens. Same hands as were held in Walter's game with the Irishman.

I'd got to the point where nothing on the trip could surprise me except if the hunters brought back game. True to prediction, they returned without so much as a field mouse. They seemed more like schoolboys on a holiday than like men accustomed to live by the chase. It struck me that if we failed on this journey, it would be want of judgment that would defeat us and if we succeeded it would be *dumb luck*.

It was the Sabbath and for once we had a day of rest. I'm sure it was accidental though, for I don't think anyone in the party except myself kept a record of time or events.

Monday it turned out was a day when I profited from the rest. The human frame, when sorely taxed during the week, is greatly the better for rest on the Sabbath.

Major had assigned the Howland brothers to our boat, and it made the *Maid* very low in the water. I didn't complain because I knew the Howlands were low in their spirits from having lost everything in the wreck, but I thought fairness demanded at least we trade off sometimes with *Sister*, or shift some cargo to the *Emma Dean* which rode pretty high.

I half expected Howland to do his mathematics, "Two rail-thin Vermonters equal one fat Englishman," but he didn't say anything for a long time, then he said, "We left not a wrack behind." I said that at least *they* weren't left behind, and Walter surprised us by saying, "God is everywhere."

Oramel said, "Wherever God was, He wasn't at the oars."

After letting the boats down two very bad rapids we started to run, and the rapids weren't too bad until we came to a place where there was a backwash off a clift. Walter and I rowed hard to get through it, but we were too heavy to get away, and the *Maid* filled and started to sink, sort of slow, like a balloon leaking air. We could hear rough water ahead and when we could see the rapids coming up—and they were big ones— I thought it was going to be the *No Name* wreck all over again. *Sister's* crew saw what was happening and by rowing hard managed to catch up with us. Frank threw us a line and they towed us to the head of the rapids where we could bail the water. We'd given up the idea of keeping the boats two hundred yards apart after Disaster Falls. Major didn't order the change, we just fell into it, wanting to be close enough to the next boat to help out in case of trouble. We speculated that if *Sister* had been closer at Disaster Falls, they could have saved the *No Name*.

Launching again, we found ourselves in a swift rapid and ran it without even thinking about it. It was reckless, but many reckless things are beautiful, and we had a beautiful ride of a half mile, racing along at railroad speed, laughing, shouting, singing, joking. Howland said it was "Merry as an Irish wake." Then there was a half mile of smooth water until we heard the tell-tale roar again and Major waved us in with his little red flag.

The next rapid was even worse than it sounded, *five times worse* than any we'd seen to that point and there was no beach, so we would have to build a road. We campt in some scrubby cedars and spent the afternoon chopping trees and carrying rocks until we had a narrow road built to where we might portage the cargoes and let the boats down and start to run again in the morning.

We'd had two opportunities to dry our clothes in the last week but we were wet again, and the constant wetting was beginning to tell. We had to strain out the lumps of the flour with a mosquito bar, or "net" as some call it. Billy's biscuits had begun to take on a sour taste and the bacon had turned fish-belly white and so near to rancid that Jack refused it. The coffee was about the only thing that had stayed dry, as Major kept it in the *Emma Dean's* forward cuddy, wrapped in his poncho.

When my boat filled with water, my notes and papers and books were soaked and my tintype albums were soggy as bog moss. I dried my notes and my discharge papers and vowed to keep them in my hat for the rest of the trip. I was afraid to open the tintypes until they dried, so I put them near the fire and set to swabbing out the *Maid* and touching up her caulking with pine pitch, as every lining takes its toll.

The next morning we lined the boats down and portaged the nearly two tons of cargo on our backs to where we could reload and line them down loaded. We got them through an eddy and then a small rapid, all of us grateful we didn't have to carry the cargoes again, but the fully loaded boats suffered more damage, being lower in the water and so striking more rocks. They were harder to hold too, five men needed to hold the line. We could have used six but Major took his brother to the clift to measure altitude, and we needed the others on the rocks or shore to fend off.

We were letting the *Maid* down and at one point gave her too much slack. She got her prow crossways to the tide where it was able to apply full force and we couldn't hold her. The rope burned through our hands and she was loose. She raced downstream like a frightened colt, smashed her stern against a boulder and began to flood. Jack and Billy jumped into the *Emma Dean* and gave chase. We watched the *Maid* disappear around a sharp bend and in a trice the *Emma Dean* was out of sight too. There was nothing I or any the six of us left there on the rocky beach could do but pray. I don't know if I did but I was hoping the *Maid* wasn't lost as ten men in two boats would hardly do. Then I realized I was being selfish as the *Emma Dean* might be gone too and I thought, "ten men in one boat." I didn't let myself think there might be only eight men.

As Jack told it, "We galloped around the bend and were brought up sharp, as if we'd been hitched to a halter rope, and there was the *Maid* turning slow in an eddy, like a colt cropping grass."

Seeing as two boats ran the rapid (and one without crew) we ran *Sister* down, easy as sleep. We were patching up the stern of the *Maid* when Major came down from the clift above, and he was steaming, face red as a raspberry. He said he'd seen Jack and Billy launch the *Emma Dean* and watched *Sister* run the rapid, and he let Jack know it was, "Damn well against orders to run a rapid I decided had to be lined."

Jack just said, "Well, Professor, we got both boats down, now didn't we?" First time I'd seen Major with nothing to say. Of course, left to me, I'd have run that rapid anyway. Its bark was worse than its bite, but of course Major didn't ask my opinion.

We campt at the top of a small rapid which I thought we could run, and I hoped and expected the worst of that canyon was over, for the soft rock was appearing nearer to the water, and when it is soft there are fewer rocks in the river and generally it behaves better. We had learned to read the river by looking at the clifts, the way you can usually tell a man's feelings by the expression on his face: dark rock is hard, and hard rock narrows the canyon, speeds up the water and makes for more treacherous, rocky rapids. Dark rock makes the canyon walls more vertical, so there may not be a beach, and we'd either have to build a road or wade. We had been in mostly dark red sandstone containing much iron. Coming up was a dirty white limestone, very shaley so, as Jack said, we had the testimony of the rocks that the future was favorable.

I'd finished the judge's book by that name and Jack had borrowed it. Frank told him that the author, Hugh Miller, must have been English, but Andy told him, "Miller was a Scot, never mind the name." Jack said, "I don't put much stock in books written by foreigners. Don't you have any other books?" "There's my Bible," I told him. "Largely written by foreigners," Oramel said.

The testimony of the rocks proved true, up to a point. We had easy running the next day, ran a number of small rapids and made about five miles between low clifts, saw beaver but couldn't get a shot at them. Then Major ordered us to let the boats down on lines in several places, and once we had to make a short portage of the freight. Then we began to strike whirlpools. Where the water can't get through it runs back upstream making an eddy. If it runs back swift enough, it may also make a whirlpool. These were alarming when we first met them but after navigating through five or six of them, we began to feel easy, sometimes rotating a time or two just for the fun of it. Then we dove over a small cataract into a huge whirlpool, and began to whirl around in circles like children on a merry-go-round until we were almost giddy with the motion and laughing that a backwards river has given us as much trouble as a roaring rapid. Major got out his flag and we beached the boats and man-hauled them through on lines, Andy pretending to drive us like oxen.

We ran rapids all afternoon, one so rocky the *Maid* was nearly stove and all the boats ended up battered and leaking. They were half full of water by the time we spotted a grove of mountain pine where we could get pitch for caulking. We got the boats in, tied them to a dead willow near the water and bailed them. We cut a path through a whole mass of dead willows and a bunch of scrub cedars that were edging the bank, and made camp in the middle of a pine grove, where there was a bed of dry pine needles that would make for soft sleeping. Major and Dunn went off with a barometer to climb the clift and measure altitude. Bill Rhoads made a fire with some tinder dry willow branches that were lying everywhere and set about getting things set up for cooking. While he and Andy were sifting some flour through a mosquito bar, a little wind sprang up and blew a few sparks from the fire to the underbrush. This sort of thing had happened before and I figured one of the boys would stamp it out and went on unwrapping my tintype albums from my poncho.

Then, with the swiftness of a rapid, a whirlwind roared up the canyon, ripped the fire from the underbrush and into the trees. It seemed like the pines were in competition with the cedars to see which could burn the fastest, each tree sounding like an explosion as its dry needles flamed all at once. The whole camp was ablaze in seconds, on the ground beneath us, in the trees above us and in the bushes around us. There was no way to put the fire out and trying to get up the clift after Major and Dunn meant breasting a wall of flame. We had to make for the river.

I grabbed my albums and the others grabbed clothing and instruments or whatever was to hand, Billy filling his arms with the meager remains of our mess-kit, and we raced for the river. We reached the bank just ahead of the fire, but when it got to the willows, the whole bank exploded in flame and our clothing began to burn. I dropped an album and when I bent to retrieve it my neckerchief caught fire. I tossed my albums into the nearest boat and tried to tear the neckerchief off. But it was knotted and I could feel my moustache and hair beginning to burn. By the time I got it off, my ears were scorched and raw, and my eyebrows and eyelashes were gone. I jumped into the *Maid* with the Howlands, and we helped beat each other's fire out.

We couldn't untie the boats from the willow, which was ablaze, so undid the mooring lines from the ringbolts, leaving the ends smoking on shore. The *Emma Dean* and *Sister* cast off, but I held my mooring line waiting for Billy, who was running with the heavy mess-kit, his clothes smoking and burning and us in the *Maid* yelling for him to hurry. He leapt for the boat but tripped over the mooring line and fell, spilling the mess-kit and himself into ten feet of rushing water. I let go the mooring line and helped him in, and we were off down the river. We landed the three boats at a small beach a few rods downstream, where we thought we were safe. But the wind had learned from the whirlpool, reversed its course and swept the fire after us. As it roared down, a dragon spitting smoke and flame, we pushed out again, into a rapid we had planned to line in the morning, managed to run it, and put in on a rocky point below, where there was nothing that could burn. We watched the fire get worse and worse, sending a plume of smoke three thousand feet in the air, rushing up the canyon walls, burning everything in sight. We were worried about Major and Dunn and hoped they'd found a cave or treeless spot to hide from the flames.

When Major and Dunn arrived they were surprised we'd had to move. They had seen the smoke but were well back from the river and hadn't seen our adventure until they saw the boats in the rapid. Bill Dunn said he figured a mutiny was in progress but Jack said we were "sullen but not mutinous." They said these in jest, but there had been more than a little grumbling and short tempers among the crew ever since we'd lost the *No Name* at Disaster Falls. Major's constant badgering of Oramel Howland left the rest of us with a bad feeling about how the trip would turn out if that kept up. Never mind our mistakes; we had to stick together or we'd fall apart, plain as that.

Major demanded to know how Billy let the fire get out of control. When he tried to explain, Major cut him off, "Why didn't you leave the mess-kit? Fire can't hurt cast iron."

"Well, now, Major, how'd I know we could get back upstream and recover it?" Major didn't dispute the point, just walked away, shaking his head and uttering a sigh audible to all.

The next morning we decided to make our way up the clift and around to where the fire had been. Jack said, "You boys go. I'll stay and guard the boats against attack by Rebel troops." Well, he'd said before, climbing wasn't in his line of work.

At the campsite, we found a black and charred landscape, burnt tree trunks sticking up like grave markers. All we recovered was a couple of blankets, scorched but usable, one teaspoon and the mooring lines, which were pretty much intact, only charred a bit where they were wrapped around the willow.

When we got back, Billy made inventory of our cooking and eating supplies and said we had:

> *One gold pan*
> *One Dutch Oven with broken lid*
> *One camp kettle*
> *One fry pan*
> *One large spoon*
> *Two teaspoons*
> *Three tin plates*
> *Five bailing cans*
> *One pick-axe*
> *One shovel*

"Lucky we got the pick-axe," Jack said. "The major might make biscuits again." Major took it all right, but he didn't laugh. Come to that, I'd rarely seen him laugh, levity not being his style.

We'd got some bacon grease on our burns, and I fear I fared worse than most. I had no eyebrows, no eyelashes, half a moustache and a black eye, not to mention scorched ears and a bruised ankle. I was a sorry sight, I know. Jack looked me up and down and said, "George, you're a sight would scare the feathers off a hoot owl."

So we had some laughs, listened to Walter sing *Old Shady* which he hopped up into quick-time, and ate the beans Billy baked in the Dutch oven using the fry pan for a lid. The beans had begun to sprout from the constant wetting, but they tasted fine. The bacon was another matter: We boiled it, but it didn't improve. Jack said it was "more over the hill than Howland," and Billy said he'd leave it for the wolves. Jack said, "No self-respecting wolf would eat it, but the coyotes will, they not having any sense of taste at all. I've seen 'em eat dried bones, deer antlers, even an old boot Bill Dunn threw out of the cabin once." Major was nodding his head as if he agreed, then he said, "I imagine the boot was quite flavorful, being Bill's."

When we got around to reckoning altitude it turned out we had descended nine hundred and seventy five feet since we left Green River City. "That's less than one fifth the descent we need to carry us to the mouth of the Rio Virgen and one-sixth that we need to get the Gulf of California," Howland calculated.

Major asked Billy how the provisions stood.

"Well," said Billy, rolling his tongue over his drooping mustache, "What we got left is about a third of our flour and beans and rice, and we just got rid of the last of the bacon. We got a goodly amount of dried apples and, Major, you needn't fear runnin out of coffee, we got bags of it."

We'd been out just twenty-four days. A blind man could see that we weren't going to last out the ten months we'd planned on, and even three months would be a stretch. Besides, we couldn't contemplate wintering over with the scant clothes we had left to us. But I told the others, "I'm sure the fishing will be good once we join with the Bear River," and Billy said, "I ain't even begun to shoot game. Just you watch my smoke when we get out of these deep canyons." Howland took his pipe out of his mouth and said, "And there's always Bill Dunn's other boot."

The soft white limestone had crept about a third of the way up the clift and the water had turned a murky grey with sediment it had torn from the stone. The river ran almost due south, the water was fast, there were few rocks and we raced along like a kite in the wind until we came to a giant surge of water coming in from the east, on our left. We knew this was the Bear River, or the Yampa as the Indians call it. The Bear had almost as much water in it as the Green, and I predicted the river would improve from then on, because more water means a wider river and less liability that the boulders that fall in would block the channel clear acrost. The Bear's water was a beautiful blue-green, and for several miles the two rivers ran parallel in the same channel, the colors staying separate as if there was a chalk-line dividing them, until they blended to a greyish-brown, the color of a possum's hide. Howland said it was like a Vermont courting couple separated in bed by a bundling board until they married.

The Bear River having two names already, Major didn't get to name it. He did get to name the canyon above, though. We had come to a clift where there were many waterfalls cascading down the side, sparkling silver in the sun. Andy said it was like "the waters of Lodore," a place in Scotland (Frank said England), and Major recited a long poem about the place, with Frank or Andy chiming in whenever Major got stuck. Jack said, "Digging into musty foreign trash for a name is un-American to say the least," but I liked the sound of the "dashing and flashing and splashing and clashing and bashing and plashing," etc. which the poem says is "the way the waters come down at Lodore." Major called the entrance to Lodore Canyon, the "Gates of Lodore," another place where a stream entered, "Alcove Brook," and the highest clift, "Dunn's Clift" because Bill Dunn nearly fell off it. It being twenty seven hundred feet high, he'd have been a goner. Major also named a place in the canyon "Triplet Falls." It doesn't take much imagination to figure why.

We campt on the east side below the junction of the Bear and the Green in a beautiful tree-rimmed grassy meadow. Acrost the river, on the west side, there was a low perpendicular clift, about six hundred feet high, grey-brown at the bottom and red on top, running for maybe a mile, where it seemed to turn to the right. The sight greatly improved our spirits which had been pretty low due to the fierce twenty-five miles of the Lodore Canyon that we had just come through, filled with hazards and dangers. Leaving that narrow deep ditch, between walls more than a half mile high, was like being released from a dark prison into broad daylight. Lodore Canyon had been the worst by far, and I predicted it was the worst we would ever meet, for what more could the river do to us than what it had already done?

An osprey soared near the top of the clift, effortless in an updraft, silver-blue wings glinting in the sunlight. I was watching the bird and didn't see Andy fire his rifle at it. He missed, of course, but I thought we were being attacked by an enemy force as the echoes came back again and again, some us said seven times but Major thought it might have been ten. The boys fired their rifles, Walter sang and Andy shouted and whistled, 'til the world was fairly ringing with sounds repeating and tumbling over one another like children in a game of leap-frog. After we settled down a bit, Major had us try different sounds and sentences, and we found that a ten-word sentence, said careful, would repeat itself before doubling.

Jack said, "That tequai's got to stay where she is, no way she can drag that many rattles around." Major laughed, remembering his story, and the laugh came back again and again as if he needed to save them up for future use. Major named the clift, "Echo Clift" and the park where we were campt, "Echo Park."

Echo Clift on the west gave us an early sunset and we all sat around the fire, smoking pipes, laying about and watching the silver disk incising the clift. "Like a harrow blade in loam," Jack said.

When we finished supper and dark descended, Walter broke into *Old Shady,* and even Andy fell silent as Walter's powerful bass voice went to the mountain and the mountain gave it back in repetitions without end:

Awayawayawayawayawayawayawayawayawayawayaway
Awayawayawayawayawayawayawayawayawayawayaway
Awayawayawayawayawayawayawayawayawayawayaway

The canyon was awash in sound. The wolves stopped to listen.

Where we were campt we could see three canyons, up the Green to Ladore, up the Bear to the east and down the Green to a canyon Major hadn't named yet, though it was probably just a continuation of Ladore. I figured with all these waters coming together there ought to be some fish, so I got out my tackle and baited up a hook. Before I'd even thrown out the line a fish a yard long came straight up out of the water, like he was hurrying me. I threw my line out, and he took the bait just as it hit the water and dove with it. I started to haul in and got him to the top of the water, but he took one look at me and broke the hook, leaving me with an empty line. I tried three more times but each time as soon as the great fellows saw me either they were off the hook or the line must break. Jack said it was my black eye and burnt mustache that did it. "Better give it up, George, they can't stand the sight of ye. Won't be fit to eat anyway."

Giving up isn't my style, so I braided four silk lines together the way Lucy taught me to do her hair braids and found a hook two inches long. I soon had a fish on shore that weighed fifteen pounds and was thirty inches long. It would make a fine breakfast for all hands. Major called it a Bear River Salmon and Jack declared it was a reptile unfit for human consumption, but the next morning he ate it same as the rest of us, there being nothing else but biscuits and coffee. We had to discard the hundred pound sack of rice, it having so much wetting it had mildewed and we couldn't eat it. I thought, "good riddance," as my boat was too much loaded to ride the waves nicely.

That night I lay listening to the three waters and thought I could tell in the dark which was which: Upriver, where the water ran against a smooth clift in Ladore, it made a sort of whirring sound much like one squirrel calling another. Near the Bear River mouth, where it was sandy, the sound was softer, a swish something like a broom on a wood floor. And downriver of our camp, where the waters joined against a ragged wall and the echo fed it back, the sound took on the voice of a hound snarling a warning.

The next morning, the 19th of June, Major and I went over to the west bank to climb Echo Clift, which is three miles long and made of white limestone. I'm not much for walls, except for the fieldstone walls of New England, but Jack said it was "the prettiest wall I ever saw." Pretty or no, it was nearly vertical so we had to walk back up the river a mile or so to where there was red sandstone mixed in and we could work our way back up the red and onto the white. We had climbed a little over eight hundred feet in whatever direction the rock let us and to our surprise came out right over the river, on an overhanging crag. I straddled it and yelled to the men in camp across the river. They yelled back or whistled and we were soon flinging sounds back and forth across the canyon like boys at a game of catch. Major had stopped to chip away at some fossils, and when he arrived and saw me sitting with my feet dangling over the edge he ordered me in, said he could sit there himself but seeing someone else in the same situation sent chills up his spine.

When we had climbed down and were waiting for a boat to collect us, I said to Major that Walter's voice at Echo Clift sounded like it was rolling down from heaven or up from the depths of the earth.

He seemed moved by my comment, grew thoughtful, then tears formed in his eyes, ran down his cheeks into his plentiful beard. Sort of looking off into space, almost as if I wasn't there, he told me this story, as best I remember it:

"I resigned from the Army in January, 1865 and was home to greet Walter when he was exchanged as disabled a month later, but I wish I hadn't been. He was nothing more than a living skeleton, greatly emaciated and had not fully half his usual weight. He was captured with thirteen other officers at the battle of Atlanta in July, 1864. A lieutenant in my command, named Xavier Picquet, came to see me after the war and told me about the experience. The Rebs moved them first to Macon, then to Charleston, then to Columbia, South Carolina, where they were stationed in an open field. They called it Camp Sorghum because it had been a grain field. They had no bedding or shelter of any kind, during months of solid rain and blistering sun. Walter took sick, most likely from sunstroke, and was taken off to what they called the hospital, just a tent without beds. Picquet and the others in the field didn't see Walter again until Thanksgiving Day. Picquet said Walter suddenly appeared before them with his arms raised aloft and his head raised towards the heavens and from his lips there poured forth an eloquent prayer. The lieutenant said he'd never forget it as it was one of the most affecting scenes he had ever witnessed. The men could see Walter was out of his head so they didn't try to talk to him, just summoned the OD and had him taken back to the hospital. Walter had escaped from the hospital and in his delirium ran across the dead line to bring prayer or salvation to the other officers."

Major's voice changed then from sadness to anger, "That was another thing our father did to us, made us recite long passages from the Bible or solemn prayers of John Wesley's or of his own making. From the time we were five years old we could rattle off texts better than most preachers. I'm sure I know the prayer Walter said at Sorghum. I can recite it to this day, though I'd like to forget it."

I said I thought we should measure the altitude and start down.

The next day was Sunday and I was glad we were to observe the Sabbath by remaining in camp. Major and his brother were taking altitudes above while Jack did the same below, Howland was putting figures in his map book, Billy was cutting off the bottoms of his buckskins as they'd stretched from the constant wetting. Dunn and Hall had wandered off looking for game, but even the animals were in repose. After I'd touched up the caulking on the *Maid* I thought it was time to see what my tintypes looked like as they seemed to have dried. I'd kept the album shut trying to save it whole but I'd of been wiser to open it at once for it fell to pieces anyway and by lying so long shut up some of the pictures were spoiled. It was painfully pleasing to see what freaks the water had cut with the tintypes. Mother had one eye missing, while all that was left of Aunt Marsh was just the top of her head. Eddie had his chin removed while Henry lost nearly all his face. One of Lucy's lost a nose but luckily it was the poorest one and I had a good one left. Though two of Chas

meal was a meager one of biscuits and coffee, and we set off again. We soon found ourselves back in red granite, the walls turned steep and closed in so it felt like approaching nightfall. The canyon just a narrow slit in the clifts, light barely entering, and with the increasing noise of the water it was about as gloomy as it gets in daylight. The noise grew so loud we knew a cataract was ahead, and there was no place to land. Jack and Dunn rowed the *Emma Dean* up against a clift on the right, keeping her there by rowing upstream with the outer oars. Major gave his landing signal so Walter and I rowed the *Maid* up against the clift in the same way, but on the left side which was nearer. *Sister* was upstream and across the river from us and couldn't see the signal, but they saw us securing a line to a rock outcrop and stopped in a small eddy they were lucky enough to happen on.

We watched while Bill and Jack eased the *Emma Dean* down along the clift to a place where there was a broken out section making a narrow shelf, maybe a foot or two wide, about ten feet above the river. The river was washing against the clift and the backwash was bouncing the boat up and down and trying to push her back into the middle, but with Dunn rowing against the tide, holding the boat near the clift, Jack stood on the bow and when the boat bobbed up he managed to grab the shelf and haul himself up on it. Major tossed him a line and he made it fast around a jutting spike of rock and pulled the *Emma Dean's* bow tight to the clift. Then Major climbed up the rope with his one arm in a way I still can't figure, didn't take any help from Jack. They crawled along the shelf in the downstream direction for about fifty feet to a place where they could stand and work their way up a crevice to a wider shelf maybe fifty feet above. Jack set out to explore the falls downstream while Major eased upriver to a point right above where *Sister* was holding in the eddy. *Sister's* crew couldn't hear his shouts over the sound of the water, so he signaled to my boat to go upstream and bring them down. We couldn't do that, the tide being too strong, but we managed to signal Andy and Rhoads and Frank to look up, which they did, with unfortunate timing in Andy's case. Just at that moment Major had elected to get their attention by tossing a small rock into their boat, so that night there were two of us with black eyes.

Major waved his flag toward the clift, and we took it to mean "come over," so we loosed the *Maid* and rowed acrost and tied up to the *Emma Dean's* stern. *Sister* made her way down to us and tied to our stern, keeping against the clift by rowing against the tide.

Jack crawled back and told us that the upper shelf crumbled to the river about a hundred yards downstream just above the head of the falls so we could line the boats to that point anyway. To do that we had to get most of the men onto the shelf to hold the lines from the boats, but the only way up to the shelf was by the *Emma Dean's* bow line, which was secured to the shelf. This meant the boys in our boat had to walk over our bow to the *Emma Dean,* then across her stern and to her bow, then climb the line, and the boys in *Sister* had to cross to the *Maid* and then to the *Emma Dean* and then to the shelf. It took some doing but we got all but Frank and Bill Dunn and me up there and tossed our lines to them. They were able to lower the boats downstream using the *Emma Dean's* bow line and *Sister's* stern line, with the boats still tied together in tandem. Those of us in the boats kept them from smashing against the clift as the waves came and washed back.

When we got them all to the head of the falls, we unloaded the cargoes and lined the boats through the chute one at a time, portaged the cargo around the falls and reloaded it. It was hard going and Jack said he felt like the fellow in Abe Lincoln's story who was tarred and feathered and ridden out of town on a rail. He said, "If it warn't for the honor of the thing, I'd of declined."

The next few miles were treacherous and we were too worn out to take chances, so we mostly lined and made one portage of the cargo, which wore us out some more. When we chanced on a stream coming in on the right, we made camp and sent Andy and Howland off to fish for trout. They brought back a mess of them, and would have caught more but they'd been startled by a grizzly bear. "He didn't stay long." Howland told us. "Andy said the bear reckoned I was more grizzled than he was. But I thought he might be going for reinforcements so, 'Exit, pursued by a bear.'"

Major said, "But you weren't pursued."

"Just an old expression," Oramel told him.

"Do you know why the bear waddles?" Major asked. It sounded like a riddle but that seemed odd coming from Major so nobody asked why. Major went on anyway and told us another Indian legend that started with the sun.

"When the earth was new, the sun came out at odd times, whenever it felt like it. So sometimes it shone for days and days and sometimes only for a few minutes. Sometimes it slept a long time and left the earth dark.

"Now, some of the animals like moles and owls and bears wanted it dark for long periods of time and others, like lizards and turtles, wanted to bask in the sun's warmth all the time. So whenever the sun appeared they were all at him, some imploring him to stay longer, others saying he should sleep longer. The sun got impatient with all this, so he told the animals to make up their minds or he would stay away altogether. Well, the animals couldn't agree so they decided to play a game, the night animals against the day animals and whoever won got to decide the hours of light and dark.

"The game was one where you had to guess the markings of four stones held in fists, so it was a long one. Sometimes one side was winning and then the other would go ahead, and nothing was being decided. Finally the sun got impatient and started to come back up from under the earth where he had been resting. The night animals were frightened of the light so they all ran away. The bear had trouble finding his moccasins and in his haste put them on the wrong feet so he went off waddling, which he does to this day. And because he was slow, he didn't get away with the night animals, nor did he stay with the day animals, and that's why he hibernates half the year and is out the other half."

Oramel said, "Exit, pursued by a bear legend," and we all went about our business, which was mostly hibernating.

The rest of us being too tired to climb, Major climbed the low clift by himself and scouted the river as far as he could. He came back and told us the next few miles at least would be easy. We were glad of the news, but even so there wasn't much singing that night, mostly just Frank with his sea shanteys, *Paddy Doyle's Boots,*

Spanish Ladies, Sally Brown... Andy tried to fit bawdy words to Sally Brown but he was less inspired than usual. When Frank got to *Shenandoah,* we all joined in, *"Oh Shenandoah, I love your daughter, Wey hey, you rolling river..."* which left us with a good feeling, and Andy did a little better with his bawdy version, which gave us a laugh. Then Frank sang:

> *My father was the keeper of the Eddystone Light,*
> *He slept with a mermaid one fine night*
> *From this union there came three,*
> *A porpoise, a porgy, and the other was me*

"A whale," Andy said.

Frank didn't say anything, just got up and walked off like he was going to his tent, like he'd done before. But instead he circled around the fire and got behind Andy, who was still laughing from his whale remark and slapping his knee. Frank was twice Andy's size and he easily picked Andy up, one hand on his shirt collar and one under his belt. Andy was caught off guard and couldn't do more than flail and yell as Frank carried him the few yards to the river and just dropped him in. We were all too surprised to give Andy any immediate help, unless laughing is help, but the water wasn't swift, just deep and cold, and Andy's dogpaddle got him to shore easy enough. He was spitting water and sputtering, mad as a wet hen, and he started for Frank, who was halfway to his tent and didn't even turn around. Major said, "Now Andy, you had it coming. Just sit down and dry out." Andy did as Major ordered, but he said he'd get even.

A small bird woke me in the morning, a canyon wren with a voice three times his size. He had the most peculiar song I ever heard, if it could truly be called a song. If you take a deep breath and then give short whistles over and over until you spend your breath entirely, you have the wren. *Wheeeeeeeee, wheeeeeee, wheeee, wheee, whee, whe...* 'til it's almost a whisper.

As Andy was still vowing to kill Frank, there was some uneasiness between the two of them, so Major switched the Howlands into *Sister,* and Walter and I won Frank. The Howlands had been good company, but they didn't say much. Frank was different: he chattered like a magpie. First he went on about the elk he hadn't killed, "Excitement, I'd judge, too nervous to shoot straight, though he was in my sights, no doubting it."

Then he got onto his parents and the wool trade, "I came over high and dry after your war, trying to get a leg up you know. There wasn't a trade I knew, just a little sheep farming for my father, but he had to sell up when we couldn't get our wool shipped to America on account of the blockade. So there was nothing there for me once my parents died and left this sphere, God bless and keep them. I took to the sea, went on a merchant for a time, but there was no future in it and it was rough life, very rough crew on the merchants, drunks, thieves, fleeing felons, and it didn't suit."

"Felt right at home in Green River City, I reckon," Walter said with that snorting laugh of his.

"That was a rough place, Captain, a rough one. I was looking for a way to leave the foul place, to get out, when I heard about the Major's expedition, this trip, and was jolly glad he took me on, let me join the crew. Jolly glad."

I asked him how it was he said everything twice, though sometimes the words were different.

"Old custom, very old, matter of necessity, really. Born of the Romans bringing law to Britain. The laws had to put everything into both Roman and Saxon, so we have things like, 'last will and testament', one's Saxon, the other's Roman. 'Deposes and says' is another one. It creeps into one's speech, don't it?"

"It do," Walter said.

Then Frank got onto the sheep he was going to raise once he found some good grazing land. "Another reason I wanted to come along is to have a look out for a place to raise some sheep after the trip is over. The land hereabouts is rather forbidding, don't you think, barren of grass and water. I thought the first need being water, a river was a good place to find it."

Even Walter didn't disagree as there was no dissenting snort.

"I was told the Uinta Basin had some fine grazing land near the river, so I've come to have a look." He went on about the kind of sheep that would be best suited for the climate, the quantity of wool they'd produce, the quality of the mutton...

Walter said, "Why don't you sing?"

So he did. A nice clear baritone, *John Anderson my jo, John,* then *Annie Lawrie.* Walter joined in and we went down the river in song, baritone and bass with my unclassifiable voice added. The song ran to the walls which gave it back as good as they got it, sometimes better, so that in one narrow place where the boulders were rolling on the bottom like a drum roll, we filled that void, filled it with song and, I have to say, joy at being in a place so beautiful God himself might feel awe.

In the days that followed, whenever we were in easy water we would sing. Frank knew most of the same Scottish ballads that Walter did, and without Andy around, we could sing them with some tune, more or less. Walter picked up Frank's sea shanteys pretty quick, so when we weren't running or lining, we learned how a *Lass Loved a Sailor,* about *Bully in the Alley, The Hog Eyed Man* and I don't know what all. My favorite was *Bounding Billows,* after *Row On,* of course, that sad lament. Walter latched on to *Strike the Bell,* because it was good and loud in the canyons I guess.

There was one shantey Frank sang that didn't please me at all. It went like this:

> *Oh Lord above, send down a dove*
> *With beak as sharp as razors*
> *To cut the throats of them there blokes*
> *What sells bad beer to sailors*

I knew the Lord would not do such a thing, and I tried to get some hymns into the repertoire starting with, *From Greenland's Icy Mountains,* but failed miserably. Frank was taken with the line, *Where every prospect pleases, and only man is vile.* He said it could apply to a lot of the western towns he'd seen, but he didn't favor the tune, "Too like to a dirge," he said.

The best times with Frank aboard were when we'd float into a canyon where the walls were close in and steep, and our voices sounded like a preacher working his sermon in a stone church.

Frank would begin, or Walter, and the canyon would fairly sound our voices back to us, sometimes with a hollow bass sound from the rocks rolling in the riverbed, so we had a regular church choir from just the three of us. Howland said the noise was so bad the boats should stay *four* hundred yards apart.

The 22nd of June found us on fast water, rocky but with clear channels, and we raced along, just using our sweep oars to steer between the rocks, the river singing its own lament along the canyon walls. We saw the red stone again and as sure as we were afloat the river began to narrow, the walls became steep and smooth and the river's song turned to a coarse hum, like it was clearing its throat, winding up for an oration. Still, the main channels stayed clear of rocks, and we raced along with the speed of a galloping horse and, truth to tell, I had a feeling just like I was riding one, and I almost missed the cavalry. That was not a feeling I was wont to cling to and it soon passed.

They tell me that men stranded in a desert see beautiful lakes or forests or cities, when there's nothing there. A "mirage" they call it, and I tell you, I thought I was seeing one when the clifts suddenly and steeply declined to low walls, and we came on a place where the river was wider than anything we'd seen, twice as wide, five hundred feet or better. The water was a flat calm and there were green islands everywhere. We were in a verdant valley of cottonwood trees and grassy fields and I half expected to see cattle grazing, but there was no sign of man anywhere when we landed.

Major took ill of a sudden and told Jack to take charge. Howland protested that he was the oldest and should take over, but Major said, "Mr. Sumner is in charge. Follow his orders."

"We'll camp here until the professor's right again," Jack told us. "Now you boys take rifles, pistols, shotguns, Bowie knives and yourselves and go fetch us some fresh meat." The men declared that they would have great success now that they had more than a few hours to ply their craft. I was pleased to have a chance to dry my clothes and to have a soft place to sleep, but I had my doubts about the hunters and so went off with bailing cans and picked about four quarts of currants, enough for a fine mess for all hands.

Jack was scornful of my berries, said he wasn't a grizzly bear, but as the men had produced no meat, he waddled over and put away his share of currants with alacrity.

Major was still sick the next morning and was taking only castor oil and coffee for nourishment. Jack sent the *hunters* out again, making sure Andy didn't follow Frank, and they fanned out, some invading different islands, others trying the main shores. I picked some more currants.

Wonder of wonders, Frank Goodman and Billy Rhoads came back to camp that afternoon with a fine buck deer. They'd spotted it on top of a high clift, and Billy dropped it with a single shot, he said. They dressed it where they shot it, and Billy brought down the two hindquarters while Frank brought in a forequarter and the rifles. They left the other quarter hanging in a tree on top of the clift.

The other hunters had had no luck but that night they were all on tiptoe, each swearing by everything he could name that some *little innocent deer* must die by his hand in the morning. I thought we'd better make the most of what we had. As Major had improved, he agreed to move camp down the river to where we'd be just underneath the clift where Rhoads had left the rest of the deer. We traveled about five miles by water around a big bend that wound along the foot of the mountain, but we went only about a half mile "as the falcon flies," Howland said, and we made camp again.

The deer was fine and fat as beef, and we had a feast. We all toasted Billy with our coffee, Howland's jug being long gone, and someone came up with the idea of naming the mountain after Billy, so we called it "Mount Hawkins," after his other name, and it was one new place that Major didn't get to put a name to.

Major was fully well the next morning and his first act was to name the place "Island Park." Major and I climbed together for a time, then I left him taking altitudes and went after the quarter of deer for I had no faith in the men killing another that day. I ascended without much difficulty and found the meat untouched by wolves. I suppose they do not climb that high (2800 feet) but I was so used to climbing then that I hardly noticed it — yet it came very hard when I was first climbing with Major.

There were many geese on the river and over it, some quite high up, and in the distance two eagles soared, but they were so far away they might have been vultures. I could see that about four miles downriver there was a spur of the mountain lying to the west and running to the southwest. The river snaked into the spur, turning northwest, then did a loop to the southeast, penetrated to the very center of the mountain and fought its way down the middle for about six miles before snaking out and heading south again on the far side. I began to believe the river followed no pattern or course that man could discern, but God could. That put me in mind of the words of a hymn, *Rock of Ages, cleft for me.* When Major caught up with me I told him my thought and suggested we might name it "Cleft Mountain." I could see he didn't hold much with hymns because he said, "We'll call it Split Mountain." At least he wasn't calling me Sergeant anymore.

Being on that plateau was like standing on top of the world. We could see fifty or sixty miles downstream to the south and miles farther than that acrost plains to the north, west and east. Beyond the next canyon, on the other side of Split Mountain, we would again be in a valley among cottonwood covered islands. To the northwest we saw the Uinta and Wasatch mountains, their slopes covered with pines merging into glittering snowfields snug below the bare windblown summits. On the plains between were whole herds of deer and a scattering of antelope. To the east we could just make out the western face of the Rocky Mountains with their vast gleaming snow fields and the Great Divide. To the southeast we saw the White River valley, placid where the White joined the Green. Back up the river we looked down on Island Park which seemed from that height to be serrated by many streams with their tributaries working their way from the center of the park, down a sloping plain to the river. Green meadows contrasted with brightly colored bands of rock formations, blue, lilac, buff and pink, vermilion and brown, all satiny and glowing in the bright sunlight. Major said we ought to rename the place, "Rainbow Park" or "Ribbon Park." I told him it was bad luck to rename a boat and maybe the same was true of parks, so he let it be.

Looking back to the slit in the rock that was Whirlpool Canyon we saw a tranquil scene: from that distance it was a rippling brook emerging from a narrow cleft. Major said, "Do you believe, Sergeant, that behind that pleasant canyon mouth lies a gloomy chasm with roaring waters and life-threatening waves?" So he was back to Sergeant again.

That night we ate more of Billy's deer, the hunters failing to kill another. Major told about how the river lay from where we saw it on the clift top, and I told my thoughts on the river's course and God's will. "Or whim," Sumner said. Then Howland gave us his views by reading out from a letter he'd been working on to send to the *Rocky Mountain News* when we got to the Ute agency:

> *I used to think that the river ran without any design. I have partially rejected that idea since leaving the mouth of the Bear River. Now I think the river goes for the highest points within the range of vision, disemboweling first one and striking for the next and serving it the same, and so on indefinitely. First it turns short and sharp into the very center of a mountain, then turns just as sharply and goes tearing down the middle, shoots out to the left again into the prairie as if in fury to think so tiny an obstacle should tower 3000 feet above it to check its progress. This makes me think it has designs on all mountains of any pretensions. Small ones are not considered worthy its notice, it seems.*

Well there we had a third opinion. Howland was endowing the river with a will of its own, Sumner said it was all an accident and I saw God's awful hand in it. Then Major chimed in saying, "It's just geology," but I'd learned from *The Testimony of the Rocks* that geology was just an expression of God's will. I believe Major had read the book in the Judge's library, for he read almost anything he could get his hands on, but it clearly hadn't changed his mind one little bit.

We started into Split Mountain Canyon the next morning but soon abandoned the effort when Jack took sick. I suspect he caught something from Major, but Jack said, "It was the deer. Wasn't cooked proper." We could have continued on down the river with Howland or Seneca manning Jack's oars, but we came to a place where we needed to make a portage and concluded to set up camp and give Jack a chance to rest and sleep, as he would take no medicine. "I want no castor oil, no ipecac and no human company."

That night as we were at supper, two coyotes came to camp and seemed to take a shine to Jack's tent, nosing all around it. Major said, "Chase them off, Billy," to Rhoads, but Howland pointed out that Jack, "did not exclude animal company," so we let them snuffle. Finally Jack yelled out, "Git you varmints, you're the nuisance of the world." The coyotes didn't seem to disagree and sidled off up a small ravine, but their bark and yodel came back so soon you'd think they were mocking him.

We had portaged all the cargoes before we bedded down for the night so as to have an early start in the morning. As Jack was taking nourishment at breakfast and had recovered enough to continue, we lined the boats, reloaded the cargoes and sailed through a broad, flaring gateway, brilliant in the sun, into a grim and sunless Split Mountain Canyon. We were able to run the first few rapids, then there were six or eight that Major said had to be lined, so we set to work letting the boats down without having to unload and portage, except in one place where there were three falls in close succession. We dropped the boats down one by one into the pools at the bottom of each falls, then did the same with the next and the next.

When we set out again we were carried along at great speed until we came to a place where the river made an abrupt turn to the right and went at right angles to the canyon, in the contrary way Howland had laid out in his letter. There was a long chute after the turn where the water ran straight to the clift and billowed back in a way like breakers do in the Atlantic Ocean. Major surely would have had the *Emma Dean* lined if he had seen the danger in time, but they were in it too quick and headed straight down the chute toward the clift.

I was following in the *Maid* and called to Walter and Frank at the oars to back water as best they could, watching to see if the little boat would be dashed against the clift. Jack and Bill Dunn were backing water too and just before the *Emma Dean* was about to smash into the clift, there came a backwash which caught the little boat's hollow bow and lifted it until the boat looked like a rearing horse, then it was turned back and thrust over a small fall, the men all soaked and just hanging on to the gunwales. We didn't know if they would gain control or be carried off downstream, but there was a small whirlpool at the bottom of the fall and they were out of danger, even recovered the oars circling around them in the pool. Major signaled us to land and line, and of course we did it, but I could see in my mind's eye how we could have run the chute, same as he did, but planned out, not accidental. Still, they were Major's boats and I surely appreciated the design when I saw the *Emma Dean's* bow rise that way.

We had a good run all morning, making in all about thirty miles with but the one portage. We came out of Split Mountain Canyon at a good speed but were soon slowed to almost nothing, finding ourselves on a river nearly five hundred feet wide, flowing through a green valley and dotted with islands. There were many geese in flight and, with Major scouting them, the men managed to kill about ten. Though they were poorly, it being the nesting season, we welcomed the change in diet.

We made camp and Major and I went in search of fossils. We chanced on some Indian dwellings, not in use at that time, each a series of loosely connected rooms. They were of varying sizes and we paced them off finding one thing that struck us odd: though the other dimensions of the rooms varied, each north-south dimension was exactly the same, about thirteen feet.

Billy baked up a batch of biscuits and spit-roasted the geese and we each ate one like we'd not known food for a week. Frank gave us his sea shanteys. Walter ran through *Old Shady* and for a change *Tenting Tonight,* and we went to bed well-fed and in fine spirits. When the wolves came, serenading us to sleep, it seemed like the canyon was singing to us.

DESERT EVENING NEWS

SALT LAKE CITY.   JUNE 27, 1869.

TRAGEDY ON THE RIVER.

By the courtesy of William B. Dougall, Esq., of the Deseret Telegraph Line, we were made aware of the imminent arrival of Colonel Jackson, who had been prospecting for silver on the north and west sides of the Green River with a company of twelve men and twenty mules. We eagerly awaited the colonel's arrival for we were forewarned that he had a story to tell that was not about silver.

Colonel Jackson has arrived here and has obliged us with an interview. It seems the muleteers had found no silver after six weeks of traversing arid, flat country punctuated by fir forests and everywhere broken by canyons, arroyos, streams and fissures. Wherever possible the party approached the river seeking to find a route where their sure-footed mules could descend to its banks. The colonel reports little success from these endeavors, finding a route to the water at Brown's Hole and only there. Everywhere else they looked down on a river roaring, rocky and impassable.

On their last night before turning north to civilization, there occurred an incident that made this editor's blood run cold in listening. We can think of no better way to convey the colonel's story than to repeat it in his own words:

"We were tethering the mules, starting a cookfire, setting up camp when one of the men shouted, "Looky there" and off to the east in the dimming crepuscular light we saw what could have been an apparition but was instead a dozen dust-covered men, bedraggled, bearded, almost skeletal, stumbling toward us. We were at first too startled to move or speak; then we heard a croak, 'Water!' Then they all picked it up until the sound of twelve men murmuring, 'Water! Water!' was like a moaning chorus in a Greek tragedy."

The colonel's crew fed and watered the poor souls who, it turns out, were the survivors of a party under the leadership of a prospector named Hook which had left Green River City a week after the widely reported departure of the Powell expedition, about which we have had no word. Hook's party came to grief after only a week on the river. Seeing the loss of Hook and his two crew in a vast whirlpool, the others prudently concluded to abandon the journey, though they nearly lost their lives as well wandering three weeks in the desert. With the Hook expedition ending in disaster and loss of life, we fully credit Colonel Jackson's assurance that the river below Brown's Hole will swallow any boat put upon it.

The next day we made thirty-three miles on flat water, but it was hard, miserable work. There was almost no tide, and we rowed like galley slaves all day. The only saving grace, aside from the distance run, was we had a chance to talk without the water drowning out our voices or keeping our attention to something other than conversation. Or rather Frank got a chance to talk. Mostly he kept at us about how we must be close to the Uinta Basin and asking how far away I thought it was. He was thinking about grazing land for his sheep, I suppose. As no man had ever before been on the river where we were, we couldn't say for certain, but we knew we were near. "Ply, ply the oars," Walter said, but Frank didn't take his meaning and started to sing us the lament. Walter joined in and it gave me a rest from listening, for sometimes Frank could make me stop thinking and wonder where I was, with his talking a steady stream. Still, it was a change from Walter's near silence. Alone with Walter, I found myself thinking too much of home.

We rowed like demons 'til late, near sunset, hoping to reach the Uinta River mouth, which everybody back in Green River City said we would never do. We were nearing it so fast on flat water that I knew we would prove them all wrong. But we weren't going to make it that day so we campt in a beautiful grassy meadow and wished we hadn't. The mosquitoes bit so badly that we spent our time waving them off or swatting at them 'til Billy got a fire going and we made some smoke by putting green grass on the fire. We were all merry at supper eating goose again, for the men shot eight that day. When I put the date (June 27th) in my journal I realized I was so elated at the prospect of reaching the Uinta that I forgot it was Sunday and that I'd worked on the Sabbath.

We reached the mouth of the Uinta near sunset the next afternoon. I was sure I would soon have mail from home, sent to the Ute Agency, hoped to get a good lot. I scribbled a few lines to Lucy but it was dark before I got very far. I wanted to send her my notes, but I'd need a couple of days to write them over, as it would puzzle a Philadelphia lawyer to read them as they were.

The mosquitoes were fierce again and we huddled near the fire where the smoke helped to keep them off. Major said to Billy, "You and Andy make up a big bonfire, see if we can attract Indians." He said he wanted to get a runner sent to the trading post which was twenty or thirty miles up the Uinta River. Frank was worried, "Major, I heard a story in Green River City about Indians killing a party led by a man named Gunnison. Don't you think we should try to avoid them, as we did at Henry's Fork?" Major laughed, "Oh, Gunnison wasn't killed near here. Anyway the Indians here are Utes; they do a little farming and mostly are hunters and gatherers, not warriors." Jack agreed with Major, said he and Bill Dunn had spent time with the Utes, "Always found them friendly," he said. Frank didn't say anything but he didn't look comfortable.

I guess Major was feeling pretty good about where we'd got to, for he surprised us all by breaking into song right after supper:

I will sing you a song of that beautiful land,
The far away home of the soul,
Where no storms ever beat on the glittering strand,
While the years of eternity roll

I was surprised and pleased at what Major was singing. He had a pleasant voice but of no particular merit. Then he rose and began to imitate an old woman at a camp meeting singing, *The dear blessed Bible, The family Bible...* and I took offense. Jack whispered, "What's got into the professor, he's as merry as a schoolgirl."

"Tain't liquor," Dunn said, "Howland saw to that. Probably expectin letters from his wife."

Walter followed his brother in song with his usual *Old Shady.* "Go to it, Captain," Andy yelled, "Sing away." Walter didn't need any encouragement, but it was the signal for me to brave the mosquitoes and gain my tent. I wrapped a mosquito bar around my head and went into a sleep suitable to Lazarus.

There were no Indians the next morning so Major decided to see if he could be rowed to the trading post. Bill Dunn and Jack "plied the oars," trying to get the Emma Dean up the Uinta River. They made about a half mile then gave it up as the tide was too swift. Major said we'd take the day to write letters and explore and we'd try again that night to attract Indians with a bonfire.

I was copying my notes over so Lucy could read them when Andy asked if I would help him write a letter to his brother. Again I told him I would look it over after he wrote it himself. I believe a man should get by on his own merits; if I wrote the letter it would be mine, not his, and if I just improved it, it would be a mongrel. I told Andy writing was no different than rowing, "Practice it enough, Andy, you'll get good at it, same as you did rowing." He said, "Well now, Sergeant, an oar is a thing you can wrap your hands around, but the writing, now, that's a thing you've got to get hold of with your head." That being the case he should be good at it with his size of head, I thought, but of course I didn't say it to him. I gave him a pencil and a piece of paper and he went off to practice writing.

After a goodly lapse of time Andy brought me a letter he'd penned.

Dear Brother:

it is with the greatest of pleasure that I now set down to write you a few lines to leet you know that I am all right yet. I wrote a letter to mother before I started with Major Powell to explore the Colorado. We had the greatest ride that was ever got up in the countenant the wals of the canone where the river runs through was 15 hundred feet in som places. I write from the Unto reservation now but I will tell you more about it when I come home. The major is from near Blumington, Ill. I suppose you never heard of him and he is a Bully fellow you bett. I have not time to write any more at present give my love to all and kiss Helen's baby fore me.

> *Be kind to our mother*
> *No more at present*

> > *Your affectionate Brother*
> > *Andrew Hall*

I knew Andy would be disappointed if I didn't say anything so I told him it was a fine letter but that there weren't two e's in "let." He crossed out "leet," wrote in "lett," and said "I knew there was two of something." I let it go; at least it matched "bett."

UTAH DAILY REPORTER

CORRINNE, UTAH.   JUNE 30, 1869.

ALL DEAD!
EXCEPT THE GUNSMITH.

We have information which we deem reliable that almost the entire Powell party, which embarked on May 1st from Green River City, Wyoming has drowned in the "Great Suck", thirty miles from Brown's Hole. Twenty men were apparently lost in a whirlpool after plunging over a twelve foot falls with Major Powell at the helm.

There was one survivor, a gunsmith named Jack Sumner, who had been put ashore to aid if possible in case of danger and to report disaster if any occurred. He told a tearful tale of Major Powell's heroism in attempting to guide their large canoe through ten miles of chutes and falls. Mr. Sumner suffered much hardship and privation on his journey to civilization through arid country populated with dangerous savages, but his huntsman's skills brought him through.

When no Indians had appeared by the time Major finished his fourth mug of coffee on the morning of 30 June, he sent Walter and Andy off to the Ute Indian Agency with a bag of fossils he thought he might barter for a horse or mule to come carry him up. He said he'd follow in two day's time if they hadn't come back. It was a strange pairing, Walter and Andy, and I told Jack I hoped Andy would exercise some judgment and not tease Walter, who was near twice his size and half as predictable. Jack said, "Oh, Major's sending Walter so's we can have two nights without *Old Shady*. He's sending Andy to keep him away from Frank." I figured he was half right, for Andy had vowed to get even with Frank for dumping him in the river, and a few days in camp might give him the opportunity.

There was a big lake a hundred yards away that was teeming with Canada geese, mallards, teal ducks and those elegant black and white grebes I'd seen our first morning on the river and hadn't seen since. We carried the *Emma Dean* over to the lake so the *hunters* could get us some fresh meat. There were some white pelicans wheeling and I hankered for a taste of something different, but they were out of range. There were flocks and flocks of ducks and geese, though, so the men were able to kill all we needed. The mosquitoes were near as large as the teal ducks and were more vicious than a rabid fox. Billy said, "I had a deer full in my sights when a mosquito swooped down and carried it off." Oramel said a mosquito asked him for his pipe, knife and tobacco. "While the rascal was loading my pipe he told me to hunt my clothes for a match."

We were on the map, for the Uinta River mouth was one place where white men had been. Major said that a Captain Berthoud had built a ferry and a road to where we were campt and that the ferry was sunk just below where our boats were moored, but nobody bothered to look. Major had Bill Dunn and me row him down to the mouth of the White River which entered across the Green from the east, about a mile and a half downstream. I asked him if that was where he had wintered over and he said it was the same river but the camp was a hundred miles away. He said that the White was also on the map. "A General Hughes has scouted the territory and reported some strange rock formations that I want to see."

When we arrived at the mouth of the White River, Bill Dunn set off with a rifle looking for deer or other game. I gave him little chance to find it for the place was one of great desolation, arid, almost treeless with bluffs, hills, ledges of rock and drifting sands. It was a world as different as night and day from the western side of the Green, which was all cottonwoods and meadow, the finest mowing land I ever saw, smooth and level as a floor, with no rocks. It would yield two tons to the acre for four miles square. That beat even the far-famed Texas.

Major and I hadn't found much in the way of fossils when we came upon an outcrop of wind-carved rocks in shapes strangely human in a grotesque way, small figures with weird body shapes, some stubby and round and others toadstool-like forms with tiny round heads. Major said General Hughes gave the place the name, "Goblin City," and it fit as well as any other, though I suspect Major would have named it something else if it wasn't on record. He wanted to poke up the river a ways but as it was all rocks and desert, I stayed in Goblin City looking for fossils. I didn't find any at first, but after a time I got a strange feeling that I was not alone there. Perhaps I'd been too long from civilization but I began to converse with the shapes and had a sense that they talked back. I imagined that I was directed to a certain hollow beyond a small rise. I went to it and I found another fish skeleton similar to one I had seen at Fort Bridger. When Major returned he said the skeleton confirmed that the whole area was once one vast inland sea. "That was on Friday, Sergeant, when the Lord made fish and fowl."

At supper Major announced that he would go to the agency on foot in the morning and that Billy would go with him. "Well that leaves us without a cook," Jack said, "so I guess Frank is elected." But Frank said he'd like to go along to the agency to get a new outfit, as all he had were handmade moccasins and my blanket to go with his shirt and long johns. Major was agreeable and that's how I got appointed cook. I protested that I'd never cooked anything, but Major said, "If I can make biscuits and boil coffee, so can you."

THE OMAHA REPUBLICAN

JULY 2, 1869.

DEATH ON THE RIVER.

ENTIRE POWELL PARTY LOST.

A trapper named Riley has just returned to Omaha from Fort Bridger in Wyoming, where he met Mr. Jack Sumner, the sole survivor of the Powell expedition on the Green River. It appears that Mr. Sumner had been sent ashore by Major Powell to explore the possibility of leaving the Green River by way of the Delaban River when the tragedy occurred. The party had made a portage around some rapids above Brown's Hole, then re-embarked at the head of a ten mile gorge with many rapids, just below Brown's Hole. As Mr. Sumner watched in horror, the boats went over a twelve foot falls and were all swamped and their occupants drowned. The river below roared and foamed through a labyrinth of broken rocks in which no boat could possibly live. Major Powell and his brave companions were seen no more.

Major and Billy and Frank set off after breakfast the next morning (July 2nd) for the agency, and I set about the task of being cook. I'd got enough currants for all hands the day before but I'd picked the bushes clean in the process. The mosquitoes had driven me away when I tried to search for more near the lake, so I determined to get ahead of them this time. I put a piece of mosquito bar over my head and fastened it at my waist and with gloves to protect my hands and a pair of boots coming to the knee to protect me from rattlesnakes, I set out. I hunted along the side of the Uinta for about a mile with the little creatures fairly screaming at me. I passed through acres of rank grass up to my hips and sunflowers higher than my head, and I thought, a goblin would have been in a forest of green and yellow trees. At last I came upon a currant bush, a single one, but a big feller. I couldn't pick the berries with my gloves on and the musical little mosquitoes wouldn't let me take them off. I broke the bush off near to the ground and carried it back in triumph. I got about three quarts of berries off of it, enough for the five of us that were left in camp.

We moved our camp to a little bluff fifteen feet or so above the river between the lake and the Uinta's mouth and the mosquitoes troubled us little there. We kept a little smoke going nearly all the time and that kept them quiet and I believe they are like the wolves in their own proportion and do not climb very high.

The bluff led to another one still higher and as it was entirely free of mosquitoes, I decided to go exploring. Jack came along saying, "It's not so high the earth will shrink." We soon came upon a number of old Indian lodges, some of them burnt. According to Jack, Indians will not live in a lodge if someone has died in it, so they burn it. I wasn't sure if this was another of Jack's facts conjured for the occasion, but I had an idea I'd heard it before, so guessed it was right. A little farther on we found a low clift, maybe fifty feet high, covered with all sorts of stick figures scratched and painted on the clift wall, mountain sheep, deer and antelope, some with Indians sticking spears in them. But the queerest thing of all was a figure of a man playing a flute and maybe dancing.

There wasn't much to keep boredom at bay in camp, especially with five of our crew away. Jack was taking barometer readings and I set about cleaning and oiling the artillery, all the guns being in bad condition from the constant wetting. Bill Dunn was checking Major's watch against the sun at noon with a care that would do credit to a librarian. Bill having Major's little silver pocket watch surprised me but that being the one they used to measure off the distance in degrees from England on the chronometer, I guessed that was why he left it. But Bill said no, Major thought more of the watch his wife gave him than he did of himself and he was afraid something might happen to it on the way to the agency.

I didn't join the others when they went out on the lake to get some ducks and currants for our Fourth of July dinner the next day. Me being appointed cook, I decided to cook up some beans. I put in what beans I thought five men could eat and set them to boiling. They boiled and swelled and I kept putting in hot water and they kept swelling until I had a large pan of ten or twelve quarts capacity solid full of beans, so full I couldn't fit in much water so they began to scorch on the bottom. I suppose it was in keeping with a poor Fourth to add burnt beans to our menu of currants and duck.

When no one had returned from the agency by supper time I began to feel some anxiety that they may have failed to find the agency or that Major was wrong about the Indians being friendly. Oramel said that they were normally friendly, but they may have sought revenge after hearing *Old Shady* a few hundred times. But I hoped for the best.

Without Walter or Frank, we were without music or song until Seneca surprised us by pulling out a Jew's harp and twanging away at *Annie Lawrie* and *Suwanee River.* We gave him a round of applause and asked for more but that just about exhausted his repertoire. After that we fell quiet for a while, just poking the fire and drinking our coffee. Then Jack got the idea that we make a list of the birds and animals we'd seen, and Howland started it off,

"Saw three kinds of bear, grizzly, cinnamon and black."

"Mule deer, white-tailed deer, black-tailed deer," Seneca said.

"Grey wolf and prairie wolf," from Jack.

"Beaver, otter, muskrat," said Dunn, and soon we were throwing animal names at each other like we were children at a game of catch, "elk, bighorn sheep, prong-horned antelope, cougar, red fox, marten, mink, lynx, wildcat, coyote, prairie dog, badger, ground hog, mountain rat, prairie squirrel, ground squirrel, shrews, mice...."

I thought to myself that out of all that the hunters had only killed a lamb, a single deer and a skinny little rabbit. "Rabbit!" I shouted and that completed the list.

We went on to the birds and the list was even longer: "Canada Geese, teal, mallard ducks, grebes, mergansers, loons, storks, bitterns, pelicans, sand-hill cranes, cormorants, bald eagles, golden eagles, falcons, snipe, woodcock, ospreys, curlews, colored raven, common crows, Clark's crows, sage grouse, black grouse, short-tailed grouse, magpie, long-crested jay, Canada jay, red-shafted flicker, blackbirds, red-winged starling, southern mocking-bird, robin, brown thrush, cross-beak, canyon wren, sparrow, sparrow hawk, sharp-shinned hawk, roose hawk, pigeon hawk, mourning dove, meadow lark, woodpeckers of every kind, buzzards..."

We decided to nominate birds for our favorite and to my surprise, the canyon wren was everybody's choice. We set to imitating his single repeated note and Bill Dunn got him off best. The first sound that came through Bill's vast black beard was a loud shrill note, then he got off one not so loud nor so high and went on that way, ending in a hoarse whisper as he ran out of breath. We were still laughing when we wandered off to our tents, the Howlands together, Jack and Bill Dunn in Major's tent, and me by myself.

CHEYENNE LEADER

JULY 4, 1869.

TRAGIC NEWS.
PARTY POWELL LOST.

We would like to bring our readers better news on this glorious Fourth of July when we celebrate the Declaration of this Great Nation as an independent Republic, but we are saddened to report the arrival in Cheyenne of the only survivor of the ill-fated voyage of Major Powell and his party of adventurers.

Captain John A. Risdon, late of Denver, has told Governor Palmer of Illinois of the sad end of twenty-one fine men and true. Governor Palmer reports that, "Mr. Risdon is an honest, plain, candid man, who told his story in a straightforward manner, and this is what he told me:"

On or about the eighth of May, the party, which consisted of twenty two persons, reached the Colorado River, in order to explore the two tributaries, the Big Black and the Delevan, about a mile and a half apart. The place of crossing was about 50 yards above a rapid, and Risdon was left on shore with the teams. The rest of the party, in a large canoe, had proceeded about four hundred feet from the shore, the whole party in excellent spirits, singing and laughing, when the canoe commenced to wheel around and around and suddenly disappeared, bow first, into the bosom of the river. Major Powell was the last man seen, his one arm firmly on the tiller.

It was a poor Fourth and a lonely one without a full crew in camp. When nobody had appeared from the agency by noon, I told the other men I thought we ought to send somebody after them, the way Major set off when the others hadn't returned. Jack said, "Give them another day, probably shooting off sky-rockets." Howland agreed so I held my peace, but it troubled me.

We had no rockets, so the best we could manage was to set our flag on a pole and fire off a few volleys, but it wasn't like home. Looking at the flag, my thoughts wandered back to other scenes and other days, to the three successive Fourths I had spent in the wilderness. Two years back I was on Lodge Pole Creek between Fort Sedgewick and Fort Sanders. The last year I was in the Uinta Mountains whose snow-clad peaks loomed up to the west and north of our camp. I wondered where I'd be on the next Fourth, whether I'd ever spend another with Mother and Lucy. I wondered about the thoughts of the other men too, but they seemed to enjoy the day as if it was normal to be in a mosquito-infested place with only burnt beans and scrawny ducks for a Fourth of July dinner. They were all down in the river, buck naked and splashing each other and playing like schoolboys. I declined the invitation to join in and as Andy wasn't here to rag me, nobody pressed the idea on me.

More geese and currants for supper and of course burnt beans. Howland suggested we call out the best Fourth of July meal we ever had. Bill Dunn and Jack talked about fresh-killed venison they'd had on the Snake River, the Howlands described a dinner of suckling pig, but I made their mouths water with my idea of a Massachusetts clambake, cooked over hot stones in a pit and covered with seaweed: sweet corn, steamer clams, lobster, butterfish, quahog chowder, watermelon. "And a touch of whiskey, I expect," Oramel said.

We knew Major wouldn't bring us watermelon or lobster or whiskey from the agency, but we wished for a few things would make the journey go better. The favorite choice was ham. We reckoned a ham would be something the agency would have and something that would keep in the heat better than bacon, but we agreed lean bacon would be a good choice, failing ham. Seneca said, "Potatoes wouldn't go amiss," and that led us to fresh vegetables that might be ripe at that season, maybe tomatoes or radishes or peas. The list went on until I so tempted my taste that I felt hungry again.

Memories of clambakes with family and friends made me melancholy and when a wind sprang up and drove the mosquitoes to ground, I took a long walk by myself along the lake and thought of home, contrasted its comforts with the privations we suffered on the trip and asked myself why I was there. But my little brother's green and flowery grave on a hillside far away seemed to answer for me and with moistened eyes I sought again my tent where, engaged with my own thoughts, I passed several hours with my friends at home, sometimes laughing, sometimes weeping until sleep came and dreams brought me into the apparent presence of those I love.

There being an over-sufficient quantity of beans, we had them cold for breakfast on the fifth. Jack said they were "mighty good, George, but not quite up to those mongrel fish you caught back up the river." We'd no sooner finished breakfast than Andy and Billy came in with two Indians with pack ponies. We gave a cheer and ran up to greet them and made our demand that they surrender the ham. "The only ham you're going to get is Andy aping Kitty Clyde's can-can," Billy told us. Then he gave us the rest of the news: the agency wouldn't take Major's letter to draw supplies so the only thing to be added to our stores was three one hundred pound sacks of flour. "All the major said he had money for," Billy told us. "They wouldn't barter for the fossils, said they could find all they wanted themselves."

"A shirt-tail of supplies," Jack scoffed, "A meager mess for ten men to make a thousand mile voyage through unknown canyons."

But Billy said, "Just nine men. Frank ain't coming back."

"More fond of bullwhacking than rowing, I expect," Jack opined and Bill Dunn said, "More likely he had all the adventure his health called for," and they had a good laugh.

"I'll miss him, though," Jack said, "He had a fine voice and knew a lot of sea shanteys. That leaves us with just *Old Shady*," and he did a poor imitation, *Ya, ya darkies, laugh away wid me...*

"There's the major, now he's decided to sing," Bill said and did an even worse imitation of Major's camp song.

"Looks like you'll have to serenade us, Andy," Jack said.

"Got a voice like a cross-cut saw, Bill Dunn said. "Still it'll keep Walter riled up. We'll have some fun." If they'd spent every day in a boat with Walter the way I did, they'd of known better, but it was their funeral.

According to the figures Oramel was keeping we had to get down almost four times the descent we'd made so far from Green River City. The three new sacks of flour were most welcome but there was no rice, no fresh beans and no mess-kit either. I was truly glad not to have to carry any more rice, for its weight exceeded its worth in my view, but I wasn't pleased that we'd have to continue to make the bailing cans do for coffee and whatever. Still, as Mother was wont to say, "Use it up, wear it out, make it do, or do without," a motto I'd lived with all my life and could do again.

Major and his brother came back that evening, traveling on foot, and bringing no mail. Of course they were without Frank. Major said Frank couldn't replace his outfit and didn't look forward to a long trip in just his shirt and drawers. I thought there might have been another reason for Frank's leaving us, besides the fear, I mean: he'd seen the fine mowing land and maybe figured he'd found what he was looking for, water and grass to raise sheep. I'd miss him in the boat and around the campfire, but at least I had my blanket back. Like me, it was scorched around the edges.

I rose before sunrise to Billy's, "Roll out! Roll out! Chain up the gaps...," anticipating an early start. I found Oramel Howland finishing up a letter to the *Rocky Mountain News* by the firelight, describing how the river had a mind of its own. He read it out to me and asked if I agreed. I didn't, as it made God out a bystander, but I did agree with the other sentiments he expressed:

> *When we have to run rapids, nothing is more exciting. Danger is our life, it seems now. As soon as the surface of the river looks smooth all is listlessness or grumbling at the sluggish current. But just let a white foam show itself ahead and everything is merry as a marriage bell. We have been nearly eaten up by mosquitoes since lying in camp here, our principal amusement having been fighting and smoking the pests. When or where you will hear from us again is hard to tell.*

THE BRECKENBRIDGE SENTINEL

JULY 6, 1869.

GRAND CANYON EXPLORATION.

———

Colonel Samuel Adams, who has graced us with his presence for nearly a month, has now declared his intent to travel down the Blue River to where it meets the Grand River and down that river until it joins the Green River and becomes the Colorado, and thence to the Gulf of California. Readers will recall from our report of June 10th that Colonel Adams was authorized by Congress to take charge of the ill-fated Powell expedition which left Green River City, Wyoming Territory in great haste, in the Colonel's view to avoid enforcement of Congress' order. It was only a few days ago that the sad news reached us of the loss of all but one member of the Powell party.

Breckenbridge lying on the western slope of the Rocky Mountains is some 3000 feet higher in elevation than Green River City, and the Blue River descends at a rate several times that of the Green.

"The rapid decline in altitude will mean a swift passage," the Colonel declared, "making our trip that much faster than that contemplated by the unfortunate Powell expedition, despite the greater distance."

There has been no shortage of volunteers to accompany him and a subscription has been raised for provisions and boats, which are only awaiting the arrival of lumber which is even now being sawn for their construction. Your editor has learned from Mrs. Silverthorne, wife of our court judge, that the good ladies of our fair community are knitting a flag for Colonel Adams boat, but as to what legend it will carry, we are sworn to secrecy. Hoorah for our ladies! And luck to the brave Colonel Adams and his fortunate companions.

A large turnout is expected for the launching in about a week's time.

PART THREE

THE GREAT UNKNOWN

Le silence 'eternal de ces espaces infinis m'affraie.

PASCAL

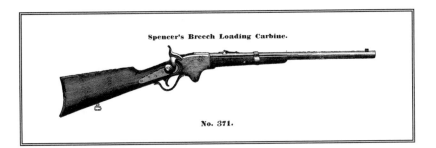

Spencer's Breech Loading Carbine.

No. 371.

JULY 6   THE DARK CANYON

It was near ten o'clock and we were still in camp, Major trying to learn Ute words from the Indians. He'd spent *three days* with the Ute Indians near the agency doing the same, while we sat around camp swatting mosquitoes. He says the Indians call this valley, "Won' sits uav," which means "Antelope Valley." Maybe it does and maybe it doesn't. "Mosquito Valley," more like. Serve him right if they told him up was down and right was left. I could see he was asking them about the river but when Jack asked him what they said, all he would say is, "Whoo-oog. Heap swallow everything." I never heard an Indian say "heap" myself, but then I haven't seen a heap of Indians.

We finally got to go and I was exceedingly glad to get away for I like to keep going. Don't like stopping. With Frank gone, my boat took on Seneca permanent. He's not a talker like Frank was, and you could see he missed his brother being by, but he was a willing rower and that gave me a rest. Though I like to keep moving, I don't mind somebody else provides the power. When it was his turn to rest and he had breath for conversation I asked him about himself and Oramel, how they came to be here on the river with Major. Seneca having nothing to do and Walter and I having a need to relieve the monotony of rowing on flat water, Seneca spun his story out:

"Oramel is my half-brother. He was born in Barnard, in the state of Vermont. His mother died in childbirth and our father married the schoolteacher in Pomfret, my mother. The local school was just down the hill from our farm. I could see the schoolyard from my window. When Oramel was in school and I was too young to go, I'd sit and watch the schoolhouse door to see Oramel the first thing he came out for recess, or to come home for dinner, I missed him that bad. With ten children and a farm to tend to, my father didn't parcel out much time to the children, so Oramel was the one to take care of me and teach me things. My earliest memory was of Oramel showing me how to take eggs from under a setting hen. To this day I can feel the sudden warmth as I poked my hand under the hen's breast and grasped the egg, as big as my small fist.

"From the time I was born we were never apart. When Oramel left Vermont and headed west just before the war, I missed him with a pain that I could feel in my arms and legs.

"I was seventeen when the war came along and a year later I enlisted, got wounded at Gettysburg and they sent me home. I went back to Vermont to get mustered out of the state militia, but there was nothing there for me, so I headed west. When I got to Denver and saw Oramel again, I was a happy man. He got me a job as his printer's devil on the *Rocky Mountain News*, where he'd hired on as printer under Mr. Byers, who's Jack Sumner's brother-in-law, you know. When Oramel became editor and I had to work for Jed Dawes, it didn't suit, and I quit. Then Jack took us to meet Major Powell and we signed on to his White River trip. We stayed a year out there, spending the winter in cabins we'd made out of green logs rough-hewn and chinked up with adobe mud. It's cold in Vermont, but I'd never been so cold as that winter at the White. You're better off to shoot yourself than suffer cold like that. We had nothing to heat the cabin with but green wood and mule dung and cedar nee-dles. You'd get more heat from a spirit lamp. Only one didn't seem to mind it was the Major, but he had his Emma Dean to keep him warm.

"It was during that winter on the White that Jack and the Major cooked up the idea of a trip down the Colorado, and that's a long answer to your question about how we came to be here. It was good company and as some of the same folks were coming down this river, we were pleased to come too. That is until we lost the boat at Disaster Falls and near drowned. Since then, Major Powell hasn't let up on Oramel..." I could see Seneca was about to get into how Major was always badgering Oramel and as Walter turned his head and got that blaze in his eyes, I cut in and told him about the canyon wren and got him to imitate its whistle. He was real good at it and after a while we heard Walter at the forward oars practicing to be a wren too.

We didn't float very far, just a little below the mouth of the White, when Major signaled to land on a big island. There was a garden there which wasn't very far along. Some carrots, just pushing up their tops, beets a little bigger, turnips, potatoes, just the tops, nothing below big enough to eat. I had read that "stolen fruit is sweet" and thought we would try and see. Major said he knew the man whose garden it was, Mr. Johnson, and was told to help himself, but I don't know where he could have met Johnson, as there are few people floating on the river. But it did ease my conscience some, taking another man's chattel.

I'd eaten beet greens and turnip greens many a time and they've tasted fine, especially with a little salt and vinegar, luxuries we'd left behind, but I wasn't sure about potato tops. Andy said, "Oh, they make fine greens. I've eaten 'em many a time," and as they were more plentiful than anything else, we gathered up a mess of them, along with the beet, turnip and carrot tops and took them aboard. When we stopped for dinner, Billy Rhoads cooked them all together, then dumped everything in Jack's gold pan and yelled, "Plunder, plunder, grub pile, come and get it!" and we all helped ourselves. The potato tops tasted so bad that I threw mine away, and Oramel did the same, but the others wolfed them down along with the other greens.

Andy had eaten more potato vines than anyone else, I guess to prove they were good eating, and he was the first to double over in pain. He retched, couldn't get anything up, then began to roll around on the ground moaning and gasping. Major was next and the others soon followed. Oramel said that if they couldn't get rid of what they'd eaten they would surely die. He grabbed the ipecac from the *Emma Dean* and made Seneca take some. It did its job and Seneca was soon expelling the potato tops like he was a small mortar firing off. We gave the ipecac to everyone who'd take it, Jack the exception, and they were all soon getting rid of the poison, but still writhing in pain. Jack was so bad we were sure we were going to lose him, and Oramel said we must make him take the medicine. Just as we approached with the bottle, nature took charge and he was able to expel the greens.

Oramel said it was like a scene out of Dante, all damned souls rolling on the ground and moaning. Andy said he coughed up a potato vine a foot long that had a potato on it big as a goose egg, but he is given to exaggeration or else it grew in his stomach. Jack said the moral was, "Potato tops don't make good greens on the sixth of July." I didn't know he knew anything about morals, but I expected we'd eat no more potato tops that season. Major named the Island, "Johnson's Island," though Oramel wanted to call it, "Purgatory." "*Purge-atory* might be more like it," I told him.

Rhoad's biscuits were tasty that night, made with the fresh flour from the agency. Major said Billy should have used up the stale and wetted flour first, but Billy said that way we were guaranteed always to have biscuits made with stale flour. Seemed right to me, make hay while the sun shines.

We got off early next morning and had a pretty little run amid rising hills. We stopped at about nine A.M. to measure them, for it seemed a place didn't exist unless it was measured and named. Where I climbed, on the farthermost hill, there was a pile of stones placed as children call "cob-house." I think it was the work of Indians for I could not find names or letters among them. I repiled them, adding a long cap rock, and made all very secure. I wrote my name and the name of the expedition and the date and fastened it up very strong. I believe it will stand for many years. It was the first time I had left my name in that country, for until then we had been in a part where white men may have been before, but we had passed below their line of travel and probably wouldn't see any more evidence of them for many more miles. Those that follow may find my writing, as we found Ashley's. Maybe some day someone will call it "Bradley's Mound," provided Major doesn't call it something else first.

Major and Bill Dunn climbed the highest hill and found it to be one thousand feet high. They said the river below ran in slow curves and would be easy running. When we ran them after dinner we discovered great terraced slopes up both sides, like an arena. One very pretty smooth one Major called, "Sumner's Amphitheatre," but did not stop to write Jack's name on it. Jack told me later that Major had promised to name the biggest canyon, "Sumner Canyon," and he thought Major was trying to get out of it, maybe call it "Powell Canyon." I told Jack we'd see when we got there, which I expected would be soon. "I'm sure the worst is over for us," I told him. "You ain't never said anything different, George," he said. "Let me know when you do and I'll quit the trip."

In the afternoon we entered rapids and ran several good ones, then more clear sailing and all day we ran about forty miles. Major said twenty-six and Jack said thirty, and Howland averaged it all out and wrote thirty-two on his map.

Billy made good sweet biscuits again and unscorched beans in quantity, so I was glad I'd be sleeping alone. There was not much singing with Frank gone, as we hadn't taken the trouble to learn his sea songs. Andy was egged on by Jack to do a duet with Walter, but it wasn't appreciated. Maybe inspired by the beans Andy gave us a song that will no doubt some day rank with America and other national anthems. All I can remember of what he rasped out was the chorus:

> *When he put his arm around her,*
> *She bustified like a forty pounder*
> *Look away, look away, look away in Dixie's land*

And he made a farting noise with his lips, as if we didn't have the wit to know what he meant.

The morning of the eighth of July was spent making observations and perfecting Howland's map with Major carping and changing the direction of the river and the placement of clifts, though Oramel had taken all the measurements except the altitudes. Major was at him for not keeping his map up to the day, even though Oramel had other duties, just like the rest of us. We were all getting pretty sick of Major's going on at Oramel and at one point it looked like Jack was going to butt in, but he didn't, probably because just then Major saw Oramel's drawing of the capsizing boat where Disaster Falls was on the map, and he fair exploded. We all got a lecture on how this was a scientific expedition and not a place for "cartooning or levity."

Andy got me aside and asked how we could get along without levity as that was what held us on the ground or made things fall from a clift. When I told him that was "gravity" he was talking about, he had another question for me, a real stumper, "How come the moon doesn't fall down with the gravity?" I told him to ask Major.

Right after dinner Major and I set out with a barometer to measure the clift height. First Jack rowed us upstream a quarter of a mile or so in the pilot boat until we found a talus of rocks with a little shelf above where we could climb. The shelf didn't get us to a very good climbing place so we descended again and were rowed up the river a ways more where we thought we could climb. Major and I started out, passed along a shelf, then started up a gulch, found a little bench and climbed that, passed along some rocks into a crevice, found another bench, and went along so.

We went on up in this fashion until we were about six hundred feet above the river where suddenly we were confronted by a sheer precipice that seemed to mock our efforts and keep us from climbing further. Major then found a place where we could wiggle up some more, but the barometer case was a problem. The case was about a yard long and maybe three or four inches square, made of hard, smooth leather. If you held it with one hand, then you had only one hand to climb with, and if you had only one hand to begin with...well, you can see the problem Major had. I suppose I should have kept the barometer and climbed the way he did, but I lacked the practice.

What we worked out was, Major went ahead and climbed four or five feet and I handed him the barometer case. He tucked it under his cut off arm, while I climbed around him. Then I reached down and took the case and he climbed around me. And so it went like a game of vertical leapfrog until Major climbed above me and found he was at a crevice a yard wide. He jumped across it onto a little ledge and grabbed ahold of a piece of projecting rock. He hadn't thought it out, though, and he found he had no place to go forward. He couldn't let go without falling sixty feet to a ledge below and then maybe tumbling the rest of the way to the river. Being a one-armed man he couldn't switch hands and jump back.

"Bradley, Bradley," he called down to me, "I need help," but as I was below I was in no position to do anything. Then I saw a place where I might inch up a crevice with my back on one side and my feet on the other, if I hadn't been burdened with the barometer case. I was about to drop the case but then figured I'd need something to hand down to Major, so I set out, holding the barometer case in one hand and pushing off the clift with the other, thinking how Major would do it, or not thinking at all, just trying to get there before he had to let go. "Hurry, Bradley, hurry." I couldn't see him but I could tell by his voice he was hanging on for dear life. Hurrying isn't a thing you can do when your shoulders are on one clift wall and your feet on another and you have only one hand to work with, but I did my best scurrying up that ragged wall like a lizard.

I could hear him calling, "Hurry, Bradley." Then just, "Hurry," then nothing, no sound but my breathing and the river gurgling below while I wormed my way up as fast as I could. I half expected to hear a thud, but there was only the river and silence. I told myself he hadn't let go but was hanging on and saving his breath. I did the closest thing to running you could do in my circumstances and finally got to a small outcropping ledge behind me that I judged to be about three feet above where Major was hanging on. I worked my head and shoulders over the ledge, then tossed the barometer case up onto it to free up my other hand. Reaching up over my head I grasped the edge of the shelf with both hands, then walked myself up so my feet and head were on the same level. I was bent down in the middle, so when I wriggled myself out straight I had most of my upper body on the shelf and was able to lever the rest onto it with my elbows. When

I could stand, I ran over to where Major was and looked down. He was still there but his arm was trembling from holding on so tight, his legs were shaking from standing on tip-toe, and his face turned red then ashen white. I reached the barometer case down to him, but he said, "I can't grasp it, Bradley," and I could see he'd have a problem all right, with only one hand and the case so big around and smooth. I looked for a pole or a stick but there wasn't a thing there but rocks. I hoped maybe to see a rattlesnake skin to serve as a rope, but there was nothing. The thought of a rope gave me another idea. As I was wearing nothing but underwear and a shirt, I yanked off my boots, slipped out of my long john drawers and lowered them down to Major, just in time I think. He let go the rock knob, grabbed the legs and slowly turned around. They made an excellent substitute for a rope, and with Major holding the legs and me the waist, he jumped back across the crevice and wiggled up the way I had.

"That must be what they mean being on your last legs," I told him. He chuckled, "No harm done except the scare."

Had it been me, I'd have rested a spell and let the shivers go away, but Major went right on to the top, took his observations with the barometer and thermometer, made me memorize them, as we'd brought no paper, then said, "I'll race you down!"

We didn't go down right away though. Instead we walked a mile or two inland then turned downriver and walked until we got beyond the camp. We were in wild and desolate desert, a succession of craggy peaks all around us and nothing living. Faraway there were pine forests but only scraggly cedars nearby in ugly clumps, like war clubs beset with spines. We could see many side canyons one after another, sometimes separated by only a few dozen feet of clift, so that wind and water were able to break holes in the walls between them. It looked like natural bridges above the holes but, of course, there were no streams under them, unless there's such a thing as a "windstream."

We could hear the river below in its endless roar and gurgle, and we could see the multicolored landscape for a hundred miles to snow-shrouded mountains. We stood there awestruck and transfixed, and Major was inspired to say, "It's the heart of America, this great river. Look at it, Bradley, listen to it, feel its pulse."

Luck favored us and we found an easy route back to camp getting down in time for supper. When we recounted the incident of my rescuing Major with my underdrawers, Jack said, "Had it been Dunn, instead of Bradley, the professor would have campt where he was."

While we were away, Seneca had been practicing on his Jew's harp and he plucked out a version of *Home Sweet Home*. It was probably a sorry affair for anybody with an ear for it, but it was good enough for us. As it was a song we all knew by heart, we joined in and made the canyon ring, or "cringe" might be more accurate, considering our musical skills.

Maybe it was the song, but that night I slept poorly, images of Lucy and Mother always in my mind, so I thought something might have happened to them, that I was a fool to put myself in such a place where they could not get word to me. In the morning I thought myself a fool for thinking that way, but I can tell you the river does something to a man with its movement that never stops, whether it's racing down a falls and spraying back up like upside-down rain, or spinning in a whirlpool like children in a game of ring-around-the-rosy, and even in an eddy when it's easing back upstream like it wanted to rest for a spell, it's never still. And it's never still in another sense with its ever-present roar or gurgle, sometimes like a thunderstorm, sometimes like a swarm of bees, and you can never separate yourself from it, even on a high plateau where it's just a distant murmur, like the soughing of wind in the trees.

Major called the canyon ahead "The Canyon of Desolation," and when we ran into it the next morning, I saw he called it right. We had a succession of very bad rapids, but Major let us run them all, and one was the worst ever run. Every boat was full of water when we got through. It was a wild and exciting game and I hoped Major would let us continue to run more and line less. Aside from the danger of losing our provisions and having to walk out to civilization, we could almost surely get ourselves to land on one side or the other, for the river generally narrows up considerably where the rapids are, so that we are never far from the shore.

We campt at the head of a rapid Major said we could not run so that we would have to make a short portage of the cargoes and let the boats down with lines in the morning. I would have run it if left to myself as the only trouble would be sunken rocks and in such swift water any rock that would injure us would show itself by roughing up the water, and we could avoid it. Major's way was safe, but as I am a lazy man, I looked more to the ease of the thing.

We got half the provisions and the little boat down and one of the big ones, leaving my boat and the other half of the cargoes for the morning, which for our force would not be a hard task. Andy said he wanted to learn some knots so I tried to teach him the bowline. It's not a particularly hard knot to learn; just takes practice, that's all. Its virtue is it won't slip, no matter how much tension or slack it's subjected to, so you can use it to make the kedge warp fast to the kedge anchor, or to bend a reefing pennant to the cringle in the leech of a sail or to make fast to a ringbolt, which was what we were doing, or a hundred other uses.

I showed Andy how you take the standing part in the left hand and the fall in your right. Then you place the fall above the standing part and move your left hand higher up and make a loop. Holding the loop with your left hand, and the fall in your right, you push the fall up through the loop, the standing part being below the loop. Finally, you pass the fall under and around the standing part and down through the loop and pull it tight.

I tried over and over to teach Andy the knot, but he couldn't seem to tell the standing part from the fall, and it didn't help his mother never corrected his wrong-handedness. After a time, I remembered a little sort of verse about the bowline, that I used once to teach the knot to my little brother, before the scarlet fever got him:

"This is the tree. This is the rabbit-hole at the base of the tree. The rabbit jumps up out of his hole, runs around the tree and dives down his hole again."

After that Andy could whip up a bowline as fast as a rabbit can jump down his hole.

I slept to the sound of a restless river rushing over every obstacle on its way to the sea. In the middle of the night I was awakened by a terrible roar which, mingled with the hollow roar of the cataract below, made music fit for the infernal regions. A hurricane of hot dry wind was sweeping our camp and tearing through the canyon; we needed only a few flashes of lightning to meet Milton's most vivid conceptions of Hell. The tremendous wind tore the sand from the beach where we were campt and with it covered our beds. When it was done with that it found more sand on a little island below and scattered it through the air of the whole canyon so that we had to bury our heads in the blankets to get breath at all.

I thought of something I'd read about nomads in the desert hiding behind their camels during a sandstorm and as our transport was the boats, I went to hunker behind them. The wind in the canyon didn't come from one direction, though, and a boat always faces into the wind to the extent its mooring lines let it. I was in a worse place than before, as the sand was picking up moisture from the river, making it stick to me like a mud-wasp building its nest, so I crawled back to where I'd been. The wind howled all night, the sand worked through our blankets into our eyes, ears, mouths and hair. By morning after five hours of shrieking wind, and scouring sand, we were covered as in a snowdrift. When we'd shaken the sand off, more or less, and went to check on the boats we found that the paint was scoured off in patches near the bow, so they suffered like my tintypes. The *Maid* was changed to *"id of the Canyon,"* and *Sister* had become *"itty Cly ister."* Only the *Emma Dean* escaped with her name intact, she being sandwiched between the other two boats.

By mid-morning, the wind moderated to an ordinary gale and we had some respite. But we set out hungry, for eating Billy's biscuits from the night before was like chewing river-bottom. Even Major's would have been preferred, limestone being softer than sand. We set off into a day of unknown dangers, but in any case to rid ourselves of sand and grit in everything we touched or tasted, Bill Dunn faring the worst with his waist-length hair and long beard looking like a porcupine's back what with the sand clinging to his copious hair.

We ran twenty miles of one continuous rapid with a succession of cataracts, our boats filling with water and the oars being torn from our hands. We would rush through a rapid like rolling thunder, the river sounding as loud, then dash over a falls into an eddy and pull for shore, if there was a shore, to bail our boats and recover the oars. Sometimes we shipped but little water and sometimes the boats were nearly full, but we bailed them either way to prepare for a new drenching. After a brief look at the next rapid to seek out the best channel, we would plunge on. If there was no shore we pulled through the eddy and into the next rapid and falls, repeating the whole thing, dashing and dancing like so many furies, our nerves drawn up to the greatest tension.

Twice we let down with ropes but could have run them had it been a necessity to do so. I realized my musing about running everything without regard to safety was foolish and vain, something Howland said the Greeks called "hubris." We needed to be careful of our provisions and our boats as the hot blasts that sweep through these rocky gorges admonished us that an attempt to walk out over a desert in search of civilization would be almost certain death, so we had better go a little slow and safe.

On Saturday I wanted to wash the grit from my clothes and copy out my notes, so I begged off going with Major to measure the mountains nearby. He ordered Howland and Bill Dunn to go instead, and though Major didn't notice, I could see both men were unhappy about it. Howland had lost the maps again in the sandstorm and wanted to make new ones from memory, and Bill was still working on scraping sand from his beard.

The canyon walls were getting lower and changing color to a dusty cream, so I guessed we were getting out of the Canyon of Desolation. As we had been in it for forty five miles, it was time it ended. When I'd finished my washing and hung my "wardrobe" to dry, I walked down the river a half mile or so and saw a very bad rapid. The waves were so heavy I knew our boats could not ride them, but there was deep water on the left which we could probably run if we were very careful.

Jack and I had figured the exploring party would return by noon and that we would start again right after dinner, but they did not appear. At five P.M. they still had not shown up, so Seneca and I set out looking for them. Jack said they had gone to "measure strata," and that he was ordered to take barometer and thermometer read-

ings every half hour at the river and they were to take the same measurements on the half hour at every strata division on the mountain.
That way they could tell the height of each layer and maybe judge
how long it took to lay down.

When Seneca and I hadn't found anybody by sunset, we built a
fire where we were, about a mile from camp, to guide them down
and climbed back in the dark ourselves, and that was a treat I'd
rather I was spared. We had to inch down step by step in some
places, feeling the way with our feet in the dark. Often we didn't
know what was below us, a sheer clift or a firm footing. The gleaming fire at camp was our only guide, and sometimes that misled us,
for we naturally wanted to head right for it, as "straight is the gate
and narrow the way." We finally worked out a method of the back-
most man holding the belt of the man in front, in case he mis-
stepped, and sort of zigzagging down, changing places every now
and then to share the danger.

We figured Major and the men would have to spend the night on
the mountain but around nine o'clock they showed up in camp.
Major explained that there were more layers than they expected,
some very thin so they had to sit and wait for the half hour to pass,
some very thick so they had to scramble to get to a division before
the half hour expired, so they hadn't finish measuring until five
o'clock, and the dark struck them before they were fairly started
down. He was sore annoyed when he learned that Jack had taken his
last measurements at noon, but he didn't go on at Jack the way he
had been going at Oramel. I suppose it was because Jack always tried
to please Major, while Howland mostly took issue.

They reported that the mountains rose to about four thousand
feet at a distance of four miles back from the river. We would find
more mountains downriver, so the coming out of the canyon was
only apparent. But I thought to myself that nothing goes on forever,
not a canyon, not a river, not a man, but I hoped we would go on long
enough to let me see family and friends again.

The Sabbath again, but Major determined that we should not rest,
and he ordered us on the river early. He listened to my description of
the rapid I had scouted and said, "If you think it can be run,

Sergeant, then we'll run it," a statement I never thought I would hear from his lips. We got all the boats across the river on the left, and the *Emma Dean* plunged into the boil, me following close with the *Maid*.

Walter was in his usual place at the forward oars, and Seneca took the aft pair. I was at the sweep, though it's often useless or worse in rapids. I saw the *Emma Dean* start into the deep water with no trouble but then she got too near the left wall and a wave pushed them into the clift, breaking one of Bill Dunn's oars. In the confusion Bill let loose the other rowing oar, so they were left with only Jack's forward pair. I could see they were trying to land but the fast water swept them into another rapid with only Jack supplying the power for steering, which is a chore from the bow.

They entered the rapid and were doing fine as it lengthened out and provided a deep channel on the right, but then the river made a sharp turn to the left and Jack couldn't turn her fast enough. A reflex wave from the clift on the right caught the starboard side of the bow, turning her downstream. Major stood up and signaled me to land, which I couldn't do. Then another wave washed over the little boat's stern, filling her with water. It caught Major standing and knocked him into the water. Bill Dunn reached over the gunwale to rescue him but that threw the little boat out of balance and when another wave lifted her, she capsized onto Major. She spilled Jack and Bill and all her cargo into the rushing water, then rolled over twice more, slow like a playful puppy. That let Major out from under but I was sure he'd drown, him having but one arm and thereby being unable to swim or maybe even to hold on to the *Emma Dean,* which the other men had managed to do. Being a maimed man, Major had a life jacket and it was always inflated in the rapids. He was staying afloat by its means, using his one arm as a sort of sweep oar to steer or row as needed for navigation but not for power, which the river was supplying in abundance.

As the little boat was carried down, the waves grew wilder and every so often one would break over Major's head and he would disappear. Each time I was certain he was a goner, he'd bob up again farther down. The boat was then twenty or thirty feet ahead of him and probably moving at about fifteen miles an hour. There is a tail at the end of every rapid where the waves grow smaller and smaller until they taper off to quiet water. When the boat reached the end of the tail and the waves stopped rolling over him, Major caught up with her. Jack and Bill were clinging to her and when Major appeared they tried to right her before they might be carried into the rapid just ahead.

They were all on one side of the boat, trying to lift her, Jack at the bow, Bill in the middle and Major at the stern, when Dunn lost his grip and went under. As he was washed downstream Jack was able to get a hold on Bill's long hair and pull him to the boat, which was still turned turtle. They were swimming as best they could and pulling the boat to get her to shore before they were taken into the next nest of rocks and rapids, but the river was carrying them downstream at a greater pace than they were moving to shore. They were nearly upon the rapid and about to be swept away when they chanced on a large pile of driftwood poking into the river from the right bank, and the little boat fetched up on it.

They should have been safe then, but Major saw their bedrolls floating toward them and let go the boat to grab them. He got hold of one but in the process was carried away again himself. Bill swam out and helped him to shore. Major clung to his bedroll, but the other two got away.

I landed with the *Maid,* and *Sister* soon followed. The rapid had not been as bad as many we had passed, but the early loss of two oars and the shipping of heavy seas had crippled the little boat so she couldn't manage it. When we talked about Jack saving Bill from drowning, Jack opined that there was virtue after all in waist-length hair. "You take a beard or a moustache now, catch ahold of that you'd drown a man."

The driftwood pile proved a blessing in another way because in it was a log big enough to allow cutting into oars, which we had to do if we were to get the pilot boat any farther without lining her. So Major was called upon to keep the Sabbath after all, but I don't think he saw the lesson in it.

The cold water had soaked every man jack of us, so we used some of the driftwood to make up a good fire to dry our clothes and warm ourselves. Jack said as he'd "already broken most of the ten commandments, a broken oar didn't amount to much." But we needed the oars for the rapids ahead, and I believe we were meant to come upon the driftwood pile for our needs just then.

When the *Emma Dean* capsized, all her cargo was lost, save the one blanket roll. The river had claimed a barometer, but we had two others. We also lost two Henry rifles with their ammunition, and that was a loss we could ill afford. We were left with just seven rifles for nine men, and if we met Indians who thought our rations were worth a fight, we might not prevail.

The oars we crafted were not things of beauty, for we had no lathe and no adze, but they would serve. We decided to make them shorter than the ones we'd lost because the chutes in the rapids seemed to be getting narrower as we progressed. We'd finished the oars by nightfall and so made an early start in the morning. We ran several fine rapids with little difficulty and I began to think the worst ones were over when we came suddenly on a thunderer. The river was full of rocks on the left and they forced the water to rush to the right where there was an overhanging clift just a few feet above river level, not high enough to get a boat and crew safely under. The *Emma Dean* went through all right, cleaving to the left, Major shouting directions and Jack and Bill Dunn rowing their hearts out, all being drenched as the waves rebounded from the rocks and filled the little boat.

I was standing at the *Maid's* long sweep oar, keeping her closer to the middle where I thought we would fare better and ship less water, but a great sea wave came off the clift and swept over our stern, knocking me into the water. My foot caught under the seat so I was being carried upside down, my head under water. With great exertion, I managed to take hold of the gunwale with my left hand and by that means was able to lift my head to breathe now and again. Seneca tried to come to my aid but he was knocked into the bottom of the boat by another great wave that filled the boat to the gunwales. That left Walter Powell at the forward oars to keep the boat from going under the clift and breaking up. He let me take my chances with the water and put his back into rowing the boat away from the clift. On one of my trips up for air, I saw that the *Maid* was being carried full-tilt to the clift which meant Walter could be knocked into the water too if the boat went under the clift's over-hang. I was pulled under again and when I bobbed back up, the danger had passed, God knows how, and Walter reached over and pulled me in, set Seneca upright and rowed to shore as if nothing untoward had happened. *Sister's* crew saw the fun from above and lined her down. We'd lost a pair of the oars we'd just made, but the crew of the little boat caught them as they floated by, so the only loss was a gash and bruise to my leg. All I feared was that the wetting and drying of my tintypes would ruin them.

I took the oars just to keep warm, rowed hard, and before long we emerged from the Canyon of Desolation into open country and warm sunshine. On a little bluff not far from the river I saw a silhouette that looked like a horse. As we came closer I saw that it was a horse, just skin and bone, spavined and lame, as I could see it hobble. Seneca speculated that it had been abandoned by Indians. The way the horse kept bobbing its head up and down, up and down, put me in mind of the deaf-mute boy in Green River City.

I hoped that we had left our problems behind us in the Canyon of Desolation, but after only a mile through flat country, we entered another canyon. Just before the entrance there was a formation made up of rocks of a dark grey color we had not seen before. Major said that the stone was lignite and was harder even than the red sandstone we feared every time we met it, so we could expect a narrow river with vertical clifts. A little farther on we came upon some seams of coal, so Major called the place "Coal Canyon." The clifts did get more vertical as we went along but, as luck would have it, only on one side at a time, so we were able to land and line on the opposite side and portage as the need arose.

At about three o'clock in the afternoon our luck gave out. We came to a narrow channel between two vertical clifts, about a thousand feet high, where there was no beach on either side. We got all three boats to a huge flat rock in the middle of the stream and held them there, the river rushing by on both sides. Major looked over the rapid ahead and said we couldn't run it, but with no beach we couldn't line it. We couldn't land, we couldn't go back and it seemed we couldn't go forward without wrecking the boats. We couldn't go on, but we had to go on.

As the river wasn't too deep there, all except Major got into the water and waded, letting our boats down on lines ahead of us until it got too deep to wade, and then we swam, holding the ropes, our bodies acting like sea anchors to slow the speed of the boats. While we were getting scraped by rocks on the river bottom, Major, in the *Emma Dean* was getting knocked about as she bounced off one rock after another. We made a hundred yards to the very head of the rapid where there was another large rock, and we managed to lash the boats to it. When we studied out the rapid ahead, we saw that while the water ran through it at a racehorse pace and that it was full of rocks, it had no great fall.

With no choice but to go downstream, Major ordered the *Emma Dean's* crew into her, and I made a line fast to her bow ringbolt. The rest of us, standing on the big rock, let her down stern-first on her line to a broken rock smack in the middle of the rapid, water rushing all around her. Jack crawled up on her bow compartment and with some difficulty managed to secure her to the rock with a short line. Then he untied the long line and we hauled it in.

Next, I made a line fast to the bow of the *Maid,* and Walter, Seneca and I got in her. The crew of *Sister* let the *Maid* down on the line in the same way we'd let the *Emma Dean* down, and we held her against the *Emma Dean* with our hands. That left *Sister* alone on the rock upstream of us, with no way to let her down on her line, so she'd have to float free. They still held our bow line, and Andy tied the other end of it to *Sister's* bow to prevent her slipping past us. Her crew got in her and let the river carry her downstream stern first. As they rode down to us, we took in the slack in the line, me praying Andy had got the rabbit in the hole when he tied the bowline. He'd done it, left-handed or no, and so in this way we got the three boats held to the big rock in the middle of the rapid, snuggling and rubbing each other like they were turtle doves, and all pointing upstream. We didn't see another sizable rock downstream that would let us repeat the process, so I figured we'd have to run the rapid, sternforemost, like it or not, as we couldn't live on that broken rock.

Howland said, "I feel like a magician who's swallowed a coin, but forgot the second half of the trick." Major said, "You've always got one problem or another, Oramel." But the rest of us laughed and it helped to ease things a bit, but I didn't feel easy sitting in a bobbing boat, water rushing all around and no way to proceed that I could figure.

When Major told us his plan, I was almost persuaded he'd taken leave of his senses, that there just wasn't a second half to the trick. I said, "Why don't we just run it, we're halfway through and if we hew to the left, I'm sure we can do it." Some of the boys were nodding their heads, which I took to mean they were agreeing, but maybe they were feeling like the hobbling horse. Major wasn't nodding though and said, "It's not safe and besides there's no way to turn the boats around. We'll do it this way." Major's plan required that a man be left on the rock who would swim or float or be dragged down after the boats, holding a rope. Major looked at Dunn who was the best swimmer. Dunn shook his head and his waist-length hair swung out so it looked like his denial was underlined, like a phrase in a book. Andy stepped forward, "I'll do it, Major, sir," so that I thought he was even madder.

First we let the *Emma Dean* down with its crew to the end of her line, keeping the other end of the line snubbed on our rock. She hung there in the swift tide, tugging at her line yawing back and forth and bobbing up and down as she tried to tear the line away. The boys in the *Emma Dean* had taken the end of the lines of the other two boats down with her, and now Bill Dunn made the *Maid's* line fast to the ringbolt in the *Emma Dean's* stern, the other end still tied to our bow. When Major signaled, I cast off and we went racing down stern first past the *Emma Dean* to the length of our line, one hundred twenty feet, so we then had two boats tethered to the rock in the middle of the rapid and swinging at the end their lines, making the *Emma Dean* one hundred and twenty feet and the *Maid* two hundred forty feet down from the broken rock where *Sister* was still moored with her crew.

Andy stayed on the rock holding the *Emma Dean's* line still snubbed while Billy Rhoads and Howland got into *Sister*. Bill Dunn made *Sister's* line fast to the *Emma Dean's* stern, and at Major's signal Andy cast off the short line and she rushed down past the *Emma Dean* the same way we had and ended up bumping gunwales with us, both our lines being tied to the *Emma Dean's* stern. Then my crew took *Sister's* line, and the men in the *Emma Dean* released it. I wrapped it around the stern oarlock, and we payed it out as slow as the river allowed until we got *Sister* downstream almost to the end of her line where her crew managed to work her into a little cove on the left. Then I took the slack out of her line and made it fast to our stern ringbolt. Now we had three boats on their lines, stretching three hundred fifty feet or so from rock to cove and tethered at each end. Andy was still on the rock upstream. He looked lonely at that remove, and small.

My heart was in my throat for that boy with the odd head, who couldn't swim any better than he could spell, standing there alone on that jagged rock, around him the roaring river, watching and waiting to catch him. He loosed the *Emma Dean's* line from the rock and jumped in.

There was nothing keeping the boy from drowning in that rushing, rocky water but a rope held by another man. If that didn't mean faith and trust, I don't know what does. Holding the line with one hand and sort of flapping and steering with the other, he was taken downstream at speed, following the *Emma Dean* and the *Maid,* both boats and him being carried down to where *Sister* was moored. Jack in the *Emma Dean* left the rowing to Bill Dunn and hauled in on Andy's line, trying to pull him into the *Emma Dean.* Jack hauled with all his strength, trying to get Andy into the boat before they got into the rocks, but the river was stronger, and Andy bounced and scraped against the rocks, helpless to do anything but just hold to the rope, with both hands now.

My boat reached the little cove where *Sister* was, and her crew hauled us in before we slipped by, and we did the same for the *Emma Dean,* which fetched up against *Sister* with a loud thump. Jack was reeling Andy in who was coughing and spitting water and clinging to his rope. He was amongst the rocks when a sidewise wave caught him and slammed him against a rock. He went limp and let go of the rope. When that happened, Jack fell backwards into his boat, then scrambled back up and out on the stern compartment, trying to reach Andy. He was too late and Andy was swept down toward my boat. I stuck the big sweep oar out in front of Andy. It stopped him for a moment or two, then he started to slip by. I felt something brush me aside and saw Seneca leap over the stern and into the water In a jiffy he had Andy by his shirt collar and with his other hand grasped the steering oar, so I was able to pull them both in. With Walter's help we got Andy held upside down and poured the water out of him. When he came to, we checked him over it seemed he'd suffered little, only a few scrapes and a bloody lip and, of course, an egg-sized lump on his sizable head. Jack was ash-white and looked more scared than Andy, but he put on his usual bluff show, saying, "I most caught a bigger fish than ever you did, George, but the big ones always get away."

Major said to Seneca, "I didn't know you could swim."

"I can't," Seneca said

And that's the way we got all three boats snugged into the little cove, pretty as you please. I'd never seen a juggler do better.

We stopped to catch our breath and to shake Andy's hand, for he was surely "the hero of the day," as Major called him, and we all agreed. But the cove was only a way stop; we still had crashing waves and broken rocks ahead of us. There was no beach at the cove so we got into the water, which was up to our waists. Holding the boats with bow and stern lines and wading, we worked them one at a time around a little point of rock to where there was a ledge on the clift, about a man's height above the water, which ran down past the worst part of the rapid. We unloaded the boats, passing their cargoes up to the ledge and carrying them down past the rapid. Then we came back and stood on the ledge holding the lines and let the boats down. It was hard and tricky work and we made only fifteen miles the whole day, Major taking my estimate maybe just to surprise me or maybe to avoid another argument with Oramel Howland.

THE BRECKENBRIDGE SENTINEL

JULY 12, 1869.

LAUNCHING OF THE ADAMS EXPEDITION.

This morning, Colonel Samuel Adams, having yesterday solemnly observed the Sabbath in the company of his fellow argonauts, successfully launched two sturdy boats on the Blue River, commencing an epic journey down the Blue to where it meets the Grand River and becomes the Colorado River, which he proposes to follow for its entire length to the Gulf of California. Such a feat has never been accomplished and only one attempt has been made, and that by the Powell Expedition which has been reported lost.

Two additional boats are nearing completion and will be hauled by wagon to a point some ten miles farther down the Blue, where they will be launched tomorrow, completing the four boat complement of the Adams party. Colonel Adams, who has spent the last six weeks gathering provisions and supervising the building of the boats, will be accompanied by nine of our most prominent citizens, whose names are given at the end of this article. The party will carry provisions for a year, but Colonel Adams believes the hunters among them will easily supplement these basic rations with fresh meat daily. For this purpose, and for protection from hostile savages, the party carries ten Spencer repeater rifles and two hundred rounds of ammunition for each.

The community of Breckenbridge did itself proud in providing an appropriate sendoff to the brave and adventurous men who set forth today, for every citizen who could walk, stumble or be carried showed up at the launching. For display on the flagship, Mrs. Silverthorne presented a knitted flag emblazoned with the message, "Western Colorado to California — Greeting"

There were many fine speeches which space does not permit us to quote here, but we would be remiss if we did not take note of Colonel Adams gracious response in which he declared, "Here, upon the extreme limits of civilization, I unexpectedly found a community which in intelligence, enterprise and moral worth were superior to that of any other I had ever met." Modesty compels us to withhold comment, but we can report that we have learned from a confidential source that upon completion of the voyage, Congress will compel us to refer to Colonel Adams as General Adams.

The next morning we came out of Coal Canyon into a long, wind-swept valley with barren, parched desert on both sides. Hot sultry winds were sweeping across it, and we were scoured with sand again. The desert seemed to go for many miles on either side, but on the right the dust and much smoke from a distant forest fire made it impossible to see any great distance. To the left we could vaguely see a horizon of buttes and mesas, buttressed in light blue or azure on the bottom, shading through grey to buff to brown at the top. The hot sun reflecting off the gleaming desert sands made all these shapes appear to be floating, sometimes upside down, just off the desert floor. Then they might disappear only to reappear and start in to dancing. I calculated that these were what made up a mirage, because with a little imagination the buttes could be cities, and the shimmering heat off the desert floor could be a lake. Desperate men see what they wish to see, despite the truth of things, and hope beyond reason makes men desperate.

After the one o'clock observations, we set out in about as deso-late a country as man could imagine or God could contrive. I won-dered why He made such a place when a verdant valley would have been no more trouble. The only saving grace was fast water. I want-ed as much of that as I could get, for I hoped we would run down our altitude before we left the Green and so have an easier time of it on the Colorado. The air was hot and the water was warm so that when we got wetted, we almost enjoyed it and had some good laughs when a boat would ship a big wave and drench the crew.

In mid-afternoon we came upon the first sign of human presence since we'd left the Uinta Basin over a week earlier. There were Indian rafts on the shore, rough logs bound together with willow withes, just used for crossing the river, I judged, for they'd never survive a full-blown rapid. Andy looked at the footprints and declared that Indians had crossed here only a few days earlier. Major got out the army maps and told us, "I'm guessing this is where Gunnison and his party crossed. They were killed some distance west of here by Indians." I was pleased to be spared the presence of the raftsmen, a feeling shared by the others, I'm sure. Jack said, "It's not a fit camping place," and Billy agreed, "No firewood for cooking, best we move on," though the log rafts would have burned just fine and there was a smooth beach for a camp.

We found more evidence of Indians the next day when we stopped at the San Rafael River, just a stream really, coming in from the west. A ways up the stream there was a place where Indians must have gathered frequently, for there were many arrowheads and flint chips scattered about. It was a place with flint in abundance, an armory you might say, but there was no sign anybody had ever lived there, and for good reason: There were no fish in the stream, and no animal could survive there. Hardly a bird save the ill-omened raven or an occasional eagle screaming over us, not even vultures for there was nothing for them to prey on.

For the first time on the trip I felt lost beyond hope and experienced a sense of loneliness looking at our little party, only three boats and nine men, hundreds of miles from civilization, bound on an errand that everyone had declared must end in disaster. Yet if an indifferent stranger were to enter our camp at night or sit with us in our boats by day, he would find a cool deliberate determination to persevere that possessed every man of our party, and he would at once predict success.

For my part I felt secure in predicting that we would reach the Grand River that week if the Green River didn't canyon badly ahead. As we were moving farther south, the weather was growing hotter, and the sun shining on the sandstone beat the whole canyon into an oven. We were nearly suffocated at night and but for a breeze that occasionally drew upon us, it would have been intolerable. Andy said he was going to find some straws for his nose and sleep under water. Billy told him the way he snored he would be drowned by midnight.

Earlier on we had stopped to examine some curious black bluffs back a ways from the river. We had not seen that type or color of rock before and wondered how it was formed and if we would see more. We did: The walls along the river grew higher and we figured we would soon be in another canyon. Numerous buttes dotted the plain before the canyon mouth, most of them symmetrical and all in beautiful colors, lilac, pink, light grey, slate, rich cream and orange. The sands on the plain were made of the stone carried from these buttes so it was a colorful desert of creams and orange running towards maroon. We soon entered the canyon and found the walls to be of the same orange color as the plain, so it looked to us like the water would not be swift or dangerous.

That turned out to be the case, so it wasn't the water that was the torment but the heat. The walls shut out the breeze, and with the river twisting like an eel, first east then west, then east again, the sun was often right overhead and beat down mercilessly, making the place Hades hot. The walls closed in and the river began to flow in great sweeping curves so that the water would wash in slow waves against the clift on the outside of the curve but leave a flood plain of silt and mud on the inside where dwarf oak and willow had taken hold. Where the water washed the clifts it undercut them so that there were vast hollow domes extending back many yards into the clift. The curves slowed the river so much we had to take up rowing again, along with cursing and sweating in the heat. When Jack took a thermometer reading down near the water it registered one hundred degrees. With hard labor in the baking heat we made twenty miles by water, less than half that land-distance, and campt on the outside of a bend where there was a little patch of shade below the undercut clift.

There was a stream opposite coming down on the inside of the bend. All but the cooks crossed over to see what lay up the stream and to see if there were any trout in it. In most places the streams that come in are so clear you can see anything that moves in them. We didn't see any fish, but when we tasted the water we found it to be almost as hot as Billy's coffee, so if there had been trout they'd have been ready-cooked.

It turned out that a little ways up the stream there were two side canyons, one on each side of the stream. It wouldn't do to have this hidden place go on without a name, so Major called it "Trin-Alcove Bend," a tongue twister for fair. The two side canyons were very twisting so we first followed the stream canyon which soon developed into high walls of sandstone with frequent caves where we found evidence of bats. Many rivulets and a few waterfalls came down the side walls and were heated by the rock before joining the stream. We searched the side canyons too, hoping for some cooler water, but found only a few caves with bat droppings.

JULY 13, 1869.

NEW LAUNCHING OF
THE ADAMS EXPEDITION.

Colonel Adams completed the first leg of his historic journey to California "without difficulty," the pilot boat being twice upset "a mere inconvenience," according to the Colonel. The Adams expedition was augmented last night by his remaining two boats, carried down by wagon to their launching site, and by a group of well-wishers who sponsored a parting celebration. They dined on fresh bread made by Mrs. Silverthorne, washed down with champagne supplied by Judge Silverthorne.

After a jolly evening of song and merriment, the boats were set into the waters of the Blue River, to wend their way northwest until they meet the Grand River, thence southwesterly to their destination. In addition to sending them off with warm wishes for success, Judge Silverthorne presented Colonel Adams with a hunting dog to further their prowess in killing game for fresh meat during the voyage. The Colonel promptly named the dog "Old Blue," after the river.

Just before their departure, Colonel Adams took the time to describe the features of the boats built to his design. They are open, made of wood and, in the Colonel's words, "Sound as a dollar." Colonel Adams suggested, "without intent to defame," that the tragic loss of the Powell party could probably be laid to faulty boat construction coupled with an unskilled crew, and he is certain he has overcome those problems. Our readers will await word from California, Colonel!

That night at supper Howland remarked that we were in the "vasty deep" and asked if anyone could summon spirits. Andy said, "No but I can call bats." Of course nobody believed him because a bat's call is a squeak almost beyond the range of human hearing. Walter said, "Be like callin' up your kin." Andy didn't say a word and he didn't make a sound. We watched him as he stuck a thumb in each ear and spread his fingers. He was looking straight at Walter and if he'd of stuck out his tongue I think Walter would have gone for him, and I could see Walter making to get up anyway. But then Andy wiggled his fingers real fast and the first thing we knew bats were flitting and buzzing all about his head. Well then we all tried it and near collapsed in hilarity as we had the whole camp abuzz with bats. Major having but one hand to work with just sat and watched the fun.

The water was calm as a lake in the morning and in some places hardly moved at all, so that in a whole day of hard, hot rowing we made but twenty five miles, river distance. At one point the river made a sharp bend to the right and kept bending for five miles, so we ended up only a quarter mile from where we started. Then it took it into its head to move to the left in a great sweeping loop of nine miles length, placing us only six hundred yards from the beginning of that loop, so we moved in the shape of a figure eight. Howland was all the time using his compass to find the direction of the curve, and he calculated that, over land, could that be done, we'd made only ten miles the whole day, so the river was teasing us or maybe just making sure we had to work to succeed in our quest. I objected to the labor but most of the other men were tickled by the river's meandering and joking about how it was tricking us. They were firing off pistols and shouting and whistling to make the walls rebound with echoes. The walls were as colorful as calico with azure and brown among the orange and maroon colors that had dominated at the entrance to the canyon.

The narrow canyon and high walls meant that the sun set early, so when we campt for the night on the west side, the river running south, in a snug little niche in the rocks, we had ample shade even though there were no trees. We were getting down on rations as the frequent filling of the boats with water had done for a quantity of our provisions. It was this, I guess, that made the cooks decide to make a pan of beans, though they were sour and sprouting. The result was a night of no sleep as we all became ill at one end or the other ("Or either or both," Howland said the lawyers would call it), and spent the night running to the river. In the morning Billy left the balance of the bad sack of beans for the crows, and that meant we had but one sack remaining. We hadn't opened it to see if it was spoiled, and Oramel said in that Vermont twang of his, "What makes you think that sack's any better than t'other?" Billy said, "Oramel, you been using it for a seat in the boat, settin on it like a brood hen. Kept it dry as her eggs." Billy poked the sack, but only a dull sound was made. We'd have to wait and see.

CHEYENNE LEADER

JULY 15, 1869.

IN MEMORIAM.

Fred Hook, former Mayor of Cheyenne, perished tragically on the Green River, in Utah Territory. Having learned of the imminent departure of Major Powell and his crew, intending to traverse the Green and Colorado Rivers, through the Grand Canyon, to Arizona Territory, Mr. Hook organized an expedition of his own. On June 1, one week after the ill-fated Powell expedition was launched, Hook and fifteen fellow miners departed from Green River City in four flat-bottomed boats built of lumber torn from abandoned shacks and recut.

One of the party's four boats was abandoned in Red Canyon, after its blunt prow met head-on an equally blunt rock. Subsequently, after portaging boats and provisions for some miles (they had not brought enough line to lower the boats on ropes more than fifty feet), Hook steered his boat into a rapid with four men, the rest of the party watching from shore.

His sweep oar snagged on a cleft rock and tore the stern out, Hook with it. His four crew members clung to the now sunken hull until it broke apart, then they clung to its body parts. Hook had nothing to cling to, having had the sweep oar torn from his grasp. Unable to swim, he quickly sank beneath the waves. The men on shore threw what lines they had to the men rotating in the boil at the bottom of the rapid and succeeded in rescuing two of them. The two others were too far away to reach with their short lines, and the men on shore could only watch in horror as the current took them over the next fall and out of sight, forever.

Hook's body was recovered and buried beneath a cairn of rocks above the high water mark. On a short pine plank, once the lintel of a shack in Green River, then a sternboard on Hook's boat, they carved a simple, "HOOK" and planted it at the head of his grave.   *May he rest in peace.*

When we started again the next morning, we followed more twists in the river, then it doubled back again and we entered another canyon on quiet water, which Major named "Stillwater Canyon." As we worked our way down, rowing all the time with clumsy hacked out oars, the river narrowed and the walls became vertical, shutting out the light. The tide grew stronger and we were borne along in an ever-gloomier, ever-narrower channel, and my heart speeded up with the water. It crossed my mind that the river might narrow up so much that our boats couldn't squeeze between the walls of the clifts. Ahead of us a huge black wall loomed up and there was no sign of a turn in the river. Seneca said it might be about to make a tunnel, that we were maybe coming upon the hole in the river we'd been warned about. There was no beach and anyway the water ran too fast for us to stop and scout ahead, so we plunged on toward the wall dead ahead, its blackness seeming to shut out the light. Just as the clifts on each side seemed to be closing in to where they'd meet each other, and just as the day was at its darkest, a lone falcon appeared from nowhere and came up the river towards us.

A minute later, the river twisted left and without warning and without the usual gradual widening of the canyon, we burst into bright sunlight, the river suddenly doubled in width and the tide became calm and strong. I felt like a gentle hand was stroking me, that another presence was looking down on us with blessed reassurance. We broke out in cheers, Hurra! Hurra! Hurra! We had come upon the Grand River quite unexpectedly at about 5 ½ P.M. on Friday the 16th of July. A "historic moment," Major called it, and he called it right.

We had been led to expect the Grand to be a rushing, roaring mountain torrent which, uniting with the Green, would give us a "Grand" promenade across the mountains. But the Rio Colorado, the river formed of the Grand and the Green, was, as far as we could see down it, calm and wide and very unlike the unpossible, unpassable succession of foaming, raging waterfalls and cataracts we had been told to expect. Our last seventy five miles on the Green a child might have sailed in perfect safety, and there we were, floating on a scene never before beheld by white men and by all regarded as impossibly dangerous of approach from any quarter and especially by water. So much so that one adventurer proposed to explore it by *balloon* if Congress would furnish the necessary greenbacks to finance the mission. Surely men do get frightened wonderfully by chained lyons.

At noon we had stopped in a place where there were beavers damming a stream and I managed to kill two. Their flesh makes only decent eating but their tails make excellent soup. So that night we had beaver tail stew, a fine change from our meatless diet. Jack said the stew wasn't fit for human consumption but I think he didn't like his story of beavers dodging bullets to be disproved.

We set up camp a short ways up the Grand, in the angle formed by the confluence of the two rivers, on a wide bank of sand deposited there by floodwaters. Trees had all but disappeared from the landscape, leaving us with just a few hackberry bushes. Not even willows, which will grow most anywhere, could take root in this desert by the river. The Grand had come in from our left, and the Colorado runs southwest from the junction. Standing at the angle and looking to my right I could see the Green, a reddish muddy flow with fast-rising volume fighting back the Grand, which was master of the field when we arrived. The Grand by contrast was as clear as the Merrimac River back in Massachusetts and moved with a strong deep tide. Its course is not much changed by joining with the Green so it is properly the Colorado and the Green is its tributary. How man delights in calling things in accordance with his desires rather than reality, for here we had a river that was green called red (Colorado) and a red river called Green.

Looking back up the Green I could see a graceful curve of clift walls where we had emerged from Stillwater Canyon and up the Grand a straighter but regular clift, but both about the same height, perhaps twelve hundred feet, the plateau behind fifteen hundred feet above river level. Looking down the Colorado I saw a river nearly a thousand feet wide with walls much broken down, which usually meant rapids and falls. It came to me then that rivers never divide, but only join one another, prizing unity over separation, for a river separates only to work around an obstacle and always rejoins itself. Rivers stick together.

From the clifts of the Grand we could see in the far distance snow-clad peaks, which Major said were the summits of a group of mountains known as the Sierra La Sal. In Massachusetts you are lucky if you can see a mile on land, but here I could see for hundreds of miles. It is not easy for an Easterner to take in such distance, and I confess I was never comfortable with it. It was like living in a big house not divided into rooms, so that the kitchen fell into the parlor and the bedrooms merged with the porch.

Our boats seemed as happy as we were to be on the Colorado at last. They were swinging lazily in an eddy, nudging one another like nuzzling puppies. We took everything out of them and hastened to start a thorough cleaning and recaulking, for we expected we would stay only a day or two to measure altitudes and latitudes and longitudes for Howland's map. But Major announced at supper that we would camp until August seventh so he could observe the eclipse that was scheduled in that day. To a man, we sat there in stunned silence. Even Walter looked at his brother as though they'd switched brains somehow. Most of the rest of us just looked at our boots or scratched an itch, and Billy stirred the fire. Finally Howland spoke up and said, "That's three weeks, John, hardly prudent. Our food supplies are low." "Yes," Major snapped, "and you know why!"

"All the same, John, we must 'arise and go or stay and die,'" I couldn't hear who Howland was quoting as just at that moment there came a thunder clap like an artillery battery firing. Lightning came with fearful brilliancy and the thunder peals were echoed and re-echoed from the four clift walls around us in a way that seemed commissioned to make doubly desolate a region set apart for desolation. The rain came down like a waterfall, drowning the campfire and soaking our provisions where we had set them on the shore. We got a tarpaulin over them but not before they got a good wetting.

The weather cleared about ten o'clock and we had a lovely night for sleep. I didn't sleep well though, my thoughts much roiled by the angry voices I'd heard at supper and a muffled conversation I couldn't entirely hear. The Howlands and Jack and Bill Dunn were huddled talking, I was sure, about the rations and Major's determination to stay for the eclipse. As Jack rose to retire, I heard him say, "I'll talk to the professor."

It was Sunday again and though a thousand spires pointed Heavenward all around us, not one sent forth the welcome peal of bells to wake the echoes of those ancient clifts to remind us of happier if not grander scenes.

We undertook to overhaul our rations and found the flour in a very bad condition, musty and full of lumps. We sifted it through a mosquito bar, took out the lumps and washed the sacks before putting it in again. We lost about two hundred pounds through this process and had only about six hundred pounds left. With only dried apples, coffee and some beans that mightn't be fit to eat, we were clearly obliged to go on soon for it would not do to be caught in a bad canyon short of provisions, no way to fish, kill game or walk out.

Thousands of men all over the globe would be squinting through telescopes at the eclipse when it came. It did not seem to me important that it be seen by a group of hungry men in a remote place. This junction of two great rivers had not been mapped nor known within one hundred miles, so I could see the importance of laying out its location and the lay of the land thereabout, but with our rations so low we should not tarry beyond absolute necessity.

Whether Jack talked to Major or Major saw the desperate state of our rations, I cannot say, but at dinner he announced that we would move on as soon as the measurements were completed, probably in two more days. Howland took his pipe out of his mouth and started to say something when Major cut him off with, "The place has to be mapped. It has to. It's the great unknown heart of America."

Howland seemed to be focusing his attention on his pipe ashes, which he was tapping out on his boot heel, one boot raised onto its toe, when he said, "If this be her heart, then America is a hard-hearted bitch." Andy giggled, but Major didn't, just shook his head and said, "We'll map it, Oramel. We'll map it and then we'll move on, not before."

When Oramel raised his foot that way, I saw that he had a round hole worn in the sole of his boot. I pointed it out to Jack who said, "Oh that's an escape route for the scorpions."

It was true we had to shake out our boots before we pulled them on, for scorpions we had in plenty. They were about the only thing alive there. It was even too hot for the pesty mosquitoes, but the not unwelcome sound of the big black cricket was heard and sometimes the shrill call of the locust. Otherwise the place was too desolate for life. So another reason to move on with some haste was the heat, for there was but scant shade in camp.

We made the most of an idle afternoon washing our clothes, which dried quickly in the heat, and washing ourselves in the clear waters of the Grand, passing our one bar of soap from hand to hand. As I had joined the boys in the water, Andy was deprived of an opportunity to rag me about not undressing, though he did make some unnecessary remarks regarding my anatomy. Billy Rhoads' buckskins had stretched some more because of the wetting, so he cut some off the legs again. "Soon you'll have nought but a belt," Andy told him.

We cleaned and caulked the boats with pine pitch and oakum, preparing them for the rigors to come. Jack cleaned the sextant and repaired the two remaining barometers; Billy scrubbed out our Dutch oven with sand; we patched moccasins and generally got ourselves shipshape for our plunge into the "Great Unknown" of the Colorado. I was writing a few notes in my journal when I heard Major call out, "What are you doing, Billy?" I looked up to see Billy down by the river with the sextant, something he'd expressed no interest in and never even held in his hand before. Billy lowered the instrument, looked at Major, then squinted through the sextant again, and said, "I'm trying to find the latitude and longitude of the nearest pie!"

THE BRECKENBRIDGE SENTINEL

JULY 19, 1869.

FIRST REPORT OF THE ADAMS EXPEDITION.

———

Mr. John Lovell has returned here this morning with our first news of the Adams expedition. It seems that on the second day after the final launching, the party came around a bend and happened suddenly on a ferocious rapid, with a fall of 250 feet in a mile and a half, by the Colonel's estimate. Three of the four boats debouched their contents and crew into the chilly waters of the Blue. While all took the ducking with humor and good sport, they suffered the loss of instruments and papers, including Colonel Adams' letters of authorization from the Secretary of War. Mr. Lovell was assigned the task of resupplying the party with instruments and a sufficiency of dry matches and will return in the morning to resume the journey to California. He will also take back "Old Blue," who earlier returned to his master, as dogs will.

At noon the next day Major and I set off to climb the mountains on the east, with the thermometer reading ninety five degrees in the shade. It got worse. I reflected that intense heat in that desert climate was not like heat in Massachusetts. My sweat did not drip but was sucked away by the dry air as soon as it left my body, so it was almost like a soft breeze was brushing my skin. We climbed for an hour up a dry gulch, which ended in a vast amphitheatre. I paced it off as seventy five yards acrost and, as it was nearly circular, it could hold many thousands of men. We couldn't find a way through it so went out and tried to climb to the left but soon came to a sheer wall. We tried the right and found a narrow shelf nearly a half mile long. We were able to walk along it about half the time but had to creep the rest. In places it was so narrow and sloping we had to lie down and crawl. I imagine this sort of thing "adds a mite to human knowledge," as Major said, but I thought humanity might survive without knowing a thing about this clift, where I could look down eight hundred feet to the river and up five hundred feet to the top and not know if I could go up or if I could get back down once I got there.

The clift was beset with fissures and crevices running toward the river and along it, crisscrossing like the web of a careless spider. Most times that we'd seen crevices they got wider near the top, so I didn't favor Major's way of climbing by hands and feet on either side of the crevice, but these ran contrary. They were narrow slits at the top and vast caves at the bottom. We wandered around in these corridors, the sun streaming in through a narrow winding skylight, trying first one direction then another, always running into dead-ends or sheer walls with no broken rocks to climb. Finally we came to a crevice that was more or less straight, narrowing somewhat at the top but still wide enough to admit our bodies. So up we climbed, the way one would climb out of a well, with our feet on one side and our hands on the other. Of course it was one hand in Major's case, but that one arm had become as strong as two. We had to play leap-frog again with the barometer passed from below and then recovered when one climber rose above the other.

When we emerged from the fissure, I changed my mind about human knowledge, for I'd never seen a vista like it, where desolation manifested itself as raw beauty. Wherever we looked there was a wilderness of rocks, deep gorges where the rivers were lost below, clifts, towers, pinnacles, strangely carved forms in every direction. We could see the course of the Colorado River for many miles, but it was a winding gorge, and we could rarely see its water. The Grand River seemed to come to us through a bottomless canyon, and the Green was only a ragged gash in the earth. To the west there were lines of clifts and rock ledges of mammoth proportions scattered as by a giant's hands. Major said it looked as though the gods had quarried them and that the clifts were such that, "The soaring eagle is lost to view ere he reaches the summit." I scanned the sky but didn't see any eagles.

While we were waiting for the time to measure altitude, I said to Major, "Walter told me about Shiloh up to the time you got on General Wallace's horse. Where did you ride to?"

"Oh, I rode back to Pittsburgh Landing." Then he grew thoughtful and said, "It was the worst time of my life."

"The wound was some painful, I guess."

"Yes, but it wasn't the wound. I had to ride by and through many wounded men, some walking, some being carried, others sitting by the roadside and waiting, calling to me to help them, or just moaning if they couldn't call out. Many were dead or dying, heroes caught by rebel fire. When I got to the Tennessee River with Walter's tourniquet working loose from the horse's trot, the blood oozing out, I stumbled somehow down the bank to the river. I don't remember how. There I saw a sight that made me forget my wound for the consuming anger: I saw a mass of beaten, frightened men, thousands of cowards, deserters, huddled against the bank. They were jeering at me, saying things like, 'If you'd been smart like us, you'd still be whole,' and they laughed like I was a fool to fight." Major's face turned red, reliving the anger, I guess, and he shook his good arm, a tight fist at the end, toward the sky, "Damned cowards, I'd have put them all on a leaky barge and sent them down the river."

All measurements having been made, it only remained for

Howland to get them onto his map. He spent the afternoon at it, Major badgering him when it didn't look the way he wanted. Seneca had taken to trying to patch up things between Major and Oramel, but that just got him on Major's bad side, too. Jack said he was sick of the bickering between Major and the Howlands, which was no different than the way we all felt. I wondered why Jack didn't speak to Major. As they were tent-mates, it would be easy, I thought. But it was never easy to talk to Major when he had an idea fixed in his mind, and Jack took care to stay on Major's good side.

Oramel made as if Major's going at him was like rain pattering on a duck's back, but you could see it was beginning to take hold: Oramel talked less, ate less, spent more time with his brother than with the rest of us and avoided Major when he could. At supper that night he read out the figures we had gathered in a droning voice that could pass for a response in a church service:

Altitude at Green River bridge, 6075 feet.

Altitude at Uinta River mouth, 4670 feet

Altitude at junction with Grand, 3860 feet

Descent achieved, 2215 feet

Altitude at Rio Virgen, 700 feet

Descent remaining, 3160 feet

Distance traveled, 539 miles.

Distance remaining, unknown

Days expired, 58

Days remaining, unknown

He said we'd come a mite more than a third of the altitude to the sea and maybe half the distance, so we had not run down the altitude as I had hoped. He calculated we'd had an average fall of four feet per mile and if the distance left was the same, we'd be having an average fall of six feet per mile for the rest of the trip.

We were none of us happy with the news. Major said we had two months rations left if we didn't lose any more. That was like saying,

THE BRECKENBRIDGE SENTINEL

JULY 20, 1869.

PROGRESS OF THE ADAMS EXPEDITION.

As we reported in this space yesterday, Mr. John Lovell returned for matches and other supplies for the Adams expedition to California. No sooner had Mr. Lovell departed with the dog, "Old Blue", to rejoin the party than Mr. Rickers returned and reported his disappointment with the progress of the journey and especially with its scientific results. We pointed out that the Colonel did not seek scientists, but able bodied adventurers for his party, to which Mr. Rickers replied, "If that's a party, I decline the invitation."

Like a coiled rattlesnake, the Colorado was lying in wait for us the next morning. After two miles of calm water and riffles just enough for us to start thinking the river was easy, the rapids began and did not end. We made two portages in the morning, carrying the cargoes on our heads and shoulders over rough broken rock, the boulders too big to let us build a road. We might have attempted to run the rapids, but our provisions being low, we could not risk their loss, so we carried them past the rapids as if they were so many tender babes. After dinner and a short portage, we began to run a rapid that looked to be passable, but the Colorado was not the Green. The pilot boat went first as usual and she'd no sooner tipped her bow over the head of the rapid than she was swamped. She couldn't sink, so she did the next worst thing, rolled over on her side like an old sow, dumping the men and the oars into the water. She kept rolling and ended bottom up. The men clung to the boat, though I couldn't see how Major managed it even in his life preserver as they were bouncing from rock to rock. After a hundred yards of such amusement they struck calm water and guided the boat to shore. We had not loaded her with cargo, so only Major's bedroll and a bailing can were lost, but three oars took their own course to the Rio Virgen.

We lined the other two boats and portaged the cargo, but as there was no beach, we were walking in water, sometimes up to our waists, carrying the goods on our heads or shoulders, slipping on the wet rocks and generally making ourselves tired and cross. Courage fades with fatigue and, truth be told, I became fearful that we had embarked on an impossible quest. There was no let-up; the rapid was continuous. We lined and portaged all afternoon, once making two portages within a hundred yards, until exhaustion forced a halt, even though there was no beach to camp on.

We made places to start a fire and to sleep by piling up rocks along the water's edge, then scraping sand from between boulders, a scanty source but all there was. In this way we made a platform of sand as wide as a man, and slept head to foot as soundly as though we were on goosedown.

We had made only eight and a half miles the first day on the Colorado and were determined to do better the next morning. Our first portage faced us only a hundred yards from our "camp". After that we lined continuously for a mile and a half. We stopped at a pile of driftwood which had timber for sawing oars, otherwise the choice was to lend oars to the *Emma Dean,* leaving a big boat shy a pair, or to line her through every rapid. So while we wanted to get on, stopping was a near necessity.

We found a big cottonwood log among the driftwood and set to work making oars with our axe and handsaw, all the tools we had. Howland stopped sawing at one point and was staring at the sky. There was nothing up there that I could see, so I asked him if was praying for a miracle to finish the job. He said, "Lookin' for a hawk, see if I can tell it from a handsaw." Jack said, "Just give us the saw, Oramel, or get on with the work."

Major wanted to determine what had so disarranged the strata there, so he went off to climb the clift, taking his brother to carry back pine pitch. We were grateful for both Walter's absence and the prospect of pitch for caulking. Although we had recaulked them only ten miles back, the boats were leaking badly from the linings and needed caulking again. When we finished the oars after dinner, we careened the boats and used up the last of my oakum filling in the worst spots. We didn't worry about caulking tools or laying it in straight, just poked it in any which way, just so the leaks stopped.

Walter brought the pitch and the Major brought the altitude, said the clifts were fifteen hundred feet high, three hundred more than at the junction with the Grand, so we were sinking deeper into the earth.

Major said he figured the strata dipped both ways from the river because part of the mountain had slid down billions of years ago. I should like to have seen the mountain slide, but from a great distance.

We made a good start on the morning of July 23rd, running the first two miles; then the fun began. We made three long, hard portages and let down the boats with ropes for three miles. The rapids got worse as we advanced so when we came to a place with flat water we stopped for dinner. At the rate the river was falling, we'd have the whole of the remaining altitude out of the way in the first hundred miles. We wouldn't be dreading rapids after that, for if it continued at that rate for more than a hundred miles, we should have to go the rest of the way *uphill*, which is not often the case with rivers.

After a meager dinner of biscuits and coffee, I went with Major and his brother up a side canyon where a little stream was pouring in. The canyon entrance was very narrow and I expected that we would have to turn back in a short while, but when we came to a cataract Major found a narrow ledge to its right, so we got around the falls by hugging the wall and shuffling along crab-wise. Suddenly the side canyon widened into a spacious sky-roofed amphitheatre. At the far end a lush green grove of cottonwoods grew and beyond and above a silver stream of shining cascades tumbled and splashed down from a height that seemed immeasurable, feeding the stream that ran across the floor of the amphitheatre and which made three little ponds on its way to the river. Major was so enthusiastic I thought he'd call the place "Eden," but he let the chance pass and it will remain unnamed until a party of strangers comes to it, for I was sure none of our crew would attempt this journey again. If it hadn't been so difficult of access, we would have campt there, for at the river it was one hundred degrees, the canyon walls were hot to the touch and the effect was like being in a bake-oven. When I told the men about the Garden of Eden, they said we should stop for the day and go swim in the little ponds, but to my surprise, Major said we should move on. While that pleased me, I couldn't figure why he'd changed from "stay" to "go." Then I thought, if it's science, it's "stay;" if it's rest or play, it's "go." Major is a determined man.

When we launched again I noticed high tide marks on the clift walls, fifteen to twenty feet above the river level. It must be fun to be on the river when the water is roaring through at that height! After a series of short falls, which we ran without difficulty, we suddenly found ourselves in a gorge of surpassing beauty. Steep, nearly vertical walls eighteen hundred feet high, rising from a swift, rockless river, the clifts reflected on its mirror-like surface. That lasted only a mile, and that mile was our last for the day as the freight train sound told us there was fast falling water ahead. The canyon walls echoed the sound and magnified it a hundred fold. We didn't need to be told there was trouble coming and so we went into camp. Major and Jack and I scouted the river a bit and saw we were at the head of a succession of furious cataracts. Major said he figured the river fell fifty feet in the next mile, and he always underestimates.

At supper we talked about the river, how we'd come through a section calm as a millpond and faced falls ahead worse than a mill dam. Jack said, "River's like a woman, loves you one minute and torments you the next." Howland said, "Torment and torrent must have the same root then." Jack said, "Oramel, you're a trial. I wasn't talking about trees."

There was general talk about where we'd been, how hard we'd worked for a few grudging miles and how it looked like there was more toil ahead. I said I thought we were lucky, that if we got all the descent over with at the beginning it would be easier later on. Billy Rhoads said, "Then we'd best pray for Niagara Falls." But finally talk ran to where we all knew it would: What if we came to a place where there was no shore, rapids we couldn't run and walls too steep to climb. Jack said it would "test the power of prayer," and there were a number of other jests, but it was Andy took the tension out by putting forward a plan: We'd sew all the tarpaulins together and make a giant balloon. Billy would "bake up a grand large mess of beans, and we'll float ourselves out."

I'd seen men in war jest in the same way, the only option being to face one's fear alone, for no man would talk of it openly. Major said he was glad to see us all in such good spirits and "indulging in badinage." Jack said, "Nothing bad about it, Professor, just joking around."

PROGRESS OF THE
ADAMS EXPEDITION.

—

Today the community was richer for the return of Messrs. Decker, O'Connor, Foment and Frazier from the Adams expedition, though Colonel Adams is no doubt poorer. Mr. Decker describes his adventure in one rapid:

"We weren't up to the speed of the water and the rocks, which we came upon suddenly. As Adams declined to adopt the safe practice of scouting the rapids in advance, we came upon one unprepared and had to experience the breaking up of the boat I shared with Mr. Lillis as well as with the loss of our outfits and firearms and ammunition, without which I was not prepared to proceed further."

In the morning we did something we hadn't done before and saw something we hadn't seen before: Every man went down to look over the rapid to see what made the fearsome noise we'd slept to and what lay ahead. We could see five cataracts running continuously for over a mile. It was a place that met two of the three tests we had laid out the night before: rapids we couldn't run, walls we couldn't climb. But there was a shore, if it could be called that, huge boulders that had fallen from the canyon walls, great angular blocks that could not roll down the talus to block the channel the way the rounder ones had. We would run down the altitude a good deal in those five cataracts, if we could get through, and perhaps there would be another beautiful stretch of calm water ahead, for even Jack's "woman" turns loving at times.

We carried our cargoes down over the first cataract and set them on a large rectangular rock, as big as a frontier cabin, that blocked the shore at the head of the second rapid. We lined the *Emma Dean* down to the rock using a long line at each end and nobody in her, because if she broke loose she'd be shattered in the next cataract like hard candy dropped on a marble floor. As it was, she sprung a plank near the bow and was taking water in the forward compartment.

The other boats went down the same way, five men holding the upstream rope and three on the downstream. We got all the boats to the head of the cataract but with serious damage to their planking, and I could see oakum strips hanging where the rocks had sprung them loose. The next challenge was the big rock. We passed the cargoes up and over and carried them to the foot of the second cataract, then talked about the boats. It seemed we'd come to a probability that hadn't entered our heads before: We couldn't run, we couldn't walk out, we had a beach, but we couldn't line. If the boats hadn't suffered so much in the first fall, we might have tried lining at least the *Emma Dean,* though there was a direct fall exceeding her length, but we didn't think they could stand more damage. "We'll have to carry them," said Major, whose role was purely supervision. But we did carry them, and it was a labor fit for Hercules as the big boats were made of oak and weighed a thousand pounds if they weighed an ounce. We practiced on the *Emma Dean,* four men on top of the big boulder, hauling on her bowline and four men hoisting her from below. We got her over with little damage, then faced the challenge of the big boats. Major said, "You can always pull more than you can push," and wanted to put five men on top of the rock, but there wasn't room for that many and a big boat too, so we put three on the rock and five below, and the same letting them down on the other side, and got them over safely, at the cost of a few bruises per man and a blue fingernail for Walter. He wailed like a banshee, swore like a trooper and threw a stone at the rock, about as futile a gesture as you could conjure. "Here," Andy said, and handed Walter a rock as big as a man's head, though smaller than Andy's! Walter threw it at Andy, but he dashed out of range, nimble as a goat.

At the third rapid we had to slide the boats along on the rocks in the river bed, standing in water to our waists. It was hard work, and after three rapids we quit for the day, about three o'clock, having had no dinner and all suffering from bruising and fatigue. We'd come only three quarters of a mile, but we had a fall of seventy five feet in that distance. The boys went to look at the next rapid and reported that it wasn't as bad as the others, but rapids don't interest me unless I can run them. That's an occupation I like, but portages don't agree with my constitution.

Looking for fossils, I came on some bones embedded in rock which Major declared to be an alligator skeleton. Since the skeleton was pointed upstream, Oramel opined that it "must have been on an independent exploring expedition in search of the junction of the Grand and the Green and failed as many do for want of breath." All I can say is the alligator was sensible to die before he attempted to ascend the last rapid we'd come down, for it had an almost direct fall of fifteen to twenty feet. We'd met nothing to compare with it before. I hoped it was our Niagara for I could do without such labor. But if the alligator was Ezekiel's "great dragon that lives in the river," we had nothing to fear, for he wasn't much over two feet long.

In spite of our general weariness, we were in good spirits, pleased to have run down our altitude so much, and looking forward to a long sleep, for the sun would not light the canyon much beyond six o'clock, the river running due south. Apparently needing still more exercise, Andy was amusing himself by throwing stones acrost the river, and I went downstream a ways to copy my notes in peace while the light lasted. By the time I'd finished, darkness was coming on but the waves below were cresting in foam so white they seemed to have a light of their own. There was a chute of water that ended up striking at the foot of a fifty foot high block of limestone, rolling half way up its front and then tumbling back in a crash of foam, like ocean breakers on a bluff shore. But the shape of the water on the river was nothing like the ocean. Where there were sunken rocks the water heaped up in mounds, or even in cones, and in places where the rocks lay just below the surface the water would strike, shoot up fifteen or twenty feet and fall back in spray like a huge fountain.

Sunday brought no rest for us, no notice being taken of it. We got the boats around the big limestone rock but with considerable collisions with their hulls and by day's end my boat was the only tight one, and I feared that wouldn't last long. At one place Major thought we could run, so the *Emma Dean* started down a steep rocky fall, taking much abuse from rocks they couldn't see and then ending up in a fast swirling whirlpool at the bottom of the fall. We'd been in whirlpools before and had managed to row out of them without troubling too much, but this one was different. We watched the little boat twist round and round and I began to wonder if they hadn't chanced on the "Great Suck" we had been warned about.

A sailboat grounded on a sandbar can sometimes be brought off by throwing an anchor out on the end of a line and hauling on it. We had brought no anchors, but Bill Dunn did the next best thing. Taking a hitch around the big sweep oar he cast it like a spear beyond the edge of the whirlpool. With Bill hauling in and Jack rowing with all his might, they broke free and made the shore, but one of Bill's rowing oars slid out of its oarlock and went beyond reach downriver. That made the second time Major's boat got in trouble on the Sabbath, but I didn't think he'd change his ways.

We lined the other two boats down and stopped there to have dinner and to cut another oar. Then we ran a short rapid, lined one, portaged and lined two more. The walls were often down to the water's edge with no broken rock to climb out on, so we had to go on, get through them running, no chance even to scout them out, and the Devil take the hindmost.

It was more toil than excitement for the falls were direct and the rapids short and we made only three and a half miles as a reward for a whole day's hard labor. Looking down from bluffs we saw that the river was still a long foaming torrent, or torment, as I had begun to think of it. We couldn't tell if we would be able to run or not, but I thought I detected a small improvement so hoped for the best. We had planned to recaulk the boats, but there were no trees and so no pitch to be had, so we would have to move on in the morning, leaks and all, though we stuffed tarpaulin strips in the worst ones.

Monday was another day wasted foolishly. We ran only a mile and a half when Major decided we should stop and look for pitch, though there was no sign of a pine anywhere and the walls were two thousand feet high. Five of us started climbing up a side canyon in one hundred degree heat and soon came upon something we'd none of us ever seen before: a disappearing brook. A freshet of a stream emerged from the right of the canyon, then was soaked up by the sand so that it just sort of petered out before our eyes.

We followed the brook up and found its source, a roofless amphitheatre with its floor a hollow basin, filled with water which overflowed into the brook. There was no way through this, even by swimming acrost, which Andy wanted to do, though a dog-paddle is the extent of his accomplishment in that area. We circled around it, found a fissure, went through that into another amphitheatre, which also had sheer walls at its back. Still moving to the right, Major said he saw a little shelf we could crawl along and maybe inch our way up a crevice on the other side. I'd had my fill of ledge crawling and crevice inching, so I said I'd go look for a better route and the other boys did the same. We scattered but I think we all had the same idea that we were on a wild goose chase and soon found ourselves back in camp, hot and tired and anxious to move on.

I figured the Major would soon see things as we did and join us. When he hadn't appeared by dinner time we began to get a little concerned, as Major had a way of getting in a fix. We could see it was clouding up and, in fact, looked to be raining already at the top of the clift, so we speculated that Major was sheltering and would start down when the showers were over. After an hour or we could see it had stopped raining on the top. In about a half hour more we heard a shout and looked up to see Major pelting toward us as fast as he could leg it. He'd rigged a strap on the barometer case, which was bouncing on his back, and he had a bundle under his arm, so I thought for a minute he'd found a whole alligator and was that excited about it. Howland said, "Look and see if he's pursued by a bear."

But Major said he was pursued by a tidal wave that was pouring down the canyon and would soon wash away our campsite. It sounded like the heat had got him, for we had had no rain in camp, but we could ill afford more loss of provisions, so we moved everything off to the side away from the canyon mouth and waited for the deluge. Jack said we'd best get in the boats taking a pair of every animal we could find with us, but Billy said he'd take the first animal to come along and cook it for us.

We waited without seeing any flood or stream or even a trickle, then Andy decided to go up the gulch and see what was going on, though Major said it was dangerous. Andy came back in five minutes and said there was a wave coming all right but it was being swallowed up by the dry sand of the canyon floor in the way of the stream we'd seen earlier, "So not to worry," says he. He'd hardly got the words out when we saw the wave coming. It was about three feet high and twenty feet wide, water and red mud. It was less a flood than a mudslide, as it was much absorbed by the sand in front of it, but still it made slow progress toward the river. We began to laugh that such a benign event could have so excited Major. We watched it trying to rush toward its goal only to be slowed again and again by the very course it had chosen. But it kept inching toward the river. Once it got there and water met water, the inch became a yard, a rod, a mile. Soon a whole wall of water and mud was coursing into the river, turning it into red turmoil. It did that for maybe twenty minutes, a half-hour, then the mud dried up in the heat, and two hours later you wouldn't know anything had happened. Nature had covered her tracks. Major said it looked like the dried mud was full of gypsum, so he called the place, "Gypsum Canyon."

Major told us he'd gotten to the top but I doubted it, as none of the rest of us found our way up. Then he gave us the bundle. He'd torn off his empty shirtsleeve, tied off the cuff end with his one hand and filled the sleeve with pitch. So he'd made it to the top after the rest of us gave up. Major is not a man for giving up.

At supper Howland said we'd now had all the elements assault us, "Earth, air, fire and water." Major scoffed at that, said he'd studied chemistry a bit and was satisfied that there were more elements than four. Later, when they were out of hearing, Jack said he wished the constant bickering between Major and Howland would stop, "Such goings on between educated men leaves a bad impression on trappers."

It was unaccountably hot that night, then it turned showery and cooled off a bit. I went hunting fossils in the morning, didn't find any but did find an Indian camp with meat bones that had been picked clean within a month or two. How was it, I wondered, that an Indian with a simple bow and arrow had the skill to find and kill game, but our hunters with repeater rifles, shotguns and revolvers couldn't kill a mouse? We were thus condemned to a diet of biscuits, dried apples, coffee and beans of speculative soundness.

We made good progress the next day, making one long portage and several times letting down with ropes, then running between narrow canyon walls that came to the water's edge. We were anxious in such places because if we met an impassable rapid, we should nevertheless have to run it, with all the risk, or abandon the expedition, and how to leave would be another question. So, barring a direct fall, we should run, and we did; we ran several very bad rapids Major would have made us line if there was a shore to stand on. The high tide marks were now thirty or forty feet above the river and often we would see driftwood caught in crevices high up on the clift, maybe a hundred feet above the river. Everywhere swallows had plastered their nests and flitted about like leaves in the wind.

Late in the afternoon we rounded a sharp point to the left with confidence, hearing no excessive noise of the water. The rocks were broken down there and about a hundred feet above the river we saw a flock of mountain sheep. For once the intrepid hunters held their fire. We put in to shore as quiet as we could, as the sheep hadn't seen us. The hunters slipped away with their guns and disappeared around the rocks at the bank. A mite later we heard rifle fire and those of us who had stayed with the boats went up to see the result. It seemed a miracle had happened: they were lucky enough to kill one sheep, and Jack and Howland had set off after the others. Soon we heard firing again, then the flock came clattering down the rocks not twenty yards in front of us. Bill Dunn lifted his rifle and killed a second sheep. We all chased the flock, but they had disappeared as if straight up the clift, for we could see no gulch or gully they could have climbed.

We lashed the two sheep across the bow of the cook's boat and started down the river. We didn't get far because some sort of message was silently passed and we went into camp early to cook the sheep. Billy didn't bother with biscuits or beans or dried apples; he just skewered the sheep quarters on a driftwood limb and set them over the fire. With considerable encouragement and urging from the rest of us, the sheep cooperated and cooked up quick and we had a feast, nothing but mutton, that and coffee, best meal of the trip.

A long portage the next morning, the longest since we reached the Colorado, then another hard portage and lining, all the boats battered on the rocks. By eleven o'clock we'd made only two miles and were hungry, or just had a hankering for more meat. When we came to a place where the walls were broken down and there was a rocky beach we stopped and Billy cooked up some more mutton. We hadn't taken altitudes since we entered the Colorado, so Major told Jack and Bill Dunn to take barometer and temperature readings at one o'clock at the river and he and his brother would do the same at the top. He gave Bill his little silver watch so they would know when it was one o'clock. It was easy enough of a climb I guess, because Major and his brother were back and we were launched before two P.M.

We had some fast water and easy running until we came to a bad place and had to let down with ropes. There were many big rocks and no clear channel near the shore, so we did what we'd done once or twice before, put a man on a rock in the river holding a boat's bow line, the end of that line being held by men on shore downstream as far as the line would let them go. The stern line was held by a man on shore and the boat was guided around the rock by the man standing on it. When the boat was in the channel on the far side, the man on the rock released the bow line and took hold of the stern line as the boat slid past. Of course, the man on shore holding the stern line had to let it go, else the man on the rock could be swept off by it.

Bill Dunn was on the rock as he was most times, and we'd got two boats down all right, but when *Sister* was being let down, Andy, who hadn't experienced the process before, didn't let go the stern line soon enough, and Bill's feet got tangled in it and he went into the water. He was able to wade to shore, and there was no serious harm done to *Sister.* The same couldn't be said for Major's watch, which Bill still had in his shirt pocket.

I once saw a man screaming mad because someone had killed his dog, and I saw a man near choler with anger when he learned about his wife lying with a neighbor man, but I'd never seen a man so angry about something wasn't a living thing as Major was about that watch. If he hadn't of been a maimed man, I'm sure he would have attacked Bill. He went on yelling at him, calling him a worthless dirty devil and worse names, so I thought Bill was going to get just as mad and there would be serious trouble. Finally Major said, "You'll pay me thirty dollars for the watch and leave the party." Bill said, "A bird couldn't get out of here."

"All right," Major said, "then you must leave as soon as you can get out. And you'll pay me a dollar a day for your board."

Bill said, "I'll take thirty dollars for the sheep I killed and fifty dollars for two month's wages."

Before Major could reply, Jack surprised us all, because he was always very deferential to Major, but he broke in and said, "Now, Professor, any man can leave the party if he wants to, provided he doesn't add to the danger of the others. But no man can be ordered out of the party."

I guess Major was surprised, too, and maybe saw that he didn't have any but his brother on his side, should things come to the boil. He said, "I'm in charge here," and that ended the conversation for the moment. We went on down the river, each man to his own riled up thoughts. As I was mulling over what had been said, it struck me that it wasn't Major, it wasn't Jack, me, nor any of our party, but the river that was in charge.

By the end of the day we'd made twelve and a half miles, most of it pretty fast. But for the last few miles the water was very still and the walls of the canyon were very low, not over one hundred fifty feet high. I feared the rapids would quit us altogether for a while and then come on again, meaner than ever, when the walls got higher. I wanted it the other way, get the altitude down early and have smooth sailing later on, but the river paid me no mind.

We came on a stream coming in from the west that was not on any of our maps. It was wider than the White River, quite muddy, and had an unpleasant odor. Jack said, "It's as filthy as the washing from the sewers of some large city but stinks more than cologne ever did."

Major named the new stream "Dirty Devil's Creek." I could see the logic as our clothes were just rags and the only water to touch our bodies since we'd entered the Colorado was rain, that and wetting by the river, our soap long gone. Never mind; as we were the only white men who had seen the stream, I for one felt quite complimented by the name. Bill Dunn said he believed Major named the river after him alone, and it's true Major had called Bill a dirty devil. Either way, it was in keeping with Major's whole character which needed only a short study to be read like a book.

Major named the canyon we'd passed through just before Dirty Devil's Creek "Narrow Canyon," though there wasn't much to be said for the name.

THE BRECKENBRIDGE SENTINEL

JULY 27, 1869.

DIRECT WORD FROM COLONEL ADAMS.

We have today received a dispatch from Colonel Adams who reports he has arrived at the junction of the Grand and Blue Rivers, a journey of 55 miles. He reports that the party has achieved a descent of 3000 feet in that distance, or 55 feet per mile. He reports the discovery of abundant crops of wild oats, wheat, barley, rye and timothy grass. If our community were not made up of miners, we would probably witness a migration to the place described, although we have never known such crops to grow at that altitude, and none of the men who returned from the expedition recalls anything but broken and rocky terrain. Colonel Adams asserts the reduced numbers leaves him with a more disciplined and better trained crew and, with fewer boats to oversee, he expects progress to speed up considerably from this point. Mr. Decker, who returned from the party earlier, believes the descent estimate to be considerably at variance with the facts, but as the barometer was lost in the early days of the trip, those facts are lacking.

We lowered our altitude a goodly amount the next day, ran twenty miles through many small rapids, or what we called small ones then but which would pass for full-grown cataracts back in the States. We liked them much for they sent us along fast and easy and ran down our altitude considerably.

We were most likely the first white men there, but we weren't the first humans in that place, for we found the ruins of Moqui Indian dwellings on the left shortly after we entered a new canyon. The ruins were about two hundred feet above the river where the clift shelved back and there had probably been a little grass and some level land on which to raise vegetables. There wasn't much left of the structure, but we calculated it had been three storeys high with four rooms on each, made of stone with adobe mortar laid in regular. When we measured the rooms we found that in one dimension they were all the same, thirteen feet, the same as we'd found at the ruins we saw earlier. Major said that they probably built in these remote and desolate area for protection from nomadic warrior tribes, and it did look like they tried to build up the place in such a way it looked like it was part of the clift. We guessed it was about two hundred years old. We kept searching around and found a single room way up on the clift side, just a cave walled across, really, and an old rickety one-pole ladder, the rungs stuck through holes in the pole. None of the men wanted to climb it, but Major did and said the room was full of corn-cobs, so it must have served for storage.

About fifteen miles farther down the canyon, we found another ruin, this one in the shape of an L, with two rooms in each leg and one in the angle. We judged this to be newer, for the mortar was quite intact in many places. In the space in the angle there was an excavation in circular form and another circle dug inside that. Major said the Indians in the Tusayan Province called these underground chambers "kivas," and that they were for religious meetings. We also found a wall with drawings on it the same as we'd seen before, but there was a handsome one of a mountain sheep with curled horns and, again, the flute player.

It was late in the afternoon, so we headed back to camp, all except Major, who went on trying to climb to the summit. We cooked the sheep, or some of it for it wasn't looking too seaworthy, and again worried about Major for he wasn't back by dark. There was no enthusiasm to go looking for him, leastways it wasn't unanimous. When we went to bed he still wasn't back, but he was with us at breakfast, said he didn't get back 'til midnight, though I don't know how he could tell without his watch working.

We had another fine run of twenty-one miles though much of the way there was little tide and we had to "ply, ply the oars," as Frank used to sing. I found myself missing Frank more and more as there had been little singing of late and he had a fine baritone voice.

We expected we were nearing the mouth of a river called the San Juan, and I couldn't wait to get there. On our Mormon map the San Juan was only fifty miles from the junction of the Grand and the Green, and we'd already come twice that distance. By the official Army Ordnance map from Washington it was put down as "probably" one hundred miles, but we had run farther west than they had placed the probable course of the Colorado. The map-makers were just guessing, as the Colorado River had not been explored where we were, nor had the San Juan been traced to its mouth. Of course, we were guessing, too, but we figured we would strike the junction in the next day or two, depending on how the river ran. The canyon walls had been getting lower and we took that as a sign we were approaching the junction. The stone was a softer gypsum shale, which provided water and wind with an opportunity to do some sculpting, and they didn't disappoint. They had carved it into mounds and columns a thousand feet high, lined up like in a Greek temple, so orderly in some places you'd have thought they were carved with a purpose.

The last day of July found us at the mouth of the San Juan River which came in from the east. It was maybe a hundred feet wide, about the size of the White River, though not so deep. It had a very rapid tide and was quite muddy. Its water would add considerably to the flow of the Colorado and increase the speed for a spell, until the canyon figured it had to get wider to let the added water through. The land along the San Juan was as devoid of vegetation as a street, not even hackberry bushes at its mouth.

We feared that Major would conclude to camp there where it was open, to observe the eclipse on the seventh. I sincerely hoped not, for to find shelter we had to crawl into the rocks under an eavelike projection of the clift, and the rocks were hissing hot. The thermometer rarely got below one hundred degrees, and that just before dawn when the heat fell off a little. Stopping there for a week would also be at serious cost to our rations; Billy had to discard the rest of the mutton, as the terrible heat had taken its toll, and there would be no game nor fish nor fowl in so desolate a place.

Sunday found us again on the move, no rest for the weary. If we were to make great progress on our journey, or if we were to seek a place where fish and game could be had, the sacrificing of our day of rest could be forgiven, but the only reason we were moving was Major found the clifts on the south side of the San Juan too smooth to climb. We moved but a mile or two down the Colorado to a little bunch of oaks and willows which with a little fixing up would afford a tolerable shelter. We saw three sheep and stopped to let the hunters chase them, but the rocks were so smooth it was impossible to follow the animals. I was not surprised that our marksmen failed to get a sheep but I was disappointed too, for they are good eating and we needed the meat very much. We were short of everything but flour, coffee and dried apples, and soon that would be our entire diet.

Beyond the willows, the grove turned to cottonwoods and box-elder. The Howlands and Dunn went into the grove in search of game. They returned empty-handed, of course, but they had found an amphitheatre of a size that would make a concert hall. We all went to see it and when we paced it off we found it was five hundred feet long and two hundred feet wide, and it looked to be about two hundred feet high at its roof, with a winding fissure going on up for another thousand feet, flooding the place with a soft light. We moved our camp inside the amphitheatre and had an evening of song for a change. Well, we had *Old Shady* and *John Anderson My Jo,* and Walter's deep bass filled the cavern with sweet sounds, and our applause afterward resounded like thunder.

That encouraged Walter to give us a response song:

I had a wee cock, and I loved it well,
I fed my cock on yonder hill;
My cock, lily-cock, coo;
Every one loves their cock,
Why should not I love my cock too?

I had a wee hen, and I loved it well,
I fed my hen on yonder hill;
My hen, chuckie, chuckie,
My cock, lily-cock, coo;
Every one loves their cock,
Why should not I love my cock too?

I had a wee duck and I loved it well,
I fed my duck on yonder hill;
My duck, wheetie, wheetie,
My hen, chuckie, chuckie,
My cock, lily-cock, coo;
Every one loves their cock,
Why should not I love my cock too?

It went on through sheep (maie, maie), dog (bouffie, bouffie), cat (cheetie, cheetie) and pig (squeakie, squeakie) which had us all making silly noises and laughing like schoolboys. When Andy helped me write out the words the next day, he naturally had a version not fit for the schoolroom. Between his spelling and mine I'm not sure I got everything right but what's down here is pretty close.

Since Dunn and the Howlands had found the place, I hoped Major would name it after them, but he called it "Music Temple," after his brother's singing, I guess. The three boys who'd found it carved their names on its wall, the best they could do.

Major kept us a second day in the same camp, and maybe we'd have to stay longer; he didn't say. He'd been taking observations ever since we came to camp and seemed no nearer done than when he started. He was right to get the latitude and longitude of every mouth of a river not before known, and we were willing to face starvation if necessary to do it, but beyond that he was wrong to ask us to wait. If we could have killed some game or caught some fish, there would have been less tension in camp, but if we didn't move on soon, I feared the consequences. His badgering of Howland continued, but now he'd added Dunn to the list, because of the watch, and that didn't help. They were two good men, and harmony was not served by Major's treatment of them, whatever the cause. Let bygones be bygones.

I guess Major had all the measurements he needed or else he got wind of the sullen mood of the men, because he announced at supper that we'd move on in the morning. I went to bed in better spirits.

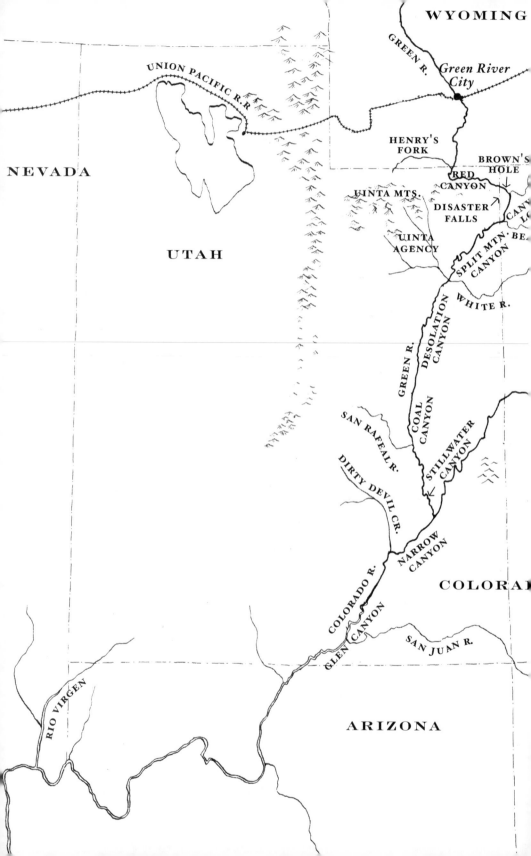

Thirty-three miles! The best distance since the Green and on fast water with easy rapids, no lining and no portages! We had lowered our altitude by seven hundred fifty feet and I thought we had probably been through the worst of the river. The walls in some places were black and shiny as though they'd been painted and then varnished over. Howland said the river gods had painted them, but Major shot back, "It's just a chemical reaction of some kind."

Jack was so fortunate as to kill a young sheep in the morning, so we would be eating well again. The sheep was quite fat and dressed weighed about eighty pounds, nine pounds of meat per man! As the hills were a little more covered with grass, it looked like our hunters might be further favored by Lady Luck. This time the cook took the precaution of drying some of the meat so we would not have to throw so much away. He sliced it in long thin strips and laid them over a framework of willow boughs with a slow fire beneath. With the hot sun above and the fire below, he soon had a mess of "jerky." I was puzzled as to how that name got stuck on dried meat until Howland told me it came from the Spanish, "charqui," meaning "charred," he thought. Jack didn't believe him, said beef jerky anyway was American. "Called that on account of the way you have to yank at it to bite off a piece," he said.

I tried my hand at fishing, but the river was covered with flies or gnats and the fish had all they wanted to eat. The gnats in turn feasted on us. Jack said the insects were "as full of venom as a politician is of tricks."

The canyon continued to have low walls of sandstone worn by wind and weather into mounds and monuments, so Major concluded to name the place "Monument Canyon." We found old pony tracks at our camp, so Indians had gotten in there, probably by following the little stream that came down at that point. If men could get in, then a man could get out, so it was possible that Major would order Bill Dunn to leave the party there. I felt like men at the front feel, waiting to see if the Rebs would attack, and I sensed an unease among the other men, too. Even if Bill could walk out there, the Indians might not be friendly, and he would face that problem in addition to finding food and water, all by himself in an unknown country. But Major said nothing, and a good thing, for I don't believe the men would have let the dismissal happen, though we hadn't talked about it, except the Howlands said if Dunn went they'd go, too.

Major said the place was called, "El Vado de Los Padres" and was "historic" because in 1776 a Spanish padre named Father Escalante and his party crossed there, the first white men to do it. If that was the test, then our party was making a whole raft of "historic" places.

On the fourth of August we made a long run, thirty eight and a quarter miles by Howland's average, hard rowing all the way. The water was very still and we had a head-wind that at times blew a perfect tornado; with lightning and rain so fierce, we thought we'd confronted the apocalypse. The canyon was narrowing up and the walls for the last twenty miles had gained much in height, though we were running down altitude but little. Despite the toil we enjoyed an occasional foray up a canyon, or glen as we were calling them if there was vegetation, and there were often willows, cottonwoods and oaks. Major called one where there were many oaks and ferns and a beautiful waterfall "Oak Glens" and he called the whole canyon "Glen Canyon." For four miles of those glens the clifts took on a variety of colors would make an artist throw away his palette. We had creamy orange at the top, then bright vermilion grading down to purple and chocolate beds with green and yellow bands.

At night we came to a place where the strata was much broken down and there was a large basin, so we campt. Jack and Bill Dunn went for a short hunt, nothing killed, and reported an extensive plain off to the south of us. There was a stream coming in which we believed was the Paria river. Back east we'd have called it a brook. There was much evidence of Indians, bones and brush beds, but quite old. Just below our camp there was a fine rapid, roaring pretty loud and showing white foam for a half mile, so we expected to make a little altitude while the rocks remained broken. We had all learned to like mild rapids better than still water, but some preferred them very mild.

THE BRECKENBRIDGE SENTINEL

AUGUST 4, 1869.

ADAMS AT GRAND CANYON.

By telegraph from Hot Sulfur Springs we have learned that the Adams party has reached the mouth of the Grand Canyon, "A slot fifty feet in breadth", according to Adams. We are surprised to find the Grand Canyon so near, as the party has traveled only 60 miles. Their descent in that distance is given as 3500 feet, but this is an estimate as the party earlier lost the instrument for the accurate measurement of altitude.

When we scouted the rapid in the light of morning, we read again the testimony of the rocks. We'd learned pretty early that hard rock meant fast water and bad rapids. Now we had come to understand the way the strata lay had a lot to do with how bad the river would be. If the strata ran horizontal, the river would be pretty quiet with few rapids, and those easy. If the strata tilted down in the direction we were headed, we'd have good fast water and but few rapids. It was when the strata tilted in the upstream direction that trouble set in, especially if the river went acrost them at a slant, and worst of all when there was hard rock above and soft rock below.

When we set out, that's just what the river threw at us. At the beginning there was a series of rapids, wet and fast, and we ran down altitude most satisfactorily. Then we came on one that satisfied us too well, a furious cataract. We passed it just before dinner by lining and portaging. In the afternoon we had a good run of two or three miles, then came to a direct fall of fifteen or sixteen feet. The little *Emma Dean* being not much longer, we had to carry her around. We hoped to line the big boats but Major said it was too much to risk, so we carried those around too, leveraging or using driftwood skids where we could, putting our backs into it where we couldn't, pull, push, pull, lever and carry, it was a hard passage. Then we had to portage the rations and other cargo the same way. It took all afternoon, time Major filled, as usual, by climbing above and calling orders while we toiled in the hundred degree heat.

The constant wetting in frigid water and exposure to the scorching sun were beginning to tell on all of us. We were less inclined to humor or to song, except for Walter, of course, who always seemed to be on a voyage of his own. Even Andy, usually full of life and pranks, was sullen and short-tempered by the time the two mile long portage was over. Major said he'd seen a nice sandy beach below which we could reach by one more lining. I'd personally had enough sand to last me a lifetime, but Major's orders were we must move on and that we must line. We were kind of looking at each other, nobody moving, when Howland said, "This'll do for a campsite, John. We're all done in." Major was determined, "We'll move on," he said.

There were many rocks and shallow water along the shore below us, so we would have to get the boats out to the main channel near the middle of the river. That meant we'd have to pass the boats around the upstream end of the rocks, the same way we'd done on the day Dunn fell in the river with Major's watch. We started with the Emma Dean. First I fixed a long line to her bow and three of the men took the end of it and walked downstream below the rapid. This left about ten yards of slack in the line. Bill Dunn being the best swimmer, Major ordered him to take the slack and wade out to a big rock on the near side of the channel. Bill climbed on the rock and, holding the line, pulled the *Emma Dean* out and around the upstream side of the rock.

When the little boat had been passed around, Bill took the stern line I was holding, and I let it go. He passed that around and payed it out until it had stretched out straight, then dropped it and it went down loose, trailing the *Emma Dean.* The men with the bow line guided the boat through the rapid and hauled her in on the little beach below it.

We let *Sister* down in the same way, me holding the stern line and Dunn on the rock. When it came to the *Maid,* I went in her, of course, to fend off. Major's practice was to supervise these operations, if he wasn't geologizing, but this time, instead of calling to one of the men to hold the *Maid's* stern line, Major took it himself. Since we were to ease the *Maid* mostly acrost the stream to get her behind the rock, there wasn't much pull on the rope so it wasn't a problem for him to hold it with one hand.

With Bill holding first the bow line and then the stern line we got the *Maid* around the rock and headed downstream. But when it was time for Major to let go the stern line, he held on to it. The *Maid* was picking up speed as the tide took her down, and the stern line grew taut. Bill was paying the line out with his back to Major, and by the time he figured out what was happening and tried to jump over the rope, it was too late. The rope caught him at the knees and he was swept off the rock into the swift water. The *Maid* was running free, and the men below were hauling in on the line as fast as they could, to keep my boat from plunging past them downstream. I yelled to them to stop, hoping to slow down enough so I could grab Bill by his long hair if he caught up to me, but the rapid drowned out my voice. By then the stern line had been yanked from Major's hand and was trailing behind the *Maid*. When Bill's head appeared above the surface I yelled and motioned for him to grab the rope. He couldn't hear me but he saw the rope as it came by and he took hold of it, and I hauled him in, letting the men on shore see to the *Maid*. Without me fending off, she took a drubbing, but nothing compared to Bill's. He ended up battered and bruised and had a cut on his leg made mine look like a cat-scratch.

Just as Andy had earlier trusted Jack to hold on to the rope while he swam behind, so Bill had faith that Major would let go the rope timely. Faith and trust disappeared that day, and from then on we were a different crew. We followed Major, of course, but the way thunder follows lightning, connected but separate.

It was some small relief to camp right at the edge of the water, the coolest place, but even that over ninety degrees. Billy and Andy went off for driftwood and Major and his brother went up to measure altitude, leaving the Howlands with Jack and me and Bill Dunn to set up camp. Bill said to nobody in particular, "That son-of-a bitch tried to drown me."

Jack said , "Oh, no it warn't deliberate, Bill, the professor'd never done it afore. He didn't know he was supposed to let go the rope."

Oramel said, "As best I recollect, the major authored the method."

At supper we naturally talked of the long day's work, how the rapids changed with the change in strata, how hot it was and generally ran back through the day's happenings, swapping stories. When we got to the last lining, Jack said to Major, "We came near to losing Bill Dunn today."

Major said, "It would have been but a small loss."

Bill jumped up, mad as a hornet, and said, "If you warn't a cripple, we'd settle that remark right now."

At that, Walter leapt to his feet, his eyes all ablaze saying, "Well, I'm not a cripple!" and he went for Bill before anybody could stop him, grabbed him by the throat and kept driving until they were both in the river. Bill was strong but Walter was stronger and he soon had ahold of Bill's long hair and was holding his head under water. Andy happened to be at the river scouring out a cast iron fry pan, and that pan seemed to fairly leap from the water to the side of Walter's head. But for his head being half under water it would have knocked his brains out, if he had any. Andy reared back to swat him again but the first shot had hit home, Walter let go of Bill's hair and went under himself. By then most of us were in the water. We pulled Bill out on the beach and stretched him out head down to drain the water out of him. Nobody attended to Walter who was floundering around in the river, dazed by Andy's blow. Major said, "For Christ's sake," and waded in to help him out. Only the third time I'd heard Major swear, and I wished he'd not used the Lord's name that way.

It struck me that Bill's waist-length hair was like the river, useful in some circumstances, dangerous in others.

Supper was doleful. Walter didn't favor us with a song, or maybe had a ringing in his ears and thought we could hear it too. Major hadn't much talk for anybody either so we had a chilly silence, should have taken some of the heat away but didn't. Of a sudden Seneca whipped out his Jew's harp and began to pluck away at *Suwanee River*. Major said he didn't see as it was a time for entertainment. But Seneca finished up the one song and swung directly into his other. When he'd finished, Oramel said, "Seneca's like General Grant who said 'I only know two songs. One's *Yankee Doodle* and the other ain't.'" It cheered me a little, that and Seneca's standing his ground with Major. Major started on a little speech about taking orders, but he'd only just got started when lightning split the sky, thunder rolled after it and heavy drops began to fall. We sprinted for shelter. First time on the trip I'd been thankful for rain.

The fight opened up something that wouldn't go away, any more than the rapids on the river go away once you've passed downstream of them. We became two camps, or maybe more. There was the Howlands and Dunn on the one hand and Walter and Major, on the "one hand", too, I guess. Jack and I were trying to be friends to both. Andy having no choice but to be against Walter Powell, though he had no quarrel with Major, and Billy Rhoads being Andy's tent-mate maybe leaning towards Andy's camp.

The next morning at breakfast Major acted as if nothing had happened, sat as usual a little distance from the men, with Walter beside him, Walter now sporting a shiner uglier than mine ever was and an ear looked like a flapjack. Billy poured coffee for those who had a bailing can and Andy handed out biscuits, nobody saying anything. After a while Major called out, "Billy, why don't you bring me my food?" something Billy had done every meal. "It's here if you want it," Billy told him, so it looked like he'd leaned all the way. From that day Walter fetched the Major's food.

Ten and three quarters miles was all we got credit for on August sixth, though it was more like fifteen by my reckoning. The walls were perpendicular and smooth, and wherever there was a side canyon, or where the rocks had fallen in, we had a rapid. Where we could run, the tide was swift and we made good speed. The altitude didn't change much in such places, though, and we had to run down altitude faster than we ran down our food.

Danger has its own sound in the canyons, and just before noon we heard danger ahead. The canyon walls rumbled with a sound like giants playing at bowls, for we could hear the boulders being rolled on the river bottom. There was no beach so we hugged the smooth walls, slipping the boats down slow as we could, the oarsmen backing water against the tide. When we saw a little nick in the clift on the other side we made for it, rowed hard over and got all the boats safely in to scout the rapid and figure out what to do next. It didn't take much figuring as the walls were too smooth to climb and the river too rocky to run. We secured the boats to a rock outcrop, carried our rations through water up to our knees, then lowered the boats on lines the same way and were away again. Three times that day we carried our goods around and lowered the boats over rapids, most of the time wading. Towards the end of the day the rapids had become less furious and we came upon the soft limestone again. The strata dipped down in the same direction as the river, so it looked like good running for the morrow.

We eased along gradual the next day, looking for a place where Major could climb the mountain and observe the eclipse. He signaled us to stop in a rocky place where he thought he could climb, but I doubted he could. Anyway, the chances to see the eclipse were small, for it had taken to raining every afternoon for the past three or four days.

Major set off to climb the mountain, taking his brother, sensing maybe that nobody else would go. They took instruments to get longitude and time as well as altitude. Nobody offered to help. We took advantage of the stretch of free time to repair the boats, which were growing old even faster than we were. I put four new ribs in mine, made from a seasoned dead oak, laying them in next to the originals in a fashion called "sister ribs." I caulked her all around with strips cut from my "holy" poncho and laid pine pitch over that, made her tight as a cup. Hoped it was the last time I'd need to repair her and was pretty sure it would be, if Major would let us run.

When Jack got out the barometer to take altitude at the river at one o'clock, he found the glass tube broken and all the mercury lost. We were down to a single barometer.

When the eclipse came, so did the rain. The moon had about half covered the sun when it clouded over and a hard, driving rain began. By the time it eased off and the clouds had passed, the eclipse was behind the bluff. If Major made the top he might have seen it and got our longitude. I suspected not. By supper they hadn't come in and one of the men (I won't say who) said he hoped "nothing trivial" had happened to them. We pitched our tents for the first time since the Uinta Basin, though they were getting so worn we might just as well have spared ourselves the trouble. I threw what was left of my poncho over the tent and hoped for the best. It rained hard all night, a regular river of rain, as if we didn't already have one. Major and his brother were still out of camp in the morning, the river red and rising.

They'd spent the night in the bluffs, in the dark and rain, came in wet at breakfast, having failed to see anything, so we still didn't have time and longitude. If we don't have the time exact, then the chronometer method isn't exact. We knew the exact time the eclipse would be total from the almanac so if Major had been able to observe it, we'd have had our longitude and our time.

It was Sunday again, but we had no rest. Made *five* portages, carrying the boats once. We'd never made so many in one day, but we'd never had so little to carry around. At ten o'clock it looked like the end of our journey, that we would get no farther at all. The river filled the entire channel and the walls were vertical from the water's edge. There was a rapid ahead that sounded like the clifts were tumbling in, but we couldn't see it from the river nor could we climb for a view from above. The *Emma Dean* rowed down a few yards, wedged itself in a notch in the clift on the right and held there. We followed in the *Maid,* and *Sister* crowded in between us, so we looked like three turtles hugging a small log. It was one time I was glad we didn't have the *No Name.*

Just over our heads was a place where the clift shelved back two or three feet. Jack Sumner being the lightest stood on Bill Dunn's shoulders and climbed to the shelf. Bill tossed him a rope and with that, Major and I got up, too. We passed along the shelf toward the fall, mostly in a crouch, to see what the rapid was made of. Then the shelf ended, or rather there was a gap in it where the rock had broken and fallen to the river. A man with spring in his legs and a running start could have jumped it, but we had neither. I went back and called to Andy to see if he could find a log or two to bridge the gap. There was some driftwood across the river and it being calm that far above the rapid, the boys in *Sister* were able to row over and fetch us two little logs. We lashed them together and made a bridge maybe strong enough to hold a small man. Jack went over it, creeping as careful as a cat stalking a bird. Soon as he was over, Major walked across and joined him, and they made their way to the fall to size it up. I waited for their advice.

What that came to was a variation on the juggling trick. There was no way we could have a man hold the boats to a rock then swim safely over the falls after letting the last boat go, the way Andy had done before, so what we did was this: Jack and Major stayed on the shelf and I returned to my boat. We eased all three boats down along the clift as far as we dared and held them there. We were still a couple of hundred feet from the head of the falls, but we'd got beyond the gap in the shelf, and that let some of the men climb a rope and join Jack and Major, leaving one man in each boat.

The *Emma Dean* was on the downstream end, *Sister* was next and I was last in the *Maid.* Bill Dunn in the *Emma Dean* tied another long line to her bow and passed the other end up to Jack on the shelf. Then Bill tied another long line to her stern and passed the end to Andy Hall in *Sister.* I could see Andy muttering something so I guess he was saying the little verse about the rabbit as he made the line fast to *Sister's* bow. He then tied a line to *Sister's* stern and passed it to me, and I made it fast to the bow of the *Maid.* With a short line, I tied the *Maid's* stern to a spur of rock. Then Andy payed out the *Emma Dean's* line, letting the tide take her down to the end of it, about one hundred twenty feet. Jack, up on the shelf, took her bowline downstream as she went.

Then I let *Sister* down, and of course the *Emma Dean* went down farther, so we had three boats strung out on the length of two lines, two hundred forty feet, the *Emma Dean* right at the head of the rapid. By this time, Jack had taken the *Emma Dean's* line down below the falls, where the other men, save Major, were waiting. Major stayed on the shelf and when he judged all was ready, he gave me a signal. I cast off the *Maid* and all three boats started on an adventure. The *Emma Dean* plunged over the falls. The men below hauled in her line as fast as they could, got her snugged against a rock at the bottom of the falls, then started hauling in *Sister's* line, not quite so adroit it seemed to me. Andy was hanging on for dear life and keeping his head down. *Sister* nosed over the falls, but by then my attention was focused on going over myself without being drowned in the process. I can tell you no child sledding on a steep hill ever had a better ride. The *Maid* didn't seem to want to go over at first, just hung on the edge as a child will before diving into a pond. Then she tipped her bow over the edge, shot straight to the bottom and dug into the wave tails there. The water-tight compartment made her pop up again like a cork; she rushed on past the men, heading downstream with a speed a locomotive would envy, and I seemed destined to run the next rapid alone and sideways and tethered to *Sister's* stern. I was in the stern with the sweep oar. I just let it go and crept forward. I was about to get out my sheath knife to cut the line when the men managed to snub it to a rock. It brought me up sharp, knocked me into the bottom of the boat, and turned her back upstream. The men were then able to haul me in next to the other boats, with the loss of an oar and a year's growth and the gain of another gashed and blackened eye.

For all our hard, hot work we made only three and a half miles when the sun began to leave us and a chill set in. We set up in an enormous cave the river had carved out of soft limestone on the outside of a bend. We figured fifty thousand people could have fit in there without squeezing. Major said it would make a fine concert hall, but as it's under water in some seasons, it might lack for comfort.

Watching Billy Rhoads stewing dried apples and cooking up a mess of beans, I saw how skinny he'd got, and cooks tend to the other extreme due to sampling their own efforts, just to check the seasoning of course. Looking at the others I saw the same. The lack of sustenance was taking its toll, for they were all thin as scarecrows. Except for Major, they were a ragged looking set, too, as the rough labor was wearing out our clothing, such as it was, Billy's costume reduced to a long tailed shirt tied in a knot between his legs. I sensed that I must look the same, they my mirror, for any who shared their labor and rations would fare the same. I said to Jack, "A few more weeks of this, we'll be naked as Adam." He said, "Be all right with an Eve or two about," but Billy said, "In this heat Eve's likely be dried as these apples."

Though the way was made difficult by the smooth canyon walls, making for fast water and no beach for lining, it was some of the most beautiful marble I'd ever seen, not excepting the capitol in Washington. Winding clifts, polished by the waves in some places and by red grit washed over the clift tops in others, rose above us almost three quarters of a mile, which made the sky narrow and twisting as a snake. It grieved me not to collect specimens of the marble, but the thought of their heft on a portage made the idea a vain pursuit. I'd even stopped collecting fossils, not wanting to carry the weight. Our only interest had become how we were to get through the canyon and once more to civilization. Our slow progress and wasting rations admonished us that we yet had a few circles of Hell before us. Major named the canyon "Marble Canyon."

Billy was sweating and swearing so much over his beans that we were sure of an ample breakfast in the morning. I should have slept better for the prospect, but fear that the rising red river would trap us in the cave kept Morpheus at bay for much of the night. After we'd eaten the beans in the morning, Billy gave us the news: it was the last of them.

The way things developed between Major and our crew, we no longer took his orders without question, and so the rapids became a subject for debate on whether we ran or lined. We wanted to conserve our scant rations and lining, which best saved them from wetting, did that. But it was slower than running, so we'd need rations for a longer period. Running ran the risk of spoiling some rations, but it was faster and we'd need less. Jack said it looked like a "Mexican standoff." But I said if we threw in the time it took to repair the wear and tear lining wrought on the boats, it tipped the scales toward running. Major said that didn't weigh, as cutting new oars to replace those often lost in running added just as much to the time, so we were back to a Mexican standoff.

It was Howland broke the deadlock, saying, "The wear on the men from lining and portaging has to be thrown into the equation" and while I don't hold much with mathematics, Major did, him being in the Engineers before he was transferred to Artillery. At first he seemed surprised at the thought. Then he looked around at us, maybe seeing for the first time the scrawny, bearded, ragged and hungry crew he depended on for his science and survival. He held a hurried conference with his brother that we couldn't hear, then said if it came to a Mexican standoff for any rapid, we'd run it. I thought then that if the trip was going to be run on the advice and consent of the demented, I'd better look for a place to walk out, but it was a victory of sorts.

With that change, we ran *thirty one* rapids in a single day, some of them bad ones we'd have lined before, the boats filling and the water drenching us again and again. Hard labor, too, with three linings needing portage of our ever lighter rations and over-worn outfits. We made only sixteen miles, but ran down the altitude so much I was no longer apprehensive on that score. The limestone was rising fast, a thousand feet above the river, and I figured that meant the river would improve. During one furious rapid that we were forced to run because of the vertical walls, we saw the prettiest sight of the whole trip. The river turned to the right just ahead and the clift at that point seemed to be enclosed in a robe of sparkling gems. When we got to the bend we saw a beautiful fountain coming from the top, bursting into mist and into a thousand smaller cascades as it tumbled down the canyon wall, the glancing sun transforming all into flashing jewels. The whole cliftside was bedecked with mosses and ferns and flowering plants of every color, in pleasing contrast with the unending barrenness of the canyon. Major named it, "Vasey's Paradise," after a botanist wasn't even on the trip.

The next day we ran *thirty five* rapids, some bad ones, one heller, the largest we had run on the Colorado. Howland allowed us thirteen and three quarters miles, and we ran down our altitude nice and sharp, until around two o'clock we came upon the "Chiquito," or "Little Colorado River" coming in from the east. It was a loathsome little stream, so filthy and muddy it fairly stank. It was not wide, thirty to fifty yards, and in many places a man could cross it on rocks, with water not over his knees, but not this man. I left that to Andy who seemed to enjoy the activity. Jack said the stream was, "too thin to plow and too thick to drink," but if you could have plowed it, it was already fertilized.

On a clift nearby there were white patches, and when we rowed down to see what caused them, we found little icicles of salt. We hadn't had salt the entire trip, and we broke them off and ate them like candy. Nearby there was an old Indian trail, so it seemed they had come to mine the salt at some time in the past.

There was a story of a man named White who claimed he'd gone down the river on a raft from the Chiquito, where we were, to Callville in Arrazona Territory. I placed but little reliance on such reports though his story had been published and Major had met the man. But if the river could be run by a man on a raft, nine men in boats should have an easy time of it, so I hoped it was a true story. Major said we would stay in that stinking place for two or three days to get latitude and longitude, because these hadn't been determined at the Chiquito's mouth before, as if anyone would want to find his way to that disgusting river of salt and mud.

There was discontent about the delay as we had had no meat at all since we finished the jerky over a week back, and scant meat ration for more than a month before that. We were willing to do all we could to make the trip a success, but felt we should not be asked to delay more than was strictly necessary.

When we got altitude, Howland said we'd run down twelve hundred feet since the Green. He said we were down to 2690 feet, leaving 2000 to go to the Rio Virgen and 2700 to the sea. He gave us total miles of 626, with an unknown distance to go. We'd conquered half our descent to the sea, and Major opined that we'd done more than half our distance to the Rio Virgen. We'd been on the river for eighty days, with an unknown time to go, but we couldn't last many days for our rations were being meted out, the cook counting the biscuits and dried apples given to each man. There was plenty of coffee, so Major didn't notice the scant sustenance for the working men.

Through all the capsizings, through fire and flood, he'd managed to hang on to Jake Field's coffee mug, and he'd managed to keep it full most of the time. The cook had always kept a little fire going while we were campt so Major could have hot coffee, but he stopped doing that the night of the fight. Major drank it cold, didn't seem to matter to him. While Howland was giving out his mileage and all, Major set his coffee mug down and a minute later I noticed a cicada of brilliant green creeping up the outside of the mug. My attention drifted from Howland's numbers as I concentrated on watching the insect move toward the rim. It had two long feelers, thinner than a baby's hair, which it kept working left and right, up and down in front as it made its way, and I thought it was a pity we couldn't scout the rapids that way, save a lot of trouble.

The other thing I noticed was the insect had some injury to a front leg that made it shorter than the others and that none of the legs was ever straight, always poised for jumping I expect. He got to the rim, his little feelers working away, and seemed puzzled they didn't touch a thing but air. Then he rounded the rim and looked down into the abyss, his neck joint bent like it was on a hinge. Some hesitation set in as though he was thinking it over, then he headed down the inside. When he got down the length of his body, he stopped, then sort of hooked his back legs to the rim and let the rest of him crawl ahead. He kept going and the hind legs kept stretching out and out until they were straight and taut. Another decision was clearly required, let go the rim and plunge on or haul back and abandon the exploration. He waved his feelers round and about, then down, for the longest time, then touched the coffee and pulled out. At that point Major picked up his mug and blew the insect off with a puff of breath like a silent whistle. It took umbrage and wing.

Howland was still reading out figures I'd lost track of while I was wool-gathering, watching the cicada. He was saying we'd had an average fall of five and a half feet per mile, made it seem like coasting down a gentle grade. Any six year old child could run a river with a five foot drop averaged out over every mile, but we'd lost a boat, many oars, pistols, rifles, ammunition, a mess-kit, blanket rolls and provisions. I didn't hold with averages even as much as I did with mathematics, and that but little. But some good news came out of all Howland's figuring: we had dropped our altitude more than thirteen feet per mile since we hit the Colorado, and it felt like it.

I was confined to camp by lack of shoes to climb with, seeing as I'd worn them out through hard travel. I had nothing left to wear on my feet but an old pair of boots of no use in climbing and which were my only reliance for making portages. In the boat and much of the time in camp I went barefoot, but I'd fashioned a pair of camp moccasins to slip into when the rocks were bad or the sand too hot. I'd given away my clothing until I was reduced to the same condition as those who lost everything in the shipwreck. I couldn't see a man in the party more destitute than me, for Job said "his children must make amends to the poor, his own hands must give back his wealth."

It began to look like we would have to stay at the Chiquito's mouth several more days to get latitude and longitude. The men were uneasy and discontented with the news and anxious to move on. I feared the consequences if Major didn't do something pretty soon, but he was, as usual, contented. He seemed to think that biscuit made of sour and musty flour and a few dried apples and coffee was ample to sustain a laboring man. If he could only study geology he was happy without food and shelter, but the rest of us were not afflicted with geology to an alarming extent.

Jack got one set of observations which gave us the time once more and if the rain held off, Major could get latitude on the north star that night and longitude by the moon and sun the next day, and we could be off. And none too soon. Our camp was under the shelving edge of a clift on the south side of the Chiquito, protected from both sun and rain by overhanging rocks, though it was filthy with dust and alive with insects. We'd killed three rattlesnakes since we arrived, and the scorpions were so mature they'd grown beards. If that was what Arrazona Territory was like, very little of it would do for me.

Well the night was clear enough, so Major got latitude by the north star. It was determined that we were as far south as Callville, making the river's course beyond generally west, though no river runs true. We should have been moving out as soon as he had the sun and moon in the morning, but instead he sent his brother to the mountains with the barometer. We had latitude and longitude and nothing else seemed absolutely necessary. There was much whispered discussion among the men and I feared they might leave Walter on the mountain, and Major too if he wanted to stay, or maybe the party would split, some moving on, some staying. I didn't know which way I'd take and decided to see how the thing broke up, if it did. I'd gotten on with Walter from the time in my boat, but there would be none other would care if he was left, except Major, of course.

Walter came down with barometer readings and it was determined that the walls there were three thousand feet high, which Howland says is "roughly" six-tenths of a mile. Rough isn't the word for it. The canyon of the Chiquito is quite as sizable as the Colorado and as high. We were in the intersection of three canyons where the walls were broken at the bottom, but only for a short ways up. From there, they were nearly vertical, with only a little patch of sky to be seen so that I felt like we were in a box. I thought prisoners must feel this way when confined in a cell where the only light comes from a small window near the roof or, come to think of it, like being in Major's hotel room in Green River City. He didn't mind that either.

We were off at nine the next morning, and none too soon for another day's delay could not have passed without some strife, especially as Major was at Howland again and would have been at Dunn had Bill not made himself as scarce as he could in a place where there was no vegetation save two nut pines and a Judas tree.

After a mile or two we felt maybe staying in camp was the best choice, for the rapids were innumerable, some of them very heavy and full of treacherous rocks. We had to let down with ropes three times but our rations were so much reduced that we left them in the boats and so made no portages. We made fifteen miles, and campt at the head of the worst rapid seen that day and the longest we'd seen on the Colorado. The river ran through a vast pile of rocks for a half mile or more. The idea of a man passing through on a raft was inconceivable, and I decided the whole White story was a hoax.

We were in red sandstone like that in Lodore, and the strata made a big dip to the west, so we felt fortunate that the granite hadn't come up again. We had a saying, "When the granite comes up, our spirits go down." Though the dark gloomy canyons were enough by themselves, it wasn't just the black walls. The roaring water and, more, the foreknowledge that there was worse roaring to come worked on our nerves and added moodiness to our other discomforts.

Then, a further mile down the canyon, the hard granite came up again and we had emphatically the wildest day of the trip to that point. We let down the first rapid in the morning, ran the heavy one at its foot, ran a succession of rough ones until near noon we came to the worst one we'd ever seen, a regular old roarer, noise like a locomotive and water just as fast. Churning foam and casting waves fifteen feet high, it ran through a narrow canyon with walls three quarters of a mile high coming right to the water's edge on both sides, so we had no choice but to run it. All being ready away, we went off, each boat tailing the next as close as it could, like a string of circus elephants holding each other's tails. The little boat was not fit for such a frightful sea and quickly filled with water, swung around with her head upriver and was almost unmanageable. We followed in the *Maid,* and the first wave struck us with fearful force, striking an oar from Walter's hand but fortunately not filling the boat nor turning her upstream. She rose to do battle with the next and with good luck I kept her head to the waves with the steering oar and rode them all, taking on water but not filling. From moment to moment we could see the little boat dancing ahead of us, stern downstream, swamped but upright, then we passed her as she swung around in a whirlpool, Jack and Bill Dunn holding her steady as they could as she whirled. *Sister* came through much as we did but got a good dunking, passed the *Emma Dean* too, and caught up with us in an eddy, a half mile from the start. For all of us it was a ride to remember, but especially for the little boat which came down swamped and unmanageable at the end, where we caught her and brought her in. The waves were frightful beyond anything we'd yet seen and it seemed to me at times we could not fail to lose all the boats. But we were a lusty set and our luck did not fail us.

It looked like Major had gone back on his word when we got to another rapid no worse than the one we'd come down, though it was dark and gloomy there between walls that rose a full mile into the sky. Starting from the river and rising up for the first thousand feet the walls were of the black granite we all dreaded so much. Black rock is hard, harsh and unforgiving, and this was harder than we'd ever seen. Major said it was "gneiss" but I didn't think it was *nice* at all. Above the black rock was red rock and, above that, void. Where the black rock tumbled into the river it made crags and spires that did not much wear away with the water and so made dams against which the waters smashed and rebounded in a foaming fall of water. The sense of looking up from a narrow canyon through black walls, up an unimaginable distance, to clifts that seemed to be aflame at the top, where the sun struck them, is one of dread of the unknown, for it seems as though the challenge is upward toward the sky rather than downward on the river.

Howland said it was like Hades turned on its head. "If that was so," I said, "We'd be in Heaven instead of Hell." In fact, the noise of giant boulders grinding along the river bottom, magnified as the sound bounced from wall to wall, could have been thunder from above. He said, "The mind is its own place and makes a Heaven of Hell and a Hell of Heaven." Well, I thought, that's the river, a place of heavenly beauty and of hellish dangers.

But for the sense of doom that the canyon created there, or maybe lacking the morning's experience, Major might have let us run it, and we could and *should* have run it, for it would have been over in a few minutes, with little damage to the boats. But he ordered us to work the boats down by clinging to the side of a granite clift and easing them along as best we could. Howland tried to start a debate about running or lining but Major just waved him off with his good arm.

The way it went was, we'd grope along, clinging to the canyon walls, find a little shelf and put a man or two on it, then we'd pass up a bow line and maybe a stern line too, whatever worked best, and neither worked very well, and inch our way down along the wall. I stayed in my boat, Walter was on the ledge with a bow line with Seneca, who held the stern line. They were doing their best to keep the *Maid* away from the wall by those lines, but it was like trying to push a wagon uphill with a rope. Being in the boat was like trying to hold a dory broadside to the surf, each wave sending the boat against the clift and its backwash carrying the boat out again, threatening to pull Walter and Seneca off the shelf into the rapid. Much damage was done and once I saw one of my new crafted sister ribs spring and break. My only defense was to fend off the clift with an oar, which broke, leaving me holding a splintered stump.

When the men reached the end of one shelf, they had to find another above or below, or to get back in the boats if they couldn't. Whenever we reached a place where the rocks had broken down and piled up at the river we made a portage. With the rations so diminished in weight, we carried the boats over the rocks loaded, or if we were lucky, slid them along on the rocks with risk of breaking their keelsons. We kept up this game until we campt, still in the middle of the rapid, only six miles made all day. If we had to continue in the same way in the morning, we would be at it for a half day instead of a run that could be over in fifteen minutes.

The camp was the worst yet, for no two except Jack and Major could find a space wide enough to make a double bed, and that on a shelf forty feet above the river. I thought if they didn't lie still we would "hear something drop" and find one of them in the river before morning. Or *not* find them for the river was swift there. Cook said he'd take bets on who got the inside berth.

I slept in a wide seam in the rocks where I couldn't roll out. Andy made his bed on a rock fragment at the water's edge, saying he preferred drowning to crushing. The rest were tucked around like eve-swallows wherever the clift offered sufficient space to stretch themselves with any degree of comfort or safety. As there was no wood to speak of on the shelves, Cook had an easy time of it, just made coffee, and that was our supper. It rained hard all night (He sendeth rain on the just and the unjust) and what with our ponchos being worn thin as veils, it was scarce a night of comfort.

We'd used what little wood there was and if we'd found more it would have been wet, so we set off early without breakfast, cross, tired and sullen about more unnecessary toil. And I feared trouble, "bubble, bubble, toil and trouble," for most of the men wanted to run the rapid. When Howland told the Major so, "We'll line, Oramel," was all he said.

It was Sunday, but it was not a place to rest, had Major been so inclined, so we set out to lower the little boat down. The only shelf that would allow two men with lines was the high one where Major and Jack had slept. We were lowering the *Emma Dean* down with much labor, Howland and Dunn on the shelf, Jack in the boat, when a backwash pushed her towards midstream and nearly took the men off the clift so they had to let the line run out, then haul it back in. With all that slack the *Emma Dean* came in on a wave like a racing sloop at the finish, ran into the clift with a crash that outdid lightning's crack, broke her cutwater and was nearly stove, Jack breaking an oar and most nearly his neck.

I knew this wouldn't do. With Jack in his boat and Howland and Dunn on the ledge way up above us, and only Billy and Andy still in their boat, it fell to me to wake Major. I knew he wouldn't listen to Billy or Andy, for he considered them too young to have an opinion, as if the rocks and falls respected grey hair and beards. And I wasn't sure I'd get a hearing on the merits of the case, so I volunteered to run the rapid with my boat. He asked his brother if he was willing to go with me, and Walter said, "Give it a go," so Major said, "Go ahead, but take the rations." We bundled up our meager stores as best we could in our last remaining tarpaulin and with Seneca sitting astride the bundle, we shoved off into a sea of rocks and foam. I'd shipped the steering oar and took up the stern rowing oars, Walter at the bow pair. We headed for the deepest, fastest water in the middle, trying to avoid the piled rocks. We took one sea at the stern, not thick enough to flood the boat but thrusting us forward with terrible force to the middle of the river. We went through a chute like an arrow shot from a bow, straight down the channel into spray and foam which concealed what was at the bottom. What was there was whirlpools, more in number in one place than we'd ever seen. We'd whirl around in one until I saw a way out; I'd shout, "Now," to Walter and we'd pull like oxen only to find ourselves in another one a minute later. But as a preacher must some time come to the end of his sermon, we came to an eddy and laid on our oars to watch Billy and Andy run it.

They pushed off from the clift, but *Sister* didn't get out far enough from shore, and a rebounding wave nearly filled the boat, then sent her sideways into a space a foot too narrow for her, between two rocks right at the head of the chute. She caught her bow on one rock, nearly breaking her cutwater, turned her bow upstream and went through the chute backwards. Billy broke an oar fending off, but saved her from being stove in. When he got into the whirlpools we threw him a line as he'd never of rowed out with one pair of oars.

When the other boys walked around the falls and carried the little boat to where we were, we totted up the score: Lining gave us some damage to the *Emma Dean* and one broken oar, while the two other boats that ran suffered only a broken oar between them. Seemed like we'd go back to running, but Major said it wasn't that simple and he was in charge, so we would line the next rapid. We didn't fight too hard, because we could see it was going to be a chore either way. The black granite had now crept almost half way up the mile-high clift. The walls didn't go straight up where we were but rose at a slight angle until the black granite ended, then shelved back a bit and then shelved again midway through the red, until I felt like we were in the spout of a narrow funnel. The sun flared the top and it being noon, we had a bit of it ourselves, most welcome as the uniforms of shirt and drawers of those were in the boats were soaking wet. We had a nice little beach at the end of a side gulch and there was driftwood, so we stopped to get dinner. We looked up a mile to the scant strip of sky beyond the walls and talked about how we might explain the height to someone who hadn't seen such an awesome thing. Major said we had to imagine it laid out horizontal and compare it to something they'd seen, and he gave us this:

"Tell them to stand on the south steps of the Treasury Building in Washington and look down Pennsylvania Avenue to the Capitol; measure this distance overhead and imagine clifts to extend to that altitude, and they will understand..."

He rattled off two more: Canal Street in New York looking up Broadway to Grace Church, and Lake Bridge in Chicago looking down to the Central Depot. I'd not been to the last two but I'd been to Washington and I could see the trick of laying the clifts out flat in your mind's eye. For me, though, they ran into the sky the same distance Lucy and I had had to walk to and from school every day, a half hour's walk in the first grade and about a twenty minute walk when I left seven years later to sign on a fishing boat. So I stretched out on my back, my feet to the walls, reached up and took Lucy's hand and walked the mile to school over the black and red rock, sometimes running a little to keep up with her longer strides.

After dinner, the clouds came again and darkened our slit of sky, and then the rains came. We'd learned by then that a camp at the end of a side gulch was a bad place to be during a storm. Freshets pour into it from the walls on both sides, cascades form from the water that drops on the rocky summits, and a dry gulch becomes a raging river, so we pulled out. We'd dropped down but a few miles when the rain stopped and the canyon bottom opened up. The walls terraced themselves back for miles on both sides and a vast panorama of reds, russets, creams, blacks and browns was before us. It was all in horizontal stripes of granite, shale, sandstone and limestone, by Major's estimate two billion years of layers laid down by seas, deserts and swamps.

It was but mid-afternoon and we'd made only seven miles, but Major signaled us to land on the right where there was a handsome weeping willow in a meadow, throwing a great shadow over a wide circle. A fine stream came in from the north, clear as crystal, swift and wide. Howland had had the misfortune to lose his maps and notes for the stretch from the Little Colorado down. Major said that we must go into camp and rebuild them from memory, hardly worth the time in my opinion, for they couldn't be right. But we needed to make oars and anyway nobody asked my opinion. Recalling the last such an occasion, I didn't fancy being present for the bickering, so I took my lines and hooks and tried to catch fish in the stream. It was so clear I could see them, but they wouldn't bite. They weren't trout but some kind of chub or whitefish. Even if they tasted like a packet of pins, as Jack had said before, it would make a change from our diet of apples and biscuits, so I got out my pistol and tried to shoot them, with no hits. That was the second time I'd failed to shoot fish, so whoever coined "easy as shooting fish in a barrel" never had the experience.

I was quite willing to stay in that beautiful glen, below brilliant terraced clifts stretching ever outward. I'd never seen such a sight to compare then or since, nor will I in this lifetime: The walls terraced themselves back for miles on each side in uneven undulated clifts, shaped like waves frozen in an ancient sea. Some were steep, some sloped back, many were rounded like ship's sterns. Back and back and back some more they sloped and terraced until they were ten miles apart at the top, maybe more, a vast broken bowl of color, reds, greens, blues, lilac, gray, beige...more colors than ever seen in any rainbow, all in horizontal tiers competing to blaze brightest in the sun.

We needed the rest for we were worn out from the rapids and portages and also needed to make oars. A few of the boys had scouted up the stream, or river as they call them in the West, and reported good timber for oars a few miles up. While I did not want to get my hopes up, I thought it possible that our peerless hunters might find game in that verdant park, for I had seen an old ram high up on a clift across the river.

AUGUST 16, 1869.

PIONEERS RETURN.

Today three more members of the Adams exploration returned to Breckenbridge with a harrowing tale. In the words of Mr. Lovell, who had earlier returned for supplies following the loss of a boat, a second boat was lost soon after the party entered the Grand Canyon. "We were letting the boats down on lines past a dangerous rapid, when one boat swung out of control and was hopelessly damaged by collision with the rocks. We lost bacon, flour, coffee, tools and most of our cooking utensils. When we tallied up our remaining supplies we were down to some two hundred pounds of partly spoiled flour, fifty pounds of bacon and ten or fifteen pounds of coffee for six men in two boats."

Mr. Waddle describes the next tragedy: "We had lost oars but we stopped and hacked some paddles out of driftwood and carried on. Our persistence was repaid by our finding a slab of our lost bacon wedged in some rocks. This greatly encouraged us to continue, but on the fifth of August another boat swamped and snagged on the rocks in a furious rapid. Though we worked diligently all morning to free it, the line parted and it disappeared in the torrent with more of our supplies."

The party had worked for four days to progress only three quarters of a mile and with but one damaged boat remaining, faced a terrible fall. "We discarded everything", Mr. Lovell reports, "clothing, tools, papers and sundry equipment and headed into the fierce foaming torrent ahead. "We came through all right and safe enough, but from there we had to portage and line the boat down a succession of rapids too rocky to run. On the seventh, we were so unfortunate as to have the line part, and our last boat went on its own way into the canyon. We had the foresight to remove some of our supplies and so were not yet on the point of starvation."

Undaunted, our heroes proceeded to build a raft and the six brave souls started again. When they camped for the night and dried their flour they found they had only a hundred pounds left and just twenty of bacon. On the ninth of August, after careful counsel, the three volunteered to leave the expedition so as not to deprive the others of sustenance. Mr. Day attributes the difficulties experienced not merely to the extreme conditions faced but also to, "faulty boat construction and unskilled seamanship."

Our prayers go with the remaining three stalwarts who, when last seen, had abandoned their raft and were walking their way down the shore.

The next morning we went to fetch the timber the men had found. It turned out to be a great pine log that must have come from six thousand feet up, for there are no pines visible below that altitude. It had been washed down the stream for many miles by the look of it, all scarred and as naked of bark as we were of clothing. The stream was too shallow to float the log, so we levered it, rolled it and skidded it the two miles or so down to camp. After days of constant running, letting down or carrying the boats and climbing up and down clifts, we found that moving the log was very wearing, especially for me for I had done so little rough work in recent years that it came hard. We had but poor tools and the great log had to be split into quarters with an axe, then each quarter had to be shaped to an oar with axe and handsaw.

While these labors got under way, Cook spread all the rations out to dry, then joined the men in making oars. While he was thus engaged, a boat swung around in the eddy tide and its rope caught the can of saleratus that was sitting on the bank and swept it into the river, never to be seen again. This was a hard loss, for we would have to eat unleavened bread from then on. After drying the flour and sifting it through a mosquito bar, it was determined that we had but ten days supply of musty flour left, some dried apples and, of course, plenty of coffee, to be drunk without sugar for that commodity had long since dissolved in the wetting of our supplies. We had not even sprouting beans to break the monotony and our wind.

There being but one set of tools, I went exploring with Major while the men made oars. The stream ran a ways back through abrupt clifts, then there was a deep, narrow canyon from which the brook emerged. Up a narrow gulch off the side of the canyon there was an old Moqui ruin with fragments of broken pottery. I collected a few for their slight weight would not add to our hardship. The foundations were all that was left, stone laid in mortar. An old grinding stone, "called a *metate*," Major said, much worn, and some trails worn deep into rock told us that this place had been inhabited for many years. Major said he believed the Indians built in such remote places because they feared the Spaniards who were conquering the territory and converting the tribes to

Christianity or, if they didn't convert, killing them. It might have been true for I'd seen a painting in the Judge's house at Fort Bridger that showed a Spanish priest baptising an Indian on one side, while a Spanish knight had a rope around the neck of another Indian on the opposite side. But I'd been told these tribes had vanished before the Spaniards arrived. They were people whose story was not even known to the tribes now in the West. Major had earlier thought marauding tribes from the north may have driven the early people to these remote places. I suspect we'll never know, for they left no writing to tell us.

Major elected to go back to camp, but I told him I wanted to explore the ruins some more. There was something about the silence of that place that made me feel the presence of those unknown people who had lived hundreds of year ago. I found myself sitting in the quiet and thinking, though neither thinking nor sitting is my usual style.

I've always been doing, the sea, the army, and, on the river, the best times for me were when we're running rapids or at least on the move. But I've never thought so much as I had on the trip. It's the constant sound of the river that does it. It takes hold of you like a child demanding attention. It's calmed Walter so he hardly prays in the boat anymore; it's kept Jack uncommon quiet, and it's made me sit and think. I no more know what's going to come into my mind next than I know what's around the next bend in the river. Sometimes these thoughts are as hard on me as running a rapid: I was uncomfortable with the idea that the world wasn't made in seven real days, but became easy with the thought; I used to think God controlled everything but every day on the river I felt his presence less; I used to think that if I did good toward man and served the Union and worshiped God, all would be well, but it turned out that my thoughts set my mind aroil the same as the rocks rile up the river, and sometimes I didn't know what to think. So far I'd always come back to faith in the Creator, but it was coming to be more and more of a chore. It occurred to me that I hadn't prayed for over a week.

Major said it was an unknown river, but God must know it well since He made it and took His time about it, it seems. And that led me to another thought, Was God leading this expedition or was Major? I hoped it was God because all Major seemed to want to do was name things and measure what he didn't name and put it all on a map. I wanted to get moving again so these thoughts would let me be. Even the waterfalls, the streams from above, the cascades fed my thoughts as they fed the river — where did all these thoughts come from and where did they lead? The water came from rain and went to the river and ran to the sea. I had no answer for the thoughts, and it left me uneasy.

But there were no cascades there in the ruins. There was no stream, no wind, no sound at all. It was the first time in the whole trip that I couldn't hear the river. There was only silence, the silence of the dead. And space, space that seemed to go on forever. Being there in that vast, unending space and that silence, I grew frightened. I hastened back to camp to help with the oars.

There were only three oars cut by nightfall, the stick being large and the tools poor and dull, but Major announced that we would be off the next day at dawn. "We haven't enough supplies to warrant further delay," was the way he put it, satisfied I guessed that none would want the latitude and longitude of that excellent stream, which he had named, "Silver Creek." My oar was left until last and was only crudely fashioned when we pulled away in the morning. It seemed to me that Major had come to think that my boat should carry all the rations, go into all the dangerous places first and get along with the least. So be it. The trip was nearly ended, and I would be as well off when it was over; still one can't help minding an imposition even in a wilderness so far from civilization.

THE BRECKENBRIDGE SENTINEL

AUGUST 18, 1869.

ADAMS EXPEDITION
ABANDONED.

Today we regret to report that the Adams expedition has ended with the return of Messrs. Lillis and Twible to Breckenbridge. Their tale of the final days on the river rounds out the story carried in our August 15th edition, where we reported on the return of three other members of the crew. After walking the river for several miles the three men remaining built a second raft of driftwood, fashioned paddles and proceeded down some rapids. In Mr. Twible's words, "We proceeded well enough for about three miles. Then we were unable to keep the raft off the rocks and it smashed one so heartily that we lost most of our remaining food and utensils and destroyed the raft. After drying what we had left, we explored down river for a mile or so and saw nothing but roaring rapids ahead, and so concluded reluctantly that we must terminate our journey where we were and join those who had deserted the party in its time of need."

When apprised of this statement, Mr. Rickers, the first crew member to abandon the expedition, said, "The only one with any sense besides me was the dog."

Colonel Adams has remained in Hot Springs to prepare his report for the Secretary of War but has promised to send a summary to the Sentinel, and we will report same to our readers.

The maps were left to be sketched out later and we had no altitude as we'd found the last of the barometers was broken and useless. Major said that if the supplies ran out we might walk out to try to find a Mormon settlement to the north. I hoped not, because I'd rather ride than walk and I was sure the worst of the river was behind us and we had only to persevere.

We ran a succession of rapids and made three portages, carrying the boats. We campt after about ten miles at the head of a mean-looking rapid we knew we would have to portage the boats around, but we were then too weary to attempt anything but sleep. There had been cold rain off and on all day, and in between, the broiling sun parched us, the thermometer once at 115 degrees. Constant, cold wetting by rain or river, followed by baking in the sun, was sucking the strength from us in the way the sand soaks up streams in side canyons.

We had some hope the river was improving for the hard granite began to get gradually lower, often as low as three hundred feet. Above that the old red sandstone set in and the marble rested on that, all stepping back to a half mile or more on either side, where at a height of four to five thousand feet there was a plateau covered with pines.

At supper the cold rain came again and, with it, the wind. Billy had just finished baking the unleavened "sinkers" when the downpour extinguished the fire and we went to try to sleep. The tents and ponchos were either ragged and useless or had been lost in capsizings, and with but one blanket apiece, the chill and the wet vied with Billy's biscuits for discomfort. I couldn't say which won but I could say when you'd eaten the biscuit, you knew you'd eaten a "heavy" meal. We'd seen the spoor of sheep, so I hoped our diet would improve, provided our hunters' aim did the same.

It seemed every time I thought we'd gotten the best of the river, it found another torment for us. It was as though it had set up a race to see which came apart first, the boats or the men. We made only four miles the next day, August 18th, all the day spent in portages, carrying the boats around great piles of rocks that had been brought down when the many side canyons were in flood. Some of the lateral canyons were near as wide as the Canyon of the Colorado, so great quantities of huge rocks had been brought down and at places literally banned up the river, making the worst kind of rapid, for we could see rocks rising above those dams and no clear channel through them. If we could have, we would have run more of them, as even Major agreed, though he said he wanted us to proceed with great care, as if care can be exercised in the midst of a roaring fall when control lies not with the boatman but with the river, or with God, or with the river gods, take your pick.

In the afternoon, just as we had finished sliding and carrying the boats around a great rapid, the heavens opened up. We had to make the boats fast to rocks and seek shelter from the wind and wet behind boulders. The rain poured down in torrents and the thunder peals echoed from crag to crag making wild music for the lightning to dance to. I thought that fatigue and hunger and discomfort would deprive a man of the appreciation of beauty, but after the shower it was grand to see the cascades leap from the clifts and turn to vapor before they reached the rocks below. There were thousands of them of all sizes, pure and white as molten silver. I wondered to what extremes a man must be driven before the idea of beauty leaves him, or if it never did, no matter what.

It was plain to me that it mightn't be long before I had a chance to test that idea, because our provisions were not sufficient for anything more than just to sustain life. Coffee and *heavy* bread cannot be called light rations but one feels quite light about the stomach after living on it for a while.

The best remedy for hunger is not to think about it, but I could think of little else. It was a nagging and constant thing, not constant like the pain of a wound but more like the sound of the river from place to place, rising and falling, sometimes roaring, sometimes gurgling, but always insistently present. At supper Cook counted up the rations we had left and said, "Flour for nine days more if we don't lose any more and eat lumps and all. After that it's eat dried apples for breakfast, drink water for dinner and swell up for supper."

In a deep voice, rough as oak bark, Andy said, "This is no time for gravity." We laughed, but the laughter had an echo that was grim.

After the shower we lowered our boats over a very treacherous rapid and campt at its foot. Just below was another one, ready to offer a man a fine chance to see what strength he had gained by a night's rest, if you could call it rest. Lying on hard ground, baking and wet by turns and thinking about feeding yourself tomorrow, the next day, next week, there is no rest. That night it rained without cease, and the morning fire made of wet wood was as meager as the fare. When we tackled the rapid we were wet, cold and hungry, snarling at one another like curs.

Howland said, "If the river is a woman, she's a G.D. shrew." I don't think God damned the river, but the river seemed bent on damming us. The waves were frightful and continuous, fifteen or twenty feet high and coming at us from all directions. I had never seen anything like it, even on the ocean. If one of our boats had shipped a sea in that fall, it would have been the last of her, for there was no still water below where she could be stopped for bailing. We ran a wild race for two miles, pulling right then left then right again to avoid the waves and escape the boulders, 'til we were fairly dizzy with the chase. Sometimes my boat was half full of water and it seemed as soon as Seneca threw some little of it out, it was replaced by double the quantity. Our heavy boat ran past the little boat, for the *Maid* was like a runaway horse, and there was no way to rein her in. We dashed on alone, whirling and rushing, looking for a place to land. At length we succeeded in checking her and floated in an eddy where we bailed and waited for the others to come up one way or another, stern first or prow, upright or capsized. We kept our oars at the ready in case we had to run out and make a rescue, of man or boat.

The other boats came through all right, the *Emma Dean's* forward compartment partly filled with water because of her broken cutwater. There being no place to land, we went on again as soon as the other boats were bailed. The rain, heavy and cold, pelted us. At one place we had to drag the boats around some rocks then line for a quarter mile, which took us 'til noon. We took dinner on the side of a clift where the cook scarcely had room to make a fire, but if it was dinner time and we came upon a place with driftwood for a fire and a spot to land we were compelled to stop, for we didn't know if either could be found ahead. Indeed, most likely we'd find ourselves in another rapid before we found quiet water again.

When we launched after our meager meal we could sense, more than we could hear, turbulent water ahead. That long word didn't do justice to the fury of the next rapid. As we were desperate men, we resolved to run it. The little boat took the lead but was swamped at once and it looked like boat and men were going under and would be lost. We were some distance behind in the big boats, but we rushed to her assistance, hardly heeding the danger we ourselves were in. My boat raced through a chute at lightning speed, *Sister* close behind. Below the chute we entered a whirlpool which threw us with furious force against some rocks. Fortunately we struck with the cutwater, the strongest part of the boat, and we rebounded, the cutwater intact, taking a sea and colliding with *Sister* which had also been caught in the whirlpool. We circled out of the whirlpool and both big boats raced side by side down to the *Emma Dean,* which had so filled with water the men had gone into the river and were holding her up. The broken cutwater had allowed the forward compartment to flood and she was going down by her head.

We took the crew aboard the *Maid,* and *Sister* towed the little boat to an eddy below, the only new damage the loss of two oars. There was a driftwood pile, so we stopped and built the biggest bonfire since Uinta to dry our clothes and the celestial instruments. This was a futile effort for the rain kept up heavy until four o'clock and the bedding was so wet from rain and river that it did not dry before we slept, or rather spent the night, in sodden blankets, arising cold and uncomfortable and out of sorts. But the sun came up clear, reaching us over the canyon wall about 8 1/2 o'clock and as all was wet, we concluded to stay where we were and dry out.

After dinner, all things dry and the men warm again, we set out, determined to make distance and altitude, having made only five and three quarters miles the day before. All the boats were leaking badly and we would need to find pitch soon. The rapids continued rough, but there was more space between them, so we weren't so pressed as the day before. We had to portage the boats once and lower them twice on ropes. We made eight and one quarter miles and when we stopped, Major got out the maps and told us, "The Mormons explored the river for sixty-five miles above Callville and I believe we're getting to that part of the river." I was sure we were, for the limestone was coming again and the black granite was getting lower. But we were still a mile in the earth.

Major and I found another Moqui ruin near where we were campt, on a terrace of trap rock. There was the usual broken pottery and milling stones scattered about and, up on a little natural shelf, a globe shaped basket that would hold maybe a peck. The willow withes were woven in a criss-cross pattern that reminded me of the timbers on the trestle bridge at Green River City. The basket had sat there in that one place for a century or maybe more, and I would have left it out of respect, but Major must have it. He took it off the shelf but didn't handle it well, and it fell apart in his hands. He pushed the broken pieces back together as best he could, but that left about a third of it broken on the ground. He put the rest back on the shelf and we went on.

August 21st, and the river changed as though my belief had been heard. It became broader, nearly three hundred feet wide, the walls sloped back, letting in more sunlight, and the black granite base of the clift was replaced by a series of huge vertical slabs like children's school slates stood on edge, sticking out into the river at intervals. The red sandstone between them was softer and had washed out in such a way that curious little bays were formed, stepping one after another down the river as though the wall was a giant washboard.

The river turned fickle and narrowed again, the water rushed against the slabs and recoiled like ocean surf on both sides of the canyon, meeting in the middle in a high, arching spume. Plunging into it was like walking into a waterfall at its base, with no knowledge of what lay beyond. But the water was clear of rocks and the tide was swift, and we ran and ran, making twenty-one miles, a day that stood first for dashing wildness. We ran all but one rapid, where the granite slabs came too far out into the river making a narrow fall, the noise like a freight train pounding by. Then the river turned slow and sweet again, and the black granite disappeared, not even giving us the usual sudden cataract where the granite ended and the sandstone commenced.

I was feeling most unwell that night. I had been wet, then cold, then baked, then cold again so often that I was ripe for any disease, and our scanty food had reduced me to a poor condition. Still I was in good spirits and was threatening all sorts of revenge when decent food was again to be had. We were in a gay mood after the good day's run and *Old Shady* was sung again with no complaints and Andy didn't cut in with his rasp, though I think he dast not, fearing revenge for Walter's fat ear. Walter followed on with his animal song:

> *I had a wee cock, and I loved it well*
> *I fed my cock on yonder hill;*

Cook said, "If I had a wee cock I'd kill it and cook it and eat it."
Howland said, "I'd leave off the cooking part."
And Jack said, "I'd leave off the killin part."
No one joined in a response to the song, so Walter left off. I said I was sure we'd be having a civilized meal soon, for I was certain we were near the end. That began a kind of round robin, much like the one we had on the Fourth of July, where each man said what he'd like to have for that first real meal. Jack proposed beefsteak, I said lobster, Howland wanted minced-meat pies, somebody else said lemon ice and I don't know what all but by the time we were through, we'd imagined a regular banquet. Bill Dunn didn't nominate anything and when I asked him later if he didn't have a dish he'd like set before him, he said, "I do: the major, dressed and skewered and roasted alive."

The cold rain came on again. Having no tent left, I took my blanket and found a protected spot in the clift and slept hard. My dreams were filled with banquets I'd never been at, with every course laid out that was said at the campfire and some more I didn't know the names of, but were most likely French. Lucy and Mother sat on either side of me and kept refilling my plate before it was half empty.

My belief that we were nearly through was short-lived. We had no sooner run the first rapid in the morning than the river made a sharp turn to the right, then turned right again so we were headed back in the direction we'd started from. The dreaded black walls loomed up before us and my heart dropped toward my feet. I thought this must be how a prisoner feels who had been told he was pardoned and had no sooner cleared the prison gates than he was led back to his cell in manacles, his freedom a mere mistake.

We ran rough rapids all day, the boats leaking and the men cursing the granite. We needed to go west but the river turned east-northeast. Oramel said, "If it keeps up in this direction we'll feel the way the old hog felt when he'd moved the hollow log so that both ends came on the outside of the fence."

We came to one rapid we could not run and made a hard, long portage of the boats, which took four hours. The river bent back west-southwest and we were cheered until the thundering loco-motive sound came again. We eased our boats down with caution until we could see the rapid, and it was a bad one, long and shallow, no water deep enough to run in. We made camp as a matter of necessity, there being no way to get down farther but a long portage. In my sorry state, I could not countenance it, though I was feeling some better. That Sunday, working like galley-slaves, we made eleven and a half miles.

As it had taken to raining every night, Major decided we should rig the tarpaulin as a sort of tent, though it was scant protection, having no sides. But rigging it would *prevent* rain, I supposed. When we took it off the supplies it had been wrapped around, we found more wetted flour, but the vote was to use it, wet, dry or lumpy, as we had no other. It was agreed that the biscuits could not be worse than the sorry hard and sour things we'd been eating.

The next morning we went on in pouring rain, skipping breakfast. The canyon changed again. The walls rose abruptly for upwards of three thousand feet, then eased off into a gently sloping terrace on both sides of the river, extending for two or three miles, then turned to clifts again that looked to be two thousand feet high, so we were in a funnel still, but with a wider mouth.

The 23rd of August was another hard day of it. We made only two miles in the morning, most of it portages, but in the P.M. we got out of the granite and made ten and a quarter miles, most encouraging seeing that the river had got back to its proper direction, mostly west. Our camp was at the head of another long rapid, and Major was talking about a portage. I hoped that he would change his mind, as it looked to be an easy and safe rapid. But I didn't say so, that being a sure way to fix a contrary idea up hard in his mind.

I might as well have spoken my piece, for we had to portage, slipping and hauling the heavy boats through the rocks along the shore. It was heavy labor, no coolie ever had worse. We should have protested but we had no leader could talk to Major, who was anyway mostly talking to his brother. Walter was a sorry case on the best days but he'd got worse. I expect the poor rations reminded him of Confederate prison, but his bulldozing ways didn't make our lot any better. At our last camp, he made Billy move his blanket so he could sleep in that spot.

Though I was somewhat recovered, the work of sliding, dragging and carrying the boats on the rocky shore came hard. After that we ran for an hour and made seven miles in near rockless water. At noon the river changed again and we had to line, with more damage to the boats and severe barking of our shins, the broken rock cruel and sharp. Major went exploring up a little creek that came in there, and was gone so long we thought we'd have to send for him, Walter being our preferred messenger, but Major showed up and brought in pitch which was badly needed. Our boats had become so damaged and leaky that we caulked every chance we got with tarpaulin strips spread over with pitch.

After dinner we picked our weary bodies up and ran again, a succession of rapids, and made 22 3/4 miles for the day. We campt at the head of another rapid, which we thought could be run in the morning. We could have gone farther but there was a singular recess in the marble rock about a hundred feet long and fifty feet wide forming a fine shelter, and as it was coming on to rain as usual at that time of day, we could stay dry for a change. We all agreed that we would "dream we dwelt in marble halls." Jack said, "Why, this is as fine as any hotel in New York." Then he looked at our cooks and said, "Though the kitchen isn't up to that standard."

When Major got out his maps, he couldn't figure why we hadn't reached Grand Wash, since the Mormon map estimated the distance from the Chiquito to Grand Wash to be seventy to eighty miles, and we had already come one hundred twenty. Howland said, "I suspect the Mormon map shows distance by land and we're traveling a river as twisted as a hangman's noose." But it was a disappointment. Of course, with the barometers broken we had no altitude, but I was sure we'd run down so much we'd have flat water the rest of the way. When we'd stopped taking altitude, we also stopped trying to fix latitude and longitude, for it had become a race for life.

"Roll out! Roll out! Roll out!..." We hadn't had Billy Rhoad's call to breakfast since the day of the fight, and I realized I'd missed it, though it was an abrupt way to wake. When we'd gathered around the fire, he opened the last sack of flour, and it was solemn as prayer in church. Nobody said anything; even Andy was quiet. Howland reached out slow, took a small handful of flour and sprinkled it on the fire, "for the river gods," he said. I tried to think of something from the Bible but it was so much like sprinkling earth at a burial that "ashes to ashes" was all that came to mind. When the cook had meted out the one-seventh portion that would make the day's biscuits, Howland said, "It'll be one-sixth tomorrow." He didn't have to go on, I'd got that far in fractions.

It was the first time I'd felt the hard gritty biscuit was satisfying, and that was probably because we made twelve miles by ten A.M., clear running, and all the way rapids. Then we came to another piece of black magic the river pulled out of its hat: lava monuments, some small but one a hundred feet high, a cone shaped black eminence rising right out of the river. As we ran down cautiously three or four miles we saw more and more of them. Looking up we saw lava patches on the south wall, and the north wall was completely lined with black basalt from the volcano. On the edge of the clift, at least fifteen hundred feet above the river, we could see where the lava had come from as there was a cinder cone with the crater intact.

I tried to think what it must have been like for millions of tons of hot lava to pour down into the icy waters, Howland's "earth, air, fire and water" all at once, steam rising who knows how far into the sky, the entire river blocked up, filled with lava for miles up and down. "And the stream thereof shall be turned into pitch and the dust thereof into brimstone, and the land thereof shall become burning pitch."

What did the river do then, I wondered, for the water must have made a vast sea, filling the canyon until it could break through. But the volcano was just an eye-blink in time, and the river had the patience of the Lord. Though it took eons, the river hammered away until it wore a channel through the lava, broke the dam, but leaving a great waterfall. We could see the vast crack under the cone that had let the lava come out of the center of the earth, a "fault," Major called it, but it was more like the "sections" Major had us make at the beginning of the trip, when we had time to care about such things. Now our attention no longer lay with the land. Our sole interest was with the river and how it was going to treat us the next hour, the next day, the day after that.

Across the river on the other wall, high up, the fault had spawned a river of its own, or maybe the sea was still draining, because a cataract of water came out so big I thought the Chiquito had followed us. Major named the place "Lava Falls".

There was a bad fall, and we had to slide the boats around it, a job of three hours on the rough cinder and lava, and my aging boots were no match for it, coming apart on the outside of one and the inside of the other. We'd learned to keep the boats in the water as much as we could, so the load was lightened, even if it meant we were in water to our waists. We'd also learned to let them down stern first. Major said the bow was supposed to point where we were going, but the bow was also the cutwater, and the water we wanted to cut was coming from upstream. We ignored Major. We were letting *Sister* down in this fashion when the metal strap holding the bow ringbolt gave way, and she was free. There were four of us in the water at the time guiding the boat and we were able to slow her down enough to get a line through the ringbolt on the stern, then turn her around and let her down Major's way. Andy got caught under the boat in the process, but the water wasn't deep and he escaped with only a scraped cheek and a torn ear. Walter looked at him and grinned, didn't say anything.

As we floated down we could see where the lava had filled side canyons, some of them still filled. We saw more and more of the cones, mostly circular at the bottom, easing off to a blunt point at the top, sometimes flattened off in one direction, sometimes in another. There was a black beauty about it, but I was so much fatigued by the portage that I couldn't take it in totally, though Major clearly did, as I heard him singing his "song of a beautiful land." No one else had breath for singing, not even Walter.

After that long fall, the river opened up, the black granite disappeared and we were surely through the worst of it, we'd taken all the river could dish out, and we'd overcome it! And we made *thirty five* miles for the day. Hurra!

The next morning we watched Billy measure out one-sixth of the remaining flour. We didn't give any to the river gods.

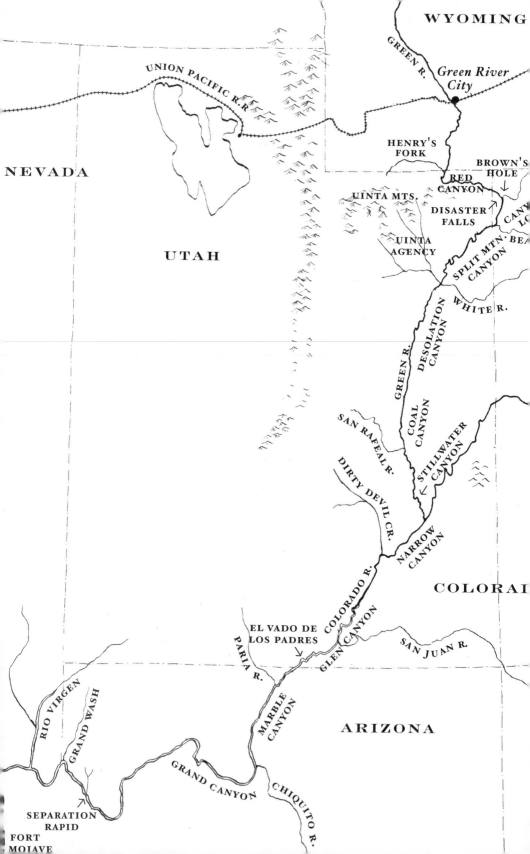

The river was benign for a time, and we saw evidence of where more volcanoes had poured lava into the side canyons and over the clifts on the right, but we couldn't see the volcanoes themselves. The lava must have entered the river through the side canyons in a slow stream like the one we saw up the river and turned solid when it hit the water. Wherever it entered, it made a dam, so that many rapids and falls were formed. We ran them one after another down, down, down all the way, rapids and calm turn by turn until we landed to scout one that looked worse than the others. We could have run it had we been on the other side of the river, but we had landed on the wrong side, so we let the boats down rather than try to cross over again.

The clifts began to be broken down in places, making rapids but not such big ones as the lava had made. Around eleven o'clock we came to a little flood plain where a stream came in from the right. We stopped to look for fish or forage for we were prepared to eat anything, even leaves. By Fortune's hand we were brought to an Indian garden. They had made a network of a central shallow ditch with side ditches so that the overall appearance was like a skeleton with ribs running off the spine. By channeling some of the water from the stream into the central ditch they had managed to grow green squashes, melons and corn in a little plot. Nearby two curious rugs were hung up, made of wildcat skins and sewn together to form a mat, but there was no other sign of habitation and we speculated that the Indians lived elsewhere.

We took a mess of the squashes, all else being too little advanced to be of use, though Andy said we could eat the corn husks if we boiled them long enough. I thought, "Thou shalt not steal," but consoled myself that we were near starvation. Then the Donner party that had eaten some of their members came to mind, and I thought, "Thou shalt not kill," and I began to wonder what use the commandments were in times of great necessity; if our situation got into worse straits, would we do the same as the Donner party? I thought not, but we were not that bad off yet, and I put the thought away, except what crept in at the last was Walter would be the first to go, or Major if Dunn had his way. We hastened away from the garden, not wanting to be found out. I wondered if we might have killed after all, if the Indians caught us, for Andy had his rifle out.

We stopped a few miles down the river and had a feast. Cook made the squash into a soup and we ate it like pigs at the trough (squeakie, squeakie). I wished we had taken more.

We no sooner had our bellies full of sweet squash and our hearts full of contentment, than we were on the river again, for one meal of green squash did not much change our difficult situation.

We were pleased with the broken rock for it meant fast water and a wide stream, so we could always find a way through the rapids or line the boats from a beach if need be. But before long the broken rock stopped and the black granite rose again, looming up in front of us as we came around a river bend, as though it had been lying in wait to punish us for our theft. The walls closed in, and the sun was pushed aside, so I felt again like a prisoner in a dark cell. The water ran swift but the rapids could be run, and we made thirty five miles again. Another day like it and we would be out of prison, I was sure.

The river was running almost due south, and the clifts were three or four thousand feet high, so it was gloomy-dark again in the morning, without birdsong, when Billy measured out one-fifth the remaining flour.

After about an hour the river turned west and we gave a cheer, for it looked like we might run around the granite and come out onto easy water, especially as the walls were getting lower and the limestone was evident everywhere. Then the river turned sharply to the south again, and the dip of the strata was to the north, the worst combination. Within an hour we saw looming ahead of us a black gate, two hard giant granite walls with a river between, like a giant mouth ready to swallow us. The very entrance gave us trouble and we had to carry the boats over a fall and into the canyon, like being your own pallbearer.

We let down on lines for another mile, then ran for two more miles, lined and ran until we got about twelve miles into the canyon and hit a wall of noise, the loudest yet, drowning out windsound, voice and, if there had been thunder, that too. We had come upon the worst rapid yet. I gave up all thought of daring to run it, of risking life and limb to prove valor. We were starving men with nothing to prove, and it would be "vanity of vanities" to work at being a hero when mere survival was so much in doubt.

We landed on the right to look over the rapid. The spectacle was appalling to us. The river dashed against the left wall of a narrow canyon and was then thrown back with tremendous force against the right, making billows so huge our boats could never ride them, even if we could steer clear of the rocks, which was about as likely. For me, running rapids had been the greatest joy on the trip, but this one brought sorrow and fear. It was more dangerous than any we'd seen, even those we had lined, and I could not contemplate running it. I had foolishly thought the worst was over but it seemed we had struck that dread place where we could neither run, line nor portage, and would have to walk out. And how did we know if we could even do that?

If we got through this first rapid, there were three more within sight beyond it, the river twisting away like flypaper pulled out of its tube. We could not see how bad they were, but with their noise like the sound of hooves in a cavalry charge and the billows higher than three men, we could tell they were huge ones. And what lay beyond those?

Major sent the Howlands and Dunn to explore the side canyon, where a little stream came down, to see if there was a route around the back of the clift, where we could carry the boats. Major and his brother set off to climb the clift itself to see if there was a place to line, although the clifts on both sides were eight hundred feet high and we had less than four hundred feet of rope.

I sat in camp, feeling about as low as ever I had on the trip, nothing to do but watch Andy and Billy set about making a fire, though there was nothing to cook, only coffee to boil. Jack just seemed to mope about camp, staring at the clifts or the rapids and falls, poking at his little boat, which was leaking badly, no pitch for repairs. To my surprise, he admitted that his "sand was about as low as it's ever been." Then I saw the fear in his eyes, first time I'd read anything in them except a sparkle of fun. I'd seen men going into battle in the same way, an expression on their faces that is no expression, except perhaps a certain fascination with an experience whose outcome is unknown. To see the fear you had to look into their eyes.

We were in a trap: if we tried to run the rapid we would surely drown; if we didn't move on we would starve; if we tried to walk out we would likely perish of thirst in the high desert. If Howland found a route for carrying the boats around the clifts, we couldn't do it. The boats were water-soaked and heavy. While our crew could carry one when we began the trip, we had become so enfeebled for lack of nourishment as to be incapable of heavy labor.

I thought it best to keep my mind occupied so as not to show my own fear. I wrote a letter to Lucy and mother, but only in my head as I was sure it could never be posted. I took a last look at my tintype albums, to say goodbye, for no matter what course we elected, I could not take them for the weight. The first picture of Lucy was completely destroyed, and the second was little better, though I could still see most of her features and could imagine the rest. Mother no longer had even the one eye, and had neither chin nor cheek. Of the rest, only Aunt Marsh could be recognized and her scarcely in human form. I put the albums in a rock cleft and covered them with a little cairn of rocks and pebbles. I took my army discharge out of my hat and read it over, though I knew it by heart, and wondered why I'd traded boredom for fear. Right then it seemed a bad bargain.

When Major returned, he reported he had found no way to line the boats as there was no ledge and no broken rock to provide a path.

Howland came in and reported that there were two other canyons besides the one the creek came down. They'd followed the stream to where it ended in a perpendicular clift. The canyon on the right they did not explore, but the one on the downstream side would permit climbing up to the top of the clift gradual enough so that we could manhandle the boats up to it, if we had the time. Major asked how much time, and Howland said he figured it would take a week to ten days. There are times when mathematics doesn't solve anything, as we had only five days' rations, even counting swelling up for supper. So we had wasted a half day's worth of rations in fruitless reconoissance. As Jack said, "Anybody with a glass eye could see it couldn't be done."

Towards sundown, after a meager supper of coffee and biscuits and a handful of dried apples apiece, Major had Dunn and me row him acrost the river to scout it from the left side. I was barefoot so couldn't climb with him and Dunn wouldn't. We watched Major creep upwards with that little hopping and hanging way he had 'til he got about four hundred feet up and stopped, looking for a way beyond, I thought. Then he yelled down, "Bradley, I need help."

I grabbed the rope and told Bill to take the oars, and we started to climb. My feet were getting cut by the rocks, but I had to go on as I knew Major's arm was getting tired holding where he was. It looked like he had his one hand jammed into a crevice with nothing solid to hang on to. He couldn't go forward, and he couldn't step back without he ended up on rocks a hundred feet below. We reached a spot just below where he was caught, and I tied a rope around the top of the long sweep oar and pushed it up above him, so the rope was dangling by his hand. But it wasn't like my drawers from above, the last time he'd got rimmed. "I dastn't let go to grasp it, Bradley," he sort of gasped, and there was anyway no place I could see for him to step back. He'd clearly made one of his little jumps to where he was, in front of him only the clift. His arm was trembling and I could see he hadn't much longer he could hold.

I lowered the long oar a few feet and jammed it in a crack

beyond him in such a way I could press it against his back and hold him to the clift. I told Bill to see if he could get up level with Major's feet and jam the shorter oar in somewhere, so Major could step back on it. Bill wormed his way up and found a horizontal crack maybe a foot below Major's feet. He pushed the blade of the oar in the crack, and when I judged it was lodged tight enough I called to Major to let his foot down slow 'til he struck the oar. It was a stretch but I thought he could manage, especially as I was holding him steady against the clift. He groped back with one foot, and I backed the big oar off gradual so he could ease himself down. I was calling encouragement and advising him how much lower he had to step, watching his foot seek the oar, the way the cicada had explored his coffee cup. His leg stretched out about as much as the insect's had and was about to touch the oar when I saw it was no longer in the crack. "Bill!" I yelled. Dunn hesitated just long enough for me to lose the power of speech, then pushed the oar back in the crack just as Major's foot touched it.

Once out of the crevice Major went on with his climb. I went down to tend my feet which were sore and bleeding from the rocks. I looked at Dunn but didn't say anything. He just grinned and shook his head, making his mane of crow-black hair waft in the wind like so much smoke.

When we crossed back over the river, and we were all assembled around a small fire, Major announced, "We'll run the rapid in the morning."

We had only his word that we could do it, for he'd climbed alone. I thought that was enough because he always took the safest course, but I could see doubt in the faces of the others, Howland's in particular. He kept shaking his head when Major explained how we'd do it. "We'll have to start from the right bank, as there's no way down on the left. We'll have to push and carry the boats over that rock," and he gestured towards a thirty foot dam of rock that was projecting into the river. "We'll let down over the first fall by wading and holding the lines."

Howland broke in, "We'll never hold them against that current, John."

Major said, a little sharp, I thought, "Of course not, we'll have to snub the lines around a rock and pay it out as we go."

Howland came back with, "I assume that's the royal 'we' you're using, John."

The tension between Major and Oramel had reached a state where listening wasn't part of talking. As if I didn't have enough discomfort with Major's plan, their distrust of one another was an added burden.

Just getting the boats over the rock would be a task for Hercules. Then to let them down over the first fall meant walking in water up to our waists, or higher. Then we'd have to scramble down the edge of the falls ourselves, again mostly in the water in order to muster the whole crew at the boats, all the while knowing we risked being swept downriver like so many twigs.

That looked to be the easy part: down to the right below the second fall, which we'd have to run, there was a huge flat rock that sloped down toward us so that the river ran up this slope, hit the clift behind it, rolled up the clift, curled over and raced acrost the river to the left in a whorl of fearsome dimensions. Major's idea was we'd run along some clear water on the right side close to the clift to the head of the fall, then turn the boats to the left, pull hard acrost it to a little chute in its middle, turn the boats to the right so they headed downstream again and run the chute. At the bottom of the fall we'd have to pull hard to the left again, crossing over the upstream end of the big rock, catching its wash which would carry us to the left wall where we'd turn right downstream again. Howland said, "An eel couldn't do it."

"We don't have a choice, Oramel, you said yourself it would take us over a week to carry the boats up to the clift tops and down below the falls, and we haven't rations for that."

"Nor strength, John. You don't carry the boats nor do you row them. We're starving and weak. We're not making maps anymore, nor taking altitudes. We can do nothing worthwhile anymore. The trip's over. We can leave the river here, and we should."

Major had never paid much attention to what Oramel said, so I was surprised when he asked, "How would we get out of here?"

"Up that little canyon, follow the creek as far as it goes, then up one of the two side canyons. We're in Mormon country, there's bound to be a settlement we can reach."

Talking over plans in front of the men wasn't Major's way, so I wasn't surprised when he said, "We'll talk about it later."

When the moon rose and the stars, Major took Jack down to the little beach with the sextant to try to determine our position. What Oramel had said was true; they hadn't been doing anything about the maps except by dead reckoning for some days. The moon had waned and then waxed some since the eclipse, and was then about half full. I watched it playing on the surface of the river, like it was beckoning me to come play too. But I'd come to a distrust in nature after the way the river had treated us. Where it shone directly in front of me the river was placid as a puddle, but thirty feet beyond it was a raging Niagara. The moon shone brilliant white on the boiling foam and made a lunar rainbow in the spray. A man without a need to travel it would call the river beautiful.

I'd spread my blanket at the edge of the beach, just beyond where the moon shone white on the sand, but I couldn't sleep. I sat up watching the moon on the water, watching Jack and Major with the sextant. When they seemed to agree on something, the fix of a planet, most likely, Jack went off to where he'd made a place to sleep, a little beyond me. The moonlight had crept up to my blanket and Major, seeing I was awake and sitting up, called to me, "Sergeant, come here, I need you."

I went down the few strides to where he was trying to lay out his plots on a paper on the sand. The moon was moving over the opposite clift and he was losing his light, so I made up a little pile of mesquite and fetched a brand from the dying campfire, where Walter was sitting and singing by himself, *Away, den away, for I can't stay any longer....*

I kept the fire up enough to let Major do his plotting, but not so much it might keep the other men awake, though they slept like the dead. Walter came by and said goodnight to his brother then spread his blanket out between mine and Jack's. Major sent me to wake Oramel, who wasn't asleep either. His brother next to him was sawing off a good stick of lumber in his sleep and I thought we should ask him to shape it into an oar. I expected Major to dismiss me, but I guess he needed the light, so he acted as though I wasn't there. He showed Oramel the plot, said we were only forty-five land miles from the Rio Virgen, but it would be seventy or eighty miles by river. Oramel said, "It's the next half mile I'm worried about, John, and the unknown rapids after that. I'd no more plunge into that maelstrom than I'd jump off that clift."

"There are unknowns either way, Oramel, an unknown desert or an unknown river."

"Between Scylla and Charybdis," Oramel said, and I guess he meant we were between a rock and a hard place.

"It's a toss-up, Oramel, six of one, half dozen of another. The party should stick together."

"Then we should all walk out, John. We've done more than any man expected us to, we've been places no white man has ever been, we've mapped an unknown river for nearly a thousand miles. We shouldn't throw success away by plunging into unknown dangers. There's a tide in the affairs of men, John. Take it here at the flood. Save ourselves and what we've got instead of risking losing all in the river."

Since Oramel had lost a few things in the river himself, I expected Major to remind him of that, but he said, "I'll sleep on it, Oramel, and you do the same."

I thought to myself that Howland had it backwards, the tide was below, not out on the desert, but nobody asked me. He was right about Major's mission though, the river's "portrait" hadn't been drawn since the last barometer broke, above Silver Creek, so if Major was willing to abandon the trip at Disaster Falls for want of barometers, he might agree to do it here. It bothered me some as I'd decided to take my chances with the river, see the trip out, though the river was treating us cruelly.

Oramel went off to his blanket and as Major didn't seem to need the light, I went to mine. I didn't drop off to sleep as I wanted to, and I suspect Oramel lay awake as well. I didn't have to suspicion about Major, for I could see him walking back and forth on the little beach, like a prisoner pacing his cell. It seemed to me if he'd made up his mind, he wouldn't be pacing, so I worried he might end up agreeing to take the party off the river, just to keep us all together, it being "six of one." Or he might let the party split, because some of us had talked this thing over with Oramel earlier, and I knew he and Dunn and maybe Seneca were determined to leave the party. In truth, Major was the last to know, along with Walter, of course, who wouldn't have known what to do with that intelligence anyway. The third choice of us all going down the river didn't figure, seeing Oramel's mindset, yet I hoped Major could find a way to move him.

It was decidedly the darkest day of the trip; even the moon was sliding away over the clift, but I didn't despair. I made up my mind to be one to try to run the river rather than take to the mountains, even if Major walked out. I was sure that Billy and Andy would come too, they being "young and foolish," as the poet said. Walter, of course, would stick with his brother, whatever he decided, and I guessed Jack would too, they being that close. So it would be a split party no matter how you looked at it; just how it would split I'd know in the morning.

I told myself, "'Tis darkest just before the day," and I was sure our day was about to dawn. Then I began to sing Frank's song to myself:

> *Ply, ply the oars and pull away,*
> *Tomorrow may shine with brighter light*

I must have dozed off while I was still puzzling over whether I'd got the words right, but I'm sure it wasn't long before I woke up. When I opened my eyes I was looking up to a sky so full of stars there was scarcely room for the dark. It was but a slit above the canyon, preening itself with the river as a mirror.

What woke me was I heard Walter wake with a snort, the way he always did, though sometimes it was a yell. I looked over to see was he coming my way and I could see Major leaning over him, sort of half whispering something. My experience was Walter didn't know how to whisper, and he said, "I'll go down the river with ye, Wes, I surely will," his voice filling the space between us as rainwater fills a gully. I wondered did it occur to Major he was testing his decision with a near madman.

Then Major woke Billy and Andy, who were nearby, and then Jack and then he came to my blanket. I was lying on my back with the blanket pulled up to my chin, pretending to be asleep. Major's figure looming over me seemed gigantic, even blocking out the sky. "Sergeant Bradley, I need your help."

"Again!" was the word came to mind. Major should have known he didn't have to ask, but there were many things he didn't know about the men. He said, "I want you to go down the river with me, please. I need my best boatman." I couldn't see his face but his tone of voice was one I'd not heard before, as I'd never heard him say "please." That made twice in one night he said he needed me. He was acting different, but I wouldn't have called him a changed man.

I guess I was put out that he'd asked near everyone else before he'd asked me, then I remembered whose advice he'd asked first and figured he was working his way up the ladder of sanity. "You can count on me, Major," I told him, and he straightened up so I could see the sky again.

Breakfast the next morning was solemn as a funeral, with two sets of mourners. The Howland brothers and Bill Dunn were together on one side of the low fire with Major and his brother and Jack on the other side, the rest of us wedged between. There was no sound save the river pounding away down at the falls, threatening or beckoning, take your pick, and a few crows urging us to get on so they could scavenge the remains of our breakfast. Thing was, there wouldn't be any. Billy Rhoads had baked up a quarter of the remaining flour, lumpy and sour, into something resembling biscuits, near hard as a rock. That and coffee was it, and we weren't about to leave even a crumb for the crows.

We stared into our coffee, served out in bailing cans, one can for two men, and gnawed at the biscuits in silence. Then Jack said to Billy, "Missouri, this here biscuit is as hard as a whore's heart."

Billy said, "Shucks, ain't nothing missing but air. Just you take a deep breath afore you bite into it." It was a good comeback all right, but nobody laughed, the mood we were in.

Finally, Major called across the fire to Oramel, "Captain Howland, are you still determined to leave the river and walk out?" I'd never heard him call Oramel "Captain" before, so there was something different between them.

"I am, Major, and if you're wise, you'll come along." He said it as though the captain intended to lead the major.

There was a pause as long as your arm when only the crows' nattering and the river's roar passed around us, and nothing moving save a hawk high up, or could be it was an eagle or a buzzard. Then Major said, very slow, like he'd memorized a speech, and I guess he had, "If you're persuaded, you're persuaded, but I'm going on. For years I've wanted to come down this river, and I'm not going to stop now that we're so near the end. We've come nearly a thousand miles and I calculate it's only forty-five miles to the mouth of the Rio Virgen, as the crow flies."

"Too bad we're not crows, John. It's suicide to go into those rapids. I've never seen the like of 'em in the whole thousand miles. They chill me to the very marrow of my bones."

Then Jack put in his two cents' worth to try and turn Oramel's thoughts around, "Lookee here, Oramel, we've only got to carry the boats over that big reef, then lower 'em on lines over the falls, row hard across into that little chute..." but his voice trailed off like a canyon wren's song, and you could see his heart wasn't in it, that he thought Oramel might have the better case.

"You might get the two big boats over, Jack, but the little one's sprung and leaking like a sieve. And that's not the half of it. There's likely a worse rapid beyond. The river runs due west right here, but yesterday I could see from the clift top that it turns south in a few miles, into that hellish black granite again. We've seen what that means, a fast river, narrow, steep walls, not even a beach to land on. If we don't walk out here, we mayn't get another chance."

He'd said what was in the minds of all of us, I'm sure, for we'd seen enough of the hard, unforgiving black clifts to know he was right. It seemed every time we thought we'd routed the river, it came at us again from another quarter, outflanked us and sent us into retreat.

"Let's just say you're right about that, Oramel, but I know this country," Major told him, "You'll have canyons to get around, and I calculate you'll have a walk of a good seventy, eighty miles over desert and rocks. You can take a fair share of our food, but you'll have no water. You don't even have canteens."

"It's been raining a lot lately, John. I'm satisfied I'll find water in holes. And if I can have a rifle, you can keep your food. Dried apples and thirst are sorry companions."

"You're welcome to the rifle, Oramel, and Billy will bake you up some biscuits." But Howland said he'd rather not have the weight, and I can't say I blamed him.

"What about your brother and Dunn?"

"They can speak for themselves," and he turned to his brother.

Seneca was for staying, "We've come this far, O.G., and we're almost there. Let's see it through." But Oramel said, "I'm walking out, Seneca."

"Then I'll go with my brother, Major."

"What about you, Dunn?"

If Bill Dunn had any thoughts of staying, Major's addressing him that way took them away, and all the pent-up wrath he must have felt for Major came out in his answer.

"I won't go another yard with ye, you one-armed son-of-a-bitch."

Before we said goodbye, Seneca told me he hadn't expected the party to split, that Oramel thought he had persuaded Major that he was exposing men unnecessarily to danger and that Major had agreed to leave the river. Seneca said he believed that his brother would have stayed if he hadn't been along, and that was why he asked Oramel at breakfast to stay with the river, though he, too, thought it was the more dangerous course.

Except between the Powell brothers and Dunn, there was good feeling for the boys who were leaving, and none of us thought they were deserting or had made a bad choice, men's minds treating circumstances as they see them, some weighing one thing, some another. But I'd been born to water, not fire, and I'd not of risked the desert if there was an abyss ahead on the river. If it was ordained that the river be the victor, so be it, but I would not surrender without a fight.

We left all the instruments, fossils, potsherds, threadbare tents, ponchos, Jack's animal traps and a lot of ammunition on the rocks, to lighten our loads to the bare minimum. Major gave the Howlands a rifle each and Dunn chose a shotgun. Oramel took a duplicate set of the scientific measurements and the maps, such as they were, and Jack gave him his watch to give to his sister, Mrs. Byers, in case he didn't make it back. I thought, if Jack thinks the river is safer, why doesn't he keep the watch? Then I remembered his eyes when we first saw those rapids.

As men in war are commanded to hold a position to the last man, we were determined to run the rapid or perish in the attempt. I didn't let my thoughts go beyond the next rapid, as Howland's had, for that way lay all the terrors of man's imagination.

We tied the little boat to the shore as she was leaking badly at the bow from the broken cutwater, and we deemed her unseaworthy. Major said, "I hate to leave my *Emma Dean*."

The three boys who were leaving helped us lift the two heavy boats over the reef, which we never could have done without them. There were long handshakes all around and not a few tears, though we pretended different, for they were as fine fellows as ever it was my good fortune to meet.

Bill Dunn was saying goodbye to Jack, his longtime trapping partner, and I couldn't help overhearing Bill say, "It's been a long time."

Jack nodded, "Yep, a long time." He added, "Is this it, then?"

"I reckon," Bill said and turned away rubbing his eyes like he'd caught a speck of dust.

We looked down at the raging, twisting, river, at the rocks and falls, and Billy Rhoads said, "If Hell was a wet place, this would be it." Yet we were willing to descend into that Hell. If you'd asked any one of us to do that when we first saw the falls, we'd have declined the honor, so something had happened in the way we looked at it, and it was this: If you look at a fearsome thing long enough, it starts to lose its power over you. You may even find a sort of comfort in it, or at least fascination or wonder. How else could army surgeons hack away around the clock amid the screams of the men and the stench of wounds and putrefying flesh, and how else could men confined in Confederate prisons survive starvation, brutality, wet and cold? And how else could men stand to go into battle time and again, but they'd seen it before. And we'd seen rapids before, if none like this.

Since we had to wade in swift water for the lining, Major wanted us to tie ourselves together with ropes, so if a man slipped he wouldn't be carried away by the river. I said, "I think not, Major. If one of the boats gets away, it'll take us all down with it."

"You're right, Sergeant," Major said, and I was as surprised he took my advice as I was I gave it.

The Howlands and Dunn climbed a crag to watch while we waded and lowered the boats on ropes over the first fall into a little cove, maybe twenty feet wide and thirty feet long, a projecting rock protecting it from the river rushing by just outside of the cove's entrance. I thought Major would come with me and Walter in the *Maid*, but he climbed into *Sister* with Billy and Andy. It seemed strange that he would trust his life to the two youngest among us, one just a boy, neither able to handle an oar when we began the trip. He was full of surprises of a sudden.

Jack shoved *Sister* off but when she reached the entrance to the cove, the tide pushed her back in. She came back to Jack, as if she was a reluctant colt being turned out of the barn. Jack said, "If you was a filly I'd give you a swat on the rump," and he slung *Sister* out again with more muscle.

Andy was at the forward oars and Billy was at the sweep, for there was more need for maneuver than power, which the river supplied in plenty. *Sister* nosed out of the little protected cove, and the current caught her, snatched her bow, turned her downstream, nearly tore the sweep oar from Billy's hands, carried the boat racing down along the right side, threatening to smash her into the clift. Billy pressed the sweep oar out to port and managed to steer her away, over to the little chute, where he turned her to the right, and she wiggled eel-like into it, plunging through boiling foam toward the big sloping rock. The boat was filling and surely Billy could not see beyond her bow for the spray that burst in front of her, but he caught the backwash off the rock and got her bow turned left acrost the stream, everything just as Major had planned.

I felt a pain in my chest and realized I'd been holding my breath, and I saw Jack wiggling his torso like he was *Sister* himself. When *Sister* got to the fall Billy was supposed to turn her bow downstream, and we could see him working the big scull oar and Andy the forward pair, trying to turn her. *Sister* seemed to have a mind of her own and started over the fall sideways.

You couldn't think of a worse way, for they were destined to be spilled out of the boat, over the fall and into the pool below, with the boat coming down right on top of them. My heart left its usual place as I watched Billy tugging at the sweep oar, pressing it out to the starboard side, which was wrong of course, the water running faster than the boat, but Billy had but little experience with the sweep, most of his time being spent on the aft oars, Oramel doing the steering. The end of the long oar snagged on a rock at the head of the falls just as *Sister* started over, and I thought Billy would be pulled out of the boat if he didn't let go. Maybe he thought that was better than staying in, or maybe he didn't think at all, but he pressed the oar out until his arms gave out, then he hugged it to his chest and laid his whole body into it and held it firm until the boat began to turn, then the oar snapped with a crack like a rifle shot. Still hugging half the oar Billy was flung on top of the rear compartment and was headed over the stern when Major let go the gunwale and caught him by the ankle as they went into the fall. The halfway turn Billy had accomplished was enough to head *Sister* somewhat downstream, and she rocked over the fall, as the bear waddles I suppose, Major and Billy loose in the rear, Andy clutching his oars like he was manning a battle station. Halfway down, her stern struck a rock on the right side and that completed the turn, so she dove straight into the pool below like she was one of those submarines from the war. The hollow bow popped her up again like a bottle, and we saw that all the men were safe, though tangled in a heap in the bow and the boat swamped.

"Well done, Jack," I said, for he had twisted and writhed with *Sister's* every movement. First time I'd caught him without words, but the fear was still in his eyes. I don't know what he saw in mine, but I hope it was confidence, for I thought I knew how to get through easier. I told myself it wasn't hubris that took hold of me then, but just that I had a better plan than Major's. I thought to pray, but the words wouldn't come. All I could think of was a child's prayer Lucy had taught me, "Now I lay me down to rest, like a birdie in the nest. If I should die before I wake, I pray the Lord my soul to take." It didn't suit. No prayer did or could. I hadn't prayed for as long as we hadn't mapped, and I wasn't sure I'd ever pray again, for I did not have Job's forbearance.

We had no one to push us off so Jack and Walter rowed hard and we came out of the little cove well enough. We entered the boiling tide with all the courage we could muster. I steered us down the right side as near to the clift as I dast, swung her bow half-left to the middle of the little chute, twisted into it and shot along toward the big sloping rock. Instead of letting the wave catch the *Maid's* bow as it had *Sister's,* I steered into it so the backwash off the rock caught us amidships and thrust us over broadside in the direction of the falls. My idea was we would already be headed downstream and wouldn't have to turn as *Sister* had. But I hadn't figured on the quantity of water nor the ferocity of the wave, and we were half swamped, the billows so great that from then on we could only hang on and hope for the best, or pray if so minded. By force of prayer or by good fortune, the wave carried us to where we wanted to descend and the fall took us from there. To say I remember the experience would be false; I only remember holding to the boat and feeling I was under water and about to drown. Then suddenly we were in the still pool at the bottom, right side up and filled with water, of course, but not even an oar lost.

We got the boats to shore, and when we'd stopped congratulating ourselves, we looked up to see the three boys standing on that crag watching us. Howland's long beard was blowing in the wind, and I thought again he could be King Lear. It only wanted rain and lightning.

I heard a crack, like my thought came true, but it was only a rifle shot. Major thought that if we fired off our rifles and motioned them to follow they might take the *Emma Dean* and come after. But I wouldn't have taken the disabled little boat on the Merrimac, let alone through that maelstrom. We'd never had such a rapid before, and I knew Howland and Dunn wouldn't essay it, though Seneca might have tried it in a sound boat. It was just possible they could walk around and join us below, but remembering what Oramel said about this being maybe the last chance to walk out and Dunn's last comment to Major, I knew that wouldn't happen either. What's Dunn is done.

A few shots were fired, Andy welcoming any opportunity to waste ammunition, and we waved our hats, the three of us still had them, but the boys just motioned us on, so we got into the boats again and started off. I looked back to see the three boys silhouetted against the sky. As we moved away and they grew smaller, and ever smaller in the distance, they did not move and could have been taken for crags themselves, part of the rock, one with the land.

The next fall was steep but straight, nothing to what we'd just come through and we easily dropped into the eddy below where we paused to catch our breath and bail our nearly sunken boats.

Major asked what we should call the place we'd come through. Jack nominated "Split-Party Falls", but I said that sounded a bit harsh and suggested "Separation Rapid." Major said that would do nicely, first time he didn't name a place himself.

We got a good little run over an almost continuous rapid until after "dinner" when we came to some more lava and a tremendous rapid, the one Howland feared we would come on. Major scouted on the left and concluded we couldn't let down there, so we crossed to the right and he climbed the clift to a shelf and walked downstream a ways. Nobody went with him as we were saving our strength for the river. When he came back he said we could let down by standing on the shelf and walking the boats down on the end of a line made fast to their bows.

It was a pretty high shelf, but we had a hundred and twenty feet of rope for each boat, so it looked all right to try it. I made the line fast to the *Maid's* bow then got in her and waited while the men took the rope to the ledge, then I shoved off. For a while it worked fine, me fending off the clift with one of the small oars and the men inching downstream along the shelf, holding the line. But the shelf got higher and the tide got stronger as I neared the head of the rapid. The boat's forward movement stopped all of a sudden, and I guessed they'd run out of rope on the ledge, for it looked to be well over a hundred feet high. Where they held me was just on the point of a crag where the tide pushed out strongest from the clift. Four feet more and I could have got in around the crag in quiet water and held the *Maid* steady, but as it was she would shear out into the tide then come in with terrible force against the rocks, then shear out again for another try at breaking up and drowning me. I couldn't make the men hear and they couldn't see me because I was under the lip of the shelf. It came to doing something or having the *Maid* dashed to pieces against the rock.

I got out my sheath knife to cut the rope, but I hoped relief would come first as they must have run for another line. One look at the foaming cataract below told me I didn't want to run it, and that thought kept me from cutting the rope. Still I had sufficient sense to look out the best channel should I have to cut loose. After what seemed like they'd gone to Green River City for the rope, and I was all the while suffering the tortures of the rack, the boat gave a furious shoot out into the breakers, the cutwater tore loose, and the rope flew thirty feet in the air, cutwater and all. The loosed boat dashed out like a war-horse eager for the fray. I didn't think about it but jumped to the stern and fitted the big scull oar into its lock. By pressing it hard to port I was able to get her head downstream just in time to meet the fall. I went straight over and through a swift chute, fastest I'd ever gone. I kept her straight by pressing the steering oar first to one side then to the other. When I'd gotten through the worst of it, I looked back and swung my hat to the boys on the clift in token of "All's well".

The men above went off in all directions, Walter and Jack running along the clift with the ropes, and Major jumping into *Sister* with Andy and Billy. They shot out into those terrible billows. In a trice, *Sister* got turned around stern foremost and went crashing through the rocks. They were washed into the chute and came down it backwards. When she hit the wave tail at the bottom of the fall, her stern plunged into it and she filled with water. Another wave caught her and rolled her over, spilling the men into the river.

As neither Billy nor Andy was a swimmer and Major a one-armed man, this was for me the most frightening moment on the river. They managed to catch hold of *Sister,* but her gunwales being under water they were having trouble clinging to her. I was watching this from an eddy where I was bailing the *Maid.* I jumped to fit the rowing oars, but when it looked like they would be swept by me, I used the big sweep oar to set my boat into the tide again. *Sister* was moving slow, being waterlogged, so I managed to cut across her path. Both boats were moving sideways, our bows pointing to the left side of the river where there was another rapid, so I had to turn them full around to get back to the eddy on the right. Billy scrambled into the *Maid,* leaving Andy to deal with Major, who was having trouble holding on to the wet hull with his one hand. *Sister* being snug up against the *Maid,* Bill could fit only one oar, but with him backing water with it and me steering with the sweep, we got the boats turned around and into the eddy. It was shallow enough so we could right *Sister* and, nobody the worse for wear except the wetting. We bailed both boats and waited for Jack and Major's brother.

We could see the two of them inching along the shelf to the top of the fall, a quarter mile away and a little beyond, but then they didn't move further. The walls were but little broken down there and that most steeply, so it looked like the men couldn't climb down. Then they started back along the shelf, and disappeared. Major hadn't scouted far enough along the shelf to know if there was a way down at the end, so it seemed they'd need to find a way around.

We were in black basalt again, and it wasn't broken down in many places, just worn away, except where the limestone or red granite beneath came to the fore and crumbled. We didn't see any way downstream where they could improve their chances, if they chose to climb to the top and walk around. We waited maybe a half hour, but it seemed like a day, Major pacing again like he'd done the night before on the little beach. I could guess what went through his mind just then: he'd never done a reckless thing the whole trip, maybe since his artillery attack at Shiloh, but he'd jumped in a boat with two greenhorn youngsters to run a rapid he'd already figured couldn't be run, and he'd left his brother and his tent-mate on a cliff without knowing if there was a way down to us. He'd done a brave and reckless thing.

We lit a fire, sat around it drying out and waited. It wasn't very long before the boys figured it out, as I guessed they would. They had the two lengths of rope they'd planned to use to let the *Maid* down and all they had to do was put them to use. With one end made fast to a rock on the ledge, they eased their way down the broken rock fall backwards, holding the rope and pressing their feet to the rocks, and they got down all right with only the loss of the ropes. I could have shown them how to fasten the line with a hitch they could release from below, but they knew only a girth hitch, being more used to mules than boats. Without ropes there would be no more lining: Every cloud has a silver lining. They'd brought the *Maid's* torn out cutwater but I didn't need it; the stempost was double on the big boats, and she wasn't even leaking.

Major said nothing gave him more joy than when he saw me swing my hat, for they all believed I had gone to the "Happy Hunting Grounds". He and I agreed totally for once: that adventure stood as "A. No. 1" of the trip. I'd made one mistake, though: when I swung my hat to tell them I was all right, my discharge papers flew out, and the river claimed them. Major said, "Except for the cutwater and the oar Billy broke, there was no damage to man nor boat." At that Billy got up and just stood there by the fire, sort of looking down at Major. Then, slowly, he untied the knot in his shirttails where they were tied between his legs We watched as he unbuttoned his shirt in the most deliberate fashion and then opened it wide. We saw a red and blue bruise running from his right nipple to his opposite hip, just exactly the shape of the steering oar that he broke at Separation Rapid.

August 29th was Sunday but I felt justified in running, for we were on the edge of starvation. I couldn't look at Walter straight on, for it seemed to me he must resemble the near-skeleton that came out of Sorghum prison. I was oddly pleased that the river was muddy, for if it was a looking glass, I'd have passed myself a penny as a poor beggar. The boys who left had refused flour or biscuits, because they "didn't want the weight," Howland had said, but I was sure it was pride, or concern for those going down the river, that made him refuse. So our provisions had expanded to six days supply for the six of us, instead of four days for nine men. Jack said it was "a miracle but not quite up to the loaves and the fishes."

We were much encouraged by the constant improvement in the look of the country, for "the walls came tumbling down," the clifts declined in altitude, the country opened up, and the sun began to stream in. We ran all the rapids we came to without even pausing to look at them, for we had no time to waste. They grew less as we advanced, and what we'd called a rapid at the beginning of the trip had become but a riffle to us. I only regretted that the three boys who left us weren't with us to share our joy and triumph. But the river had teased us cruelly before, and I had a suspicion it wasn't done with us yet.

We ran out of the black granite the next day, and that made me believe the river had run out of tricks. But it came up with one more I hadn't figured on: it turned northwest, and we wanted west, or even west-southwest. Then it turned due north. If it turned again, we'd be headed back to Green River City and back into the granite. Jack told Major if the river made another turn or two in the same direction, we'd be the first to chart a circular river, "A full three hundred sixty degrees, Professor." When we stopped for the day we'd made forty two miles, no more fractions with Oramel gone.

We talked 'til midnight, mostly worrying about the three boys who'd left, because the northward course of the river meant they'd have to go easterly to get around the lateral canyons, and that could add considerable miles to their trip. More than that, we wondered if they were finding water, or even if they'd been able to climb to the top, side canyons often being box canyons, leading to a dead-end. Andy had been an Indian fighter so it was natural he should ask about a danger from that quarter, which nobody had thought about up 'til then. Major and Jack talked it over some, then agreed that the Indians there would most likely be friendly farmers and gatherers and not warriors.

Major announced that the big canyon we'd just come through was the "Grand Canyon," and we would keep that name, as "befitting its size and grandeur." I looked over at Jack but he just bowed his head. He'd have to be satisfied with "Sumner's Amphitheatre". Later he complained, "There's lots of 'grand' canyons. It's a poor name and may confuse the stranger."

THE BRECKENBRIDGE SENTINEL

AUGUST 30, 1869.

COLONEL ADAMS REPORTS.

As he promised, Colonel Adams has sent us a summary of his report to the Secretary of War concerning his abbreviated expedition in search of a water route to the Gulf of California with nine local men. The story has been reported to our readers as members of the party returned to Breckenbridge with news. Suffice it to say that the expedition was forced to terminate after traveling 95 miles on the Blue and Grand Rivers and losing all four boats and nearly all their provisions and supplies. We recite here verbatim Colonel Adams' reflections on the journey.

"I am fully satisfied that we had come over the worst part of our rout in 95 miles we had descended about 4500 feet. The vallies were open up river, the mountains bec smooth the pine and cedar larger everything indic that a prosperous passage was ahead of us had we been in a position to have gone on. Three years before as I stated in my Report to the Sec of War, I looked up the Colorado River from a point 650 miles from its mouth and could then see a vally exten 75 miles to the NE. I could now (on Aug 13) look to the SW & almost see the narrow gap which divided us."

We asked some of the members of the expedition why they had reported to us a somewhat different conclusion. We quote one of them, "My name is 'Waddle', not 'twaddle'!"

We were off at sunrise, rowed twenty six miles, hard labor on a flat river, so we almost regretted the rocks and rapids being gone. We were passing through low canyons and weren't satisfied we were yet out of prison, for we'd been told there was flat country before the Rio Virgen and Callville. We passed some clifts we thought might be called "Grand Wash" on the Army map, so had hope we were in known territory. The river had settled on a northwesterly direction, then did another little dance all the way round to the south-south-west, the way we wanted to go.

When we launched again after dinner, such as it was, the river turned again, first west then, in a long loop, north-northwest, until we felt we were in a giant whirlpool. Then we followed a sudden veer to the west, the country opened up as if a curtain had been raised and, in front of us, as if by a conjurer's trick, there appeared three men in the river with a seine and a boy on the bank building a sand castle.

They were Mormons, Joseph Asa and his two sons, sent to start an encampment at the mouth of the Rio Virgen. Mr. Asa said he'd been asked to look out for us, which surprised us no end until he told us we'd been reported drowned and they were looking for broken boats or, "something worse." They immediately took us to their one room cabin and gave us fish and squash and whatever else they had to hand. We sat on the dirt floor and ate like starved dogs, threw down our blankets, slept and ate again, slept and ate some more.

That evening Billy spread out the provisions we had left: ten pounds of mouldy flour, fifteen pounds of dried apples and seventy or eighty pounds of coffee. Major could probably have lived on that coffee for another month or two, but the rest of us were about played out.

One of the three men at the Mormon camp was a Paiute Indian, and Mr. Asa sent him up to St. Thomas, a Mormon settlement about twenty miles away, to get some more provisions and our mail, as none of us had had a letter for three and a half months. I wrote a line and sent it to Lucy to assure Mother that I was all right, but I was so intoxicated with joy at getting through so soon and so well that I don't know what I wrote to her.

That night we sat and talked until the morning star could be seen. We again devoted most of our conversation to the three boys who had left us at Separation Rapid. We all felt we had made the right choice to stay on the river, though my experience in the next rapid, where I lost the cutwater, gave me some doubts at the time. I told Major what I'd thought at Separation Rapid when Howland talked about the flood tide, that he'd got it backwards.

"In more ways than one, Sergeant. It goes like this:

> *'There is a tide in the affairs of men,*
> *Which, taken at the flood, leads on to fortune;*
> *Omitted, all the voyage of their life is bound*
> *in shallows and in miseries.*
> *On such a full sea are we now afloat;*
> *And we must take the current when it serves,*
> *Or lose our ventures.'*

"Oramel knew that. He was trying to turn the meaning around just as he was trying to turn the party from the river."

"He was afraid to run it," Andy said.

"Don't you believe it," Major said, and Jack agreed, "I'd never seen fear in Oramel in all the years I've known him. He had another reason for leaving."

I thought back to what Seneca had told me, that Oramel always took care of him and told the boys about it.

"It rings true," Jack said, "he thought he was protecting Seneca, taking him off the river."

"Then why did he tell Seneca to make up his own mind?" Andy asked.

Jack said, "He knew Seneca would choose to stay with him, no doubt of that."

But Andy stuck to his guns, "I think he was afraid." We were too tired to argue the point.

As I was drifting to sleep, I heard Major singing:

> *I will sing you a song of that beautiful land...*

Yes, it was beautiful where we were, what with a sunset you could watch all the way down, and now the stars, crisp in the dark. We'd had just as good, I'm sure, back on the river, but beauty is different on a full belly.

The next evening around sunset a Mormon bishop named Leithead arrived in a wagon with our mail and some fresh flour and melons. He embraced Major, treated him like a long lost brother or maybe a prodigal son. "My dear Major Powell, we had heard that you were lost," the bishop said, "but you're here, and you've conquered the river."

"Yes," Major said, "I made it. The river is mine."

"And he can have it," Billy muttered.

Again we sat up most of the night and talked, all hungry for news of the outside world. The bishop told us how we'd been declared drowned numerous times in numerous places and that such was the true fate of the Hook expedition and nearly that of an attempt by Sam Adams, the man Major sent about his business at Green River City.

One of the papers the bishop brought was the *Rocky Mountain News,* where Howland used to work. It had a full account of how a man named Risdon had claimed to be with the party and was the only one wasn't drowned. The paper recited all his lies and told how he made up names for twenty people he said were in the crew, that we were all in a twenty five foot long birch "yawl" built by an Indian named "Chick-a-wa-nee" who was along, etc. Risdon told some whoppers would make Jack blush. The paper set out many of them. All these were swallowed hook, line and sinker by Governor Palmer of Illinois, and spread all over the country. The best thing about the paper was what the editor wrote:

TO OUR READERS, FROM THE EDITOR.

———

The articles in this and earlier editions of The News recite the despicable lies told by one of the most scurrilous rascals ever to appear on God's green earth. He is by name, John Risdon, proclaiming no less than a hundred lies concerning the voyage of Major John Wesley Powell down the Green River. Among the lies are: pretense at being among the Powell party, being the only survivor thereof, witnessing the demise of Major Powell and his entire crew in a whirlpool, placing the number of the party at double its actual number, stating the date of the imagined tragedy to be two weeks before the party began its voyage and claiming himself to be a captain (of what he does not say). If he is the captain of any company, it is the Liar's Brigade, and he is a deserter from the Battalion of Truth, not even a human being and if Governor Palmer of Illinois has a compassionate bone in his body he will have Risdon strung up on the nearest tree and left for the crows to peck at for the crime of causing anguish and concern among the relatives and loved ones of Major Powell and his brave band and for assaulting Fact with a broad axe and murdering same.

The bishop offered to carry Major and his brother to St. Thomas, where they could get transportation to Salt Lake City, so Major decided to end the trip there at the mouth of the Rio Virgen. He said the river had been explored from that place to the Gulf of California and that further exploration "would not add to the store of human knowledge".

Jack told us he'd asked Major for wages and for payment of beaver traps that had been lost. Major said the traps were Jack's loss and he'd have to send the wages later because he had lost three hundred dollars in the river. Jack said later, "I lost my temper, having nothing else to lose," but there was nothing he could do. You can't get blood from a stone.

In the morning we wrote out some letters for Major to post. Andy told me he'd taken my advice, was going to learn writing same as he'd learned rowing, knowing little about it when we started and running every rapid at the end. He started with a letter to his brother:

> *Dear Brother:*
>
> *It is with the greatest pleasure that I once more sit down to write to you that I am still alive and well after coming through a hard and perilous voyage. I turned up al rite at last. We have been reported all drowned by some lying scoundrel by the name of John Risdon from Illinois and he reported he was the last survivor of the party. There was no such man ever was with the party. Who ever he is he is a liar and a scoundrel and it wont do for him to let any of us see him.*
>
> *We came through in from Grene river City in ninety seven days to the Rio Virgen. The Major is going to leave us here with his brother Walter. Of the 10 men that started from Grene river only six came through. Just before we came out of the canyon three of the men left us on the head of the rapids. They were afraid to run it so they left us in a bad place. We were then short of hands and we had to abandon the Major's boat. The name of it was the "Emma Deene." Then we still had one left for each three men. The first boat that run the*

*rapid was the "Sister" as we called her. It is the boat that
Bill Rhoads and I started from Greene river with.
The Major was in the boat with us. We ran the rapid all right
and gave a loud cheer. Next came the "Maid of the Canyon"
named by J.Y. Bradley and the Major's brother. Now I will
give you the names of all the boats. "The No Name" wrecked
on the Greene river, the "Emma Deene" abandoned in the
canyon, the "Maid of the Canyon" and "Kitty Clyde's Sister"
that was given to Bill Rhoads and me. The other was given
to Bradley and Sumnar.*

*Write to me at Fort Yuma, California. Must close.
Give my respects to all. Write soon.*

*Yours till death
Andrew Hall*

I told him it was a fine letter and he'd soon be a scholar, but my
first initial was "G", not "J". He said, "But they call you 'Jawge'." He
had a point, but I could see it was a going to be a while before he was
running rapids with his pencil.

As Andy wrote, Major gave the two boats to the four of us that were left, and we set out to complete the trip to the Gulf of California, travel the river from one known end to the other, which no man, white or red, had ever done before, and certainly would never do again. Our leave-taking with Major was brief and friendly but mine was the only handshaking with Walter. Jack summed up the feeling most had for Major's brother when he said, "He was about as worthless a piece of furniture as you'd come across in a day's travel." But he was a good rower and had given me no trouble if you didn't mind the prayers.

Andy and Billy in *Sister* and Jack and me in the *Maid,* we floated easy on flat water, no rapids, no rocks, no clifts, and to tell the truth, I didn't miss them. For much of the journey I thought I would like to run every rapid, show the river that we could beat it, that the danger to life was but trifling. Maybe it was hubris, as Howland called it when he said that man could press too far and the gods would punish him. I didn't know about that, but it did seem that every time we thought we'd come through the worst of it, the river came up with something worse, so I thought the river had been testing us.

The river was wide and quiet, so the boats floated side by side, the men chaffing back and forth. Jack said, "This is a capacious boat, George. Not like being all cramped up in the little one."

I said, "There's something I've been meaning to ask you, Jack. Why do you always call her 'the little boat' or 'the pilot boat', instead of *Emma Dean?*"

"Shucks," he said, "If you knew the Major's wife as I did, you wouldn't have to ask. I was afraid if I called her, she'd come."

Andy burst out with another of his "classic" songs in a voice would tear the bark off a tree, had there been any in sight:

> *They were floatin down the mizzen*
> *They both were in the stern*
> *She had ahold of hisn*
> *And he had ahold of hern*

Billy told him to shut up or he'd drown him.

We campt at Black Canyon, Billy and Andy cooked up some fish we'd taken along, and we set ourselves to talking about the trip. We'd about exhausted the subject of the three boys who had left and we started on the Mormons and how they treated us like long lost brothers and took care of us so well, even to providing the fish we were eating.

Jack said he'd always wondered if their religion was the reason they were immune to snake venom. I bit, "What do you mean?"

"They didn't have a drop of snake medicine, and I'm told they don't take it at all."

We agreed snakes were a serious threat and we'd better lay in some medicine first chance we got as we hadn't had any whiskey since Disaster Falls. Finally, when it seemed we could put it off no longer, our talk turned to Major, a subject we'd been circling around the way a dog does before he'll lie down in an unfamiliar place.

One thing we agreed on all around was the way Major treated Oramel and Bill Dunn wasn't fair. Jack said, "Now, it was the accidents the Major didn't like. It was careless of Bill to keep the watch in his pocket when he went to the rock, and maybe Oramel was careless at Disaster Falls, but they were still accidents."

I asked Andy if he still thought Major was a "bully fellow".

He didn't seem comfortable with the question or maybe it was his answer gave him some unease, but finally he said, "Well, the bully part anyway."

Billy said, "I'll say this truthfully about the Major - that no man living was ever thought more of by his men up to the time he wanted to drive Bill Dunn from the party."

No man disagreed, and Jack said, "He had no right to order Bill out."

"Nor to try to drown him," I said, which provoked a lively discussion of whether that was the case, until Andy pointed out that I was the only one to see what happened, the others being downstream and some distance away.

Jack said, "Still, it could have been an accident. And I'll say this, he got us here, not a man lost. The Hook and Adams expeditions came to grief almost before they started. You have to give the Major that. He was more careful than he needed to be at times, maybe, and he didn't treat Howland and Dunn right, but he got us through."

"Half starved," Billy said.

"But safe," Jack said, "He was never reckless."

"Well not until the end," I said, "when he got into Billy's boat."

"Whoa now. Whoa," Billy said, and puckered up his mouth some. "He just wanted to improve his chances of gettin through alive." and Andy said, "Taking the safest course, as always, Sergeant Bradley."

Jack said, "Shucks, it was just that he didn't want to ride with Walter, and who could blame him."

"Didn't want two deaths in the family," Billy added.

When I said, "He saved your life, Billy," we all got quiet, reliving the moment, I guess. Anyway I was. The sight of Major letting go the gunwale with his one hand so he could hold Billy in the boat is with me today.

"He's a bully fellow," Andy said, "you bet," and there was no disagreement.

We came to the old town of Callville and found it deserted, a great disappointment, "I thought it would be our first glimpse of civilization," I said.

"And whiskey," Jack said.

"Same thing," Billy told him.

We camped at the head of Black Canyon, and there we saw the strangest bird of the trip. He was a little brown and grey feller, could have been a fledgling of many birds we knew, but he did the most peculiar thing. He dove into the water and disappeared for about five minutes, then came up *upstream*. He hovered over the water for a few minutes, then did it again, even swimming into the rapids. We were watching the bird's antics and laughing when Jack said, "He's a determined little feller. I wonder what he's called."

Nobody knew and I said, "Everything else on this trip was given a name. Why don't we name him?"

Just then the bird flew out from under a falls. "Nothing stops him," Jack said, "best we call him 'Major.'"

The next morning we were off early for we were anxious to get to civilization. We drifted down to a mining camp which wasn't the place to find it. We had to listen again to the story of James White coming down the river on a raft. Jack told them it was "Plain silly; he was probably a some renegade horse thief that had to leave town between two days and struck the river at Grand Wash."

One of the miners knew White and didn't take too kindly to that remark, so we bought some whiskey and set out the same day, made camp again, then pressed on for two more days. When we reached the army post at Fort Mojave, there was a telegram, and Jack read it out:

Howland brothers and Dunn killed by Indians — Powell

Well that just took the heart out of me, and my spirits sunk lower than a snake's belly. I decided then and there I wasn't going on the river any more. Billy felt the same way, so we sold the *Maid* for twenty-five dollars, spent most of it on new outfits for the four of us and set out to drink up the rest. We didn't need to, though. All the local roughs and cavalrymen kept buying us drinks and slapping us on the back until I feared our new shirts would get worn out.

Then Colonel Stacy, who was in charge of the post, got up on a chair and made a little speech, telling everyone how we'd come through great perils and dangers and calling us "Heroes, who had conquered the 'Great Unknown.'"

But I wasn't so sure. While the men around us were clapping their hands and stomping their feet and whooping and cheering, I looked at Jack and Billy and Andy, saw how their new clothes hung on them like scarecrows dressed, and in my mind's eye I could see those other three boys lying dead in the desert, and thought, maybe the river had won.

ORAMEL and SENECA HOWLAND and WILLIAM DUNN never reached a Mormon settlement. A few days after the party reached the Rio Virgen, the Mormon pioneer, Jacob Hamblin, received word from an Indian runner that three white men had been killed by members of the Shivwit Indian tribe, and that they had come from the river. A newspaper report on the eighth of the September reported that the men had shot an Indian woman and that three Shivwits had then killed the men. Another report had it that the men had been mistaken for three prospectors who had raped one of their women.

Years later a Shivwit Indian named Toab claimed that he had participated in the murders as part of a robbery. Sumner[1] believed that white men had been responsible and suspected that a watch he saw in a white man's possession was the one he had given Howland to take to his sister.[2]

JOHN WESLEY POWELL began a second trip down the same route in 1871 in the company of students and intellectuals, including a brother-in-law. Sumner was invited to join the crew but was prevented by snowstorms from doing so. Powell left the trip twice, once to visit his wife who was expecting their first and only child. He ended the trip at the Kanab Creek well above Separation Rapid. In the process of combining the experiences of both trips as if they had all happened on the first trip, he renamed some of the places. In particular, he changed the name of Silver Creek to Bright Angel Creek, probably to offset the naming of Dirty Devil River.[3]

Powell became one of the towering figures of the West, mapping it as Director of the U.S. Geological Survey, determining water needs, befriending the Indians and learning their languages and customs (for which he was named Director of the Bureau of Ethnology of the Smithsonian Institution). Had Congress heeded his recommendations on the use of land and water, many hapless homesteaders would have been spared the misery and deprivation of drought. He spent much of his career in Washington, D.C., a popular and deservedly famous man. He retired to Maine where he died in 1902.

When he died, his wife EMMA DEAN POWELL was denied a widow's pension by the bureaucracy and had to have a special act of congress passed to obtain it.[4]

ANDREW HALL and JACK SUMNER continued down the river to the tidewaters of the Gulf of California where, in Sumner's words, "Not wishing to locate a ranch there, we stayed only two hours." The river there was largely tidal mudflats and today no longer reaches the Gulf, its waters absorbed by irrigation and other diversions. Sumner and Hall were able to jury rig a sail from a wagon sheet to help propel them back up the river, where they separated.

Sumner died in 1907, bitter about Powell's fame and his own failure to be recognized for his part in the voyage. He was especially angry about Powell's failing to honor their contract to pay wages, complaining that he had spent over a thousand dollars of his own money and had received only $75 for two year's work. Nearly four decades after the river trip, Sumner wrote, "As for myself, I have heard it said, 'Success is a virtue and failure is a crime'. As I shared the blankets with Major J. W. Powell for two years, I believe I knew him – perhaps not. He gave scant credit to any of his men. He was vastly over-estimated as a man. As a scholar and scientist he was worthy of all praise."[5] The gnawing pain of failure over so many years had colored Sumner's recollections, and he took credit for nearly everything that happened on the voyage, from the design of the boats to the naming of many places that had been named by Powell. With unconscious irony, Sumner wrote, in tribute, "Nearly all my companions have passed over the range, and I am still left behind."[6]

Hall died young. He took a post riding shotgun on the mail

stage and was killed in a robbery in 1882 at age 31 or 32. His three killers were apprehended and at least one was hanged in Globe, Arizona.

GEORGE YOUNG BRADLEY spent much of his life in California, but returned to Newburyport to live, and to die, in the home of his beloved sister Lucy. He died in 1885.

FRANK GOODMAN lived out his life near the Uinta Basin, where he had left the party, raising sheep until he was forced out by cattlemen. He died in Vernal, Utah in 1913.[7]

WALTER POWELL tried farming, but his mental problems grew worse and he was unable to carry on any occupation. He ended up in California living with his sister, supported by a disability pension based on mental incompetence. He died in an Army hospital in 1915.

WILLIAM HAWKINS, or Missouri Rhodes, became a successful rancher in Arizona. He lived into his 70's, dying in 1919. He, too, felt some bitterness toward Powell for not sharing the glory. Powell had given Rhodes his life preserver which, in turn, Rhodes donated to the Smithsonian Institution.

SAM ADAMS, after hearing of the conclusion of Powell's river trip, wrote a diatribe in the *Omaha Republican* in which he poo-poohed the accomplishment, claiming he had "ascended and descended [the canyons] several times within the past three years." He spent most of his life trying to compete with Powell in land surveys and seeking compensation from Congress for his (unauthorized) reports. He returned to his home town of Beaver Falls, Pennsylvania where he practiced law and died in 1915 at the age of eighty-seven.

JOHN RISDON's fabrications about the loss of the Powell party were published in newspapers across the country, including the *Rocky Mountain News,* the *Chicago Tribune,* the *Detroit Post* and the *New York Times*. The publicity so garnered and the concomitant concern for a war veteran all across the young nation made Powell a national figure. When he reappeared he was greeted as a hero returned from the dead in every place he visited, and his career was launched. For his part, Risdon was exposed as a liar but one with glib invention, bordering on charm, which disarmed his accusers until the law caught up with him in Lincoln, Illinois where, according to the *Springfield Journal*:

> *John A. Risdon, alias Miller, alias Clark stole a horse from Mr. William Bowman...went a little distance...and stole a blanket, overcoat, quilt and shawl [from J. C. Jones]...He found the Kickapoo [River] too high to cross, and left the horse and proceeded forward on foot to Atlanta where he was captured.*

Notes

[1] Letter to R.B. Stanton ca 1906-07... *Colorado River Controversies*, Stanton, Dodd Mead, 1932, reprinted by Westwater Books, 1982

[2] For a brilliant discussion and reconstruction of the Howland/Dunn journey and murders, see *The Dunn-Howland Killings, A Reconstruction,* by M. Belshaw, The Journal of Arizona History, Winter 1979, pp. 409-422.

[3] In Powell's reports and lectures, he ascribes the naming of Dirty Devil River to Dunn. Bradley ascribes it to Powell, and Sumner, forty years later, claims authorship himself.

[4] National Archives, Washington, D.C

[5] Stanton, *op cit*

[6] ibid

[7] Webb, Roy. *If we had a Boat*. Salt Lake City:University of Utah Press, 1986

The Journal of Arizona History. Martin Anderson. *First Through the Canyon: Powell's Lucky Voyage in 1869,* Winter 1979. *John Wesley Powell's Explorations of the Colorado River,* Winter 1983. Michael Belshaw. *The Dunn-Howland Killings: A Reconstruction,* Winter 1979;

Cooley, John. *The Great Unknown.* Flagstaff: Northland Publishing, 1988.

Crumbo, Kim. *A River Runner's Guide to the History of the Grand Canyon.* Boulder: Johnson Books, 1981.

Darrah, William Culp. *Powell of the Colorado.* Princeton: Princeton University Press, 1951.

Dellenbaugh, Frederick S. *A Canyon Voyage.* New Haven: Yale University Press, 1962 (originally 1908).
——— *The Romance of the Colorado River* New Haven: Yale University Press.

Dary, David. *Red Blood and Black Ink: Journalism in the Old West.* New York: Knopf, 1998.

Goetzman, William H. *Army Exploration in the American West 1803-1863.* New Haven: Yale University Press, 1959.

Levy Collection, *American Folk Music,* Milton Eisenhower Library, Johns Hopkins University. Music and Lyrics to *Kitty Clyde's Sister, Old Shady, Annie Lawrie, etc.*

Miller, Hugh, *The Testimony of the Rocks.* Boston: Gould and Lincoln, 1872.

Marriott, Alice and Rachlin, Carol K. *American Indian Mythology.* New York: New American Library.

Powell, John Wesley. *The Exploration of the Colorado River and Its Canyons.* New York: Dover, 1961. (Originally 1875)
———— *Canyons of the Colorado.* Golden: Outbooks, 1981. (Originally Flood and Vincent, 1895)
———— Notes on the Exploration in Bell, Wm A, *New Tracks North America.* London, 1870.

Archives, *Rocky Mountain News,* Letters of O.G. Howland, articles on Powell, etc.

Silber, Irwin. *Songs of the Civil War.* New York: Dover Publications

Stanton, Robert Brewster. *Colorado River Controversies.* Boulder City: Westwater Books, 1982 (Originally New York: Dodd, Mead, 1932)

Stegner, Wallace. *Beyond the Hundredth Meridian.* New York: Houghton Miflin, 1954.

Utah Historical Quarterly, vols. 15,16,17, 37 (Bradley's Diary, Hall's letters, Sumner's "lost" journal, W. Powell's letters, etc.) 55 Smith, Melvin T. *Before Powell: Exploration of the Colorado River.*

Webb, Roy. *If We Had a Boat, Green River Explorers, Adventurers and Runners.* Salt Lake City: University of Utah Press, 1986.

ACKNOWLEDGEMENTS

It is hardly enough to dedicate this book to Ruth Dupont, teacher, librarian and wit, whose patient review and criticism kept the narrator from changing personality and the narrative from strolling from its appointed route. Her encouragement and advice were major contributions to the novel.

John Freeman Gill, a professional editor, was responsible for my discarding a present tense, third person version, and for urging me to let the men speak their minds and otherwise helped shape the narrative.

Anna Hannon, a dedicated reader, not only helped improve the narrative but more importantly, gave decided and firm advice on choice of narrator.

Tracy, a magazine editor, provided both insight and editorial assistance. Diana, a whiz at genealogy, tracked down Bradley and the Howlands for me.

Brad Dimmock, river guide and author, who played Walter Powell in a National Geographic recreation of the 1869 trip, and ran a sixty-seven day expedition of his own following Powell's route (and took me on part of it), gave immeasurable help. In particular he was my expert on rivers, boats, oars, cliffs and everything else pertaining to the Powell trip. I can't thank him enough.

I wish to thank the Huntington Library for access to the Marston Collection and for a copy of Bradley's journal with both annotations by W. C. Darrah and notes by "Doc" Marston.

I am grateful to the New York Public Library for access to its vast resources, which include the original contract between Powell and some of his men.

Mary Campbell, Curator of the Lester S. Levy Collection at the Milton Eisenhower Library of Johns Hopkins University was invaluable in furnishing or helping me to find words and music for the period songs.

The National Archives and the Map Collections of the Library of Congress were also valuable resources.